P9-DJK-599

THE MERCIFUL GOD OF PROPHECY

THE MERCIFUL GOD OF PROPHECY

His Loving Plan for You in the End Times

Tim LaHaye

with Steve Halliday

Warner Faith

WARNER BOOKS

An AOL Time Warner Company

Unless otherwise noted, Scriptures are taken from the NEW KING JAMES VERSION. Copyright © 1979, 1980, 1982, Thomas Nelson, Inc., Publishers.

Scriptures noted NIV are taken from the HOLY BIBLE: NEW INTERNATIONAL VERSION®. Copyright © 1973, 1978, 1984 by International Bible Society. Used by permission of Zondervan Publishing House. All rights reserved.

Scriptures noted KJV are taken from the King James Version of the Bible.

Scriptures noted TLB are taken from *The Living Bible,* copyright © 1971. Used by permission of Tyndale House Publishers, Inc., Wheaton, Illinios 60189. All rights reserved.

An AOL Time Warner Company

Printed in the United States of America
First Warner Books printing: October 2002
10 9 8 7 6 5 4 3 2 1

Text design by Stanley S. Drate/Folio Graphics Co. Inc.

Library of Congress Cataloging-in-Publication Data

LaHaye, Tim F.
    The merciful God of prophecy : his loving plan for you in the end times / Tim LaHaye.
        p. cm.
    ISBN 0-446-53024-7
    1. Bible—Prophecies—End of the world. 2. End of the world—Biblical teaching. 3. God—Mercy—Biblical teaching. 4. Bible—Prophecies. I. Title.

BS649.E63 L345 2002
231.7'45—dc21

                                                                    2002025890

To the merciful God of prophecy, who lovingly designed Bible prophecy to prove his existence and true nature. His boundless mercy and love moved him to send his only begotten Son (in fulfillment of prophecy!) into this world to die for our sins, making it possible for us to enjoy eternal life with him. And to his Son, Jesus Christ our Lord, "the spirit of prophecy."

We also dedicate this book to the millions of readers of the Left Behind series of prophetic novels (written with Jerry B. Jenkins), and to all others who have yet to appreciate how merciful our heavenly Father really is. May they discover soon what he has done and what he plans to do to demonstrate his amazing love!

The LORD, the LORD God, merciful and gracious,
longsuffering, and abounding in goodness and truth,
keeping mercy for thousands,
forgiving iniquity and transgression and sin.

Exodus 34:6–7

Contents

PART THREE

WHY DOES IT MATTER?

PART FOUR

APPENDICES

Introduction

So many people have a distorted view of God. Whether their confusion results from a legalistic background or because skeptics in school or at work have turned them against God, the God they envision either does not exist or he looks nothing like the God revealed in the Bible.

It is crucial that all of us get a clear idea of the God who actually exists, for the day will come when all of us will look to him for mercy and help. I hope that day will not come for you in the form of a major life crisis, especially nothing like the 9/11 terrorist attack that, without warning, claimed approximately three thousand innocent lives and left an entire nation grieving, bewildered, and groping for answers.

Those who gain a good understanding of the merciful God of the Bible are quick to turn to him, where they find comfort in their time of desperation. Those who do not know God—or who have the wrong understanding of what he really is—have to face their time of tribulation alone. Consequently they find themselves facing both the present and the future with fear and dread.

Knowing the true God—as he is revealed by the Hebrew prophets and by his Son, Jesus Christ—can be the most comforting experience of life. When our youngest daughter, Lori, was five years old, she had double pneumonia twice within two months. I shall never forget the experience of standing at the side of her hospital bed, her body enveloped by an oxygen tent. As I watched her little chest rise and fall in desperate gasps for breath, the doctor turned to my wife and me and said, "If you folks know how to pray, you'd better do it now. I have done everything for her that I possibly can!" Beverly and I immediately bowed our heads and prayed to our heavenly Father and put Lori's plight in his strong hands.

As we finished our prayer, a deep sense of peace and assurance washed over us. No one can understand such an experience except those who have walked through something like it. Even then we knew that whether she lived or died, she remained in God's loving care and that someday we would see her again. Two days later, Lori was out of the oxygen tent and well on the road to recovery. Today she is the busy mother of four of our nine grandchildren.

But the story doesn't end there. Next to us in that room so long ago sat a couple about our age with a daughter in the same plight. They wept uncontrollably. Though I tried, I could not console them, for God was obviously a stranger to them. That is when I began to realize how very important it is to gain the right understanding of who and what God really is before we face that unknown tragedy or circumstance that will come inevitably to every life.

That is what this book is all about—getting to know the real God, just as he has revealed himself through the most spiritual men in the Bible: the Hebrew prophets and the apostles of Jesus. Even though "God is Spirit" (John 4:24) and "no one has seen God at any time" (John 1:18), God has given us many ways to come to know him. As the Psalmist said, "the heavens declare the glory of God" (Ps 19:1). Certainly the marvels of creation prove that he exists, that he is all-powerful, and that he is the Master Designer of all things. But creation does not tell us much of *who* God is—what he is like, how he feels, and whether he is for us or against us. Somehow we all know he is holy, while we are sinners who have fallen short of his standard of holiness. But it is only in the Bible that we learn what he is really like and what kind of relationship we can have with him.

The apostle Paul spoke of two ways to know God: through

the revelation the Lord has given of himself through the Hebrew prophets and through God's only begotten Son, Jesus Christ, who came into this world not only to die for the sins of mankind but also to reveal God as Father.

> God, who at various times and in various ways spoke in time past to the fathers by the prophets, has in these last days spoken to us by His Son . . . the express image of His person. (Heb. 1:1–3)

Think of it! The Bible calls Jesus Christ the "express image" of God. When Jesus walked on this earth, everything he did expressed the true nature of God. His attitude toward children reflected the heavenly Father's attitude toward the totally dependant of our world. Jesus said, "Suffer the little children to come unto me" (Mark 10:14 KJV), which shows God's love for children. We learn that when the Savior felt the hurt and sorrow of his friends, "Jesus wept" (John 11:35). He saw the sorrow of Mary and Martha at the death of their brother, Lazarus, and he revealed himself to be completely in tune with human sorrows, grief, and hurts. By doing so he revealed how God the Father responds when we hurt.

While in this book we shall examine the life of Christ as the crowning illustration of God's character, we shall also explore the writings of the most spiritual men of the ancient world: the Hebrew prophets. From Enoch, Moses, Samuel, and the twelve minor and four major prophets, we learn things about God that would otherwise remain unknown. No other religion or philosophy in the world gives anything that will convince us that we do not have to quake in fear before God, afraid of what he may do next. But in this study we will learn that he is a merciful God, longsuffering, compassionate, and forgiving. We will learn that God loves us and is for us—a welcome thought in times of need!

Sooner or later we will all face our own personal time of crisis. Your time of need may be self-inflicted. Or it may occur simply because you are a human being living in a fallen world. I pray you will see that, whatever the cause of your misfortune, you can turn from wherever you are, like the Prodigal son, and return to your heavenly Father.

As we begin, I must declare that I cannot view God as a cruel taskmaster, standing at the gate of heaven to keep people out. Instead, I see him as the loving, merciful heavenly Father—just as described by the prophets and Jesus Christ, his Son—who stands at the gate of heaven, seeking to draw the greatest possible number of men and women in. While all those who enter must come through faith in his Son's sacrifice for our sins on the cross and his subsequent resurrection, we can be certain of this: if there is any way to get someone through the pearly gates, God will make sure it happens!

Where did I ever get such an idea of God? The Bible! The Word of God remains the only reliable source of who and what God is—and only there can we discover the wonderful plan he has in store for humanity. I invite you now to join me and make that delightful discovery for yourself.

PART ONE

THE GOD OF PROPHECY

1

God Has Gotten
a Bad Rap

When someone speaks of "Bible prophecy," what images come to mind? What pictures do you see? More important, how do these images influence your concept of God? What sort of scenes do they paint in your consciousness?

If you're like many people, "Bible prophecy" conjures up frightening images of doom, of fireballs raining from heaven, of mountains crashing into the sea, and of the sky turning a deep, blood red (before it grows dark and inky black altogether). It makes you think of an angry God bent on destruction. It scares you, and you'd just as soon not think of it at all.

Although I'm no movie buff, I think two scenes from the 1984 blockbuster film *Ghostbusters* probably sum up as well as anything the picture most folks have of biblical prophecy.[1] In the first scene, Winston and Ray are driving across the Brooklyn Bridge in New York City when Winston asks, "Hey, Ray. Do you remember something in the Bible about the last days, when the dead would rise from the grave?"

"I remember Revelation 6:12," Ray replies. "'And I looked, as he opened the sixth seal, and behold, there was a great earthquake, and the sun became as black as sackcloth. And the moon became as blood.'"

"And the seas boiled and the skies fell," whispers Winston.

"Judgment Day," Ray concludes.

"Judgment Day," agrees Winston.

A little later in the film, all of the ghostbusters appear before New York's mayor, trying to convince him and other city officials to allow them to handle the crisis. "This city is headed for a disaster of biblical proportions," says their leader.

"What do you mean, 'biblical'?" asks the mayor.

"What he means is Old Testament biblical, Mr. Mayor," replies Ray. "Real wrath-of-God-type stuff. Fire and brimstone coming from the sky! Rivers and seas boiling!"

"Forty years of darkness!" cries another. "Earthquakes! Volcanoes!"

"The dead rising from the grave!" shouts Winston.

"Human sacrifice, dogs and cats living together, mass hysteria!" sneers their leader.

The movie plays these scenes for laughs, of course—it's supposed to be a comedy, after all—but nevertheless I believe it accurately captures the general public's attitude toward biblical prophecy. When many folks ponder the Bible's predictions about the future, they often dredge up mental images of terrifying calamities, as well as grim scenes of a furious God flinging one bolt of judgment after another at trembling sinners. Even many Christians feel this way.

Frightened of Prophecy

Shortly after they were married, Tom and Carol[2] very publicly declared to friends at their church that they did not intend to have children. When asked how they had made such an important decision, they both pointed to Bible prophecy.

"The Bible tells us that the world is going to get worse and worse," Carol explained. "There are going to be awful wars and terrible earthquakes. Thousands, maybe millions, of believers are going to be martyred for their faith. Why would I want to bring any children into a world like *that*?"

Tom wholeheartedly agreed. "It just doesn't make any sense to subject your own children to the awful time that's coming," he would say. "I mean, the apostle Paul says in 2 Timothy that 'there will be *terrible* times in the last days.' God says, 'People will be lovers of themselves, lovers of money, boastful, proud, abusive, disobedient to their parents, ungrateful, unholy, without love, unforgiving, slanderous, without self-control, brutal, not lovers of the good, treacherous, rash, conceited, lovers of pleasure rather than lovers of God—having a form of godliness but denying its power.' Paul even says to 'have nothing to do with them.' So why would we want to expose our own flesh and blood to something so atrocious as that?" (2 Tim. 3:1–5 NIV).

A longtime friend of this couple, Barb, expressed similar feelings. "I haven't studied any of the 'end times' stuff and I don't read any of the novels on prophecy that are so popular right now," she said. "I don't read them because when you talk about the devil, that scares me. It's not like sci-fi, which is make-believe; Satan is a real power, not some scary monster. Also, because I am such a visual person, it's hard for me to get those images out of my head. So I have avoided prophecy, although I know I probably should study it so that I'm more prepared for the future and so that I can recognize some of the 'signs of the times' when they happen."

Barb's avoidance of Bible prophecy comes down to what we might call "the fear factor." Prophecies of hard times and coming judgment don't comfort her, they frighten her. They make her wonder what terrifying events might happen in the next minute, what might be lying in wait around the next corner.

"Prophecy makes me feel the way you do when you're watching a horror movie and something bad happens in the bathroom—after that you don't want to go in your *own* bathroom!" she explained. "I tend to want to avoid both conflict and fear; that's been my M.O. I also don't like thinking about the spiritual battle between evil and good. A few days after the terrorist attack on the World Trade Center towers, my family attended a service in our community. One speaker talked about how we're really not battling an army, we're battling evil itself. And that kind of gives me the creeps because it is so less concrete than the other thing, which we could dominate."

When unspeakable acts of violence strike our world—like the September 11, 2001, attacks on the World Trade Center and on the Pentagon—it's almost impossible *not* to recall biblical images of future judgment. More than one witness to the destruction caused in New York City and Washington, D.C., described it to television reporters in these words: "It looked like Armageddon."

Jesus himself, speaking of "the end," told his disciples that when that time comes, "Nations will be in anguish and perplexity . . . Men will faint from terror, apprehensive of what is coming on the world, for the heavenly bodies will be shaken" (Luke 21:25–26 NIV).

Now, I freely admit that such terrifying imagery doesn't bring comfort in the usual sense (in fact, I don't think it's meant to). But I *am* convinced that even such knee-knocking terminology is designed to communicate God's immeasurable mercy, grace, and love. God is not some celestial ogre who delights in inflicting catastrophe, but a loving Lord who does everything he can to help us *escape* divine judgment. He uses Bible prophecy not to frighten us, but for at least three other purposes: to prove beyond a shadow of a doubt that he exists; to warn us of the real dangers that lay ahead; and to encourage us into accepting his gracious offer of life, happiness, and ultimate satisfaction—forever.

From my perspective, the popular images of prophecy as a "downer" are all wrong. They completely misrepresent the loving nature of God and what he plans to do with the inhabitants of planet earth.

Of course, I can well understand how such a huge misunderstanding can take place. Why? Because many years ago I shared the very same viewpoint.

Who Wants to Go to Heaven?

At a summer camp when I was fifteen years old, I dedicated my life to the gospel ministry. Even from that early age, I knew I wanted to serve Jesus Christ and tell as many people as possible about his amazing love.

Five years later, after serving two years in the Air Force, I entered a Christian college to study to be a minister. Shortly after classes began, I met a beautiful young woman named Beverly. I fell in love with her almost immediately and eventually married her, but I almost missed the opportunity to discover what a real gem she truly is. On our very first date, I nearly torpedoed any chance I had at winning her heart. Truth be told, I just about scared her off.

At our school, students on dates couldn't hold hands or do anything really exciting. We were allowed to talk and that was it. So in two hours of conversation—with eagle-eyed chaperones lurking nearby with rifles and telescopes (or so it seemed to me)—she asked a few questions about the future and about heaven.

Without much thought, I blurted out, "I really am not too nuts about going to heaven—you know, floating around on a cloud, strumming a harp. I'm musically tone-deaf, anyway. It just doesn't grab me."

My lovely date looked at me with incredulity in her eyes and stammered, "Well, don't you love God?"

"Do you want me to be honest?" I asked.

She nodded.

Understand, I came from a background where God had been pictured as an angry taskmaster who sat glumly on the judgment seat, eagerly waiting for us to do something sinful so that he could zap us with a lightning bolt. I grew up thinking that God just couldn't wait to condemn all kinds of people to hell.

So I flatly told Bev, "To tell the truth, I really don't even *like* God."

Today, of course, I realize how close to blasphemy such a statement is—but it's exactly how I felt at the time. Fortunately, God knows the condition of our hearts and he judges according to our hearts, not necessarily by some of the stupid things we say.

After recovering from the shock, my gracious wife-to-be sat up straight and asked me in her very direct and spiritual way, "Well, if you don't like God and you don't want to go to heaven, *then why are you here?*"

A sensible question from a most sensible and practical woman. But I thought I had a perfectly logical answer.

"You don't understand," I said. "I love *Jesus.* He saved me, he called me to preach, and he's the reason I'm here."

So far as I was concerned, that answer explained everything. I loved Jesus with all my heart. I knew that Jesus loved me and that he had died for my sins so that I might live forever with him. I felt excited, even thrilled, about the opportunity to win people to Christ. I went to that school so that I could more effectively tell others about Jesus.

But I had no idea how Jesus and God connected. To me, they seemed as different and as contrary to one another as could be imagined. Therefore I could enthusiastically declare that while I loved Jesus, I disliked God.

Do you know what was wrong? I knew practically nothing of what the Bible actually teaches about God. I had not rejected God, but rather a grotesque caricature of him that has become very common in our world.

I'm convinced that one of the main reasons so many men and women in our society feel such aversion toward God is that they have no idea how gracious and merciful and loving he really is. They suffer under a *Ghostbusters* view of God, a distorted picture that sees the Almighty as dour, angry, ill-tempered, and eager to mete out horrific judgment. And amazing as it now seems to me, I once was a card-carrying member of that nervous club.

After our unusual date, Bev returned to her dormitory—you

might even say she fled—and told her roommate, "I just had a date with the craziest guy I've ever met. I will never date him again." (So much for *that* vow, after fifty-five years of marriage!)

This sad event occurred a long, long time ago, and today I can say that I truly love God with all my heart. Once I studied every verse in the Bible about who and what God is, I gained a completely different view of him. Once I discovered the truth about God—that he is really merciful and gracious and looks on us with such inexhaustible love that he sent his Son, Jesus Christ, to become the Savior of the world—my whole world changed. To bring about this change and to open my eyes to his true nature, God especially made use of a famous story from the lips of Jesus.

Discovering the Truth

When Jesus wanted his audience to grasp the passionate love of God for them, he told them three short but powerful stories (Luke 15). All of them memorably illustrate the Father's longing to find and bring home all of his lost children.

In the third of these stories, a young man from a wealthy family demands and gets his inheritance long before the death of his father (the time when custom said he ought to receive the money). He leaves home and spends his entire fortune on wild living, eventually winding up broke and friendless and working in a pigpen. One day, surrounded by hogs that eat better than he does, he comes to his senses. He realizes that even his father's servants enjoy a better life than the one he is enduring. So he picks himself up and sets off for home, determined to ask his father for work as a hired hand.

Meanwhile, his dad sits patiently on the veranda, scanning the road and praying each day to see his wandering son return home at last. On this day, while the son is still a long way off, the father recognizes the tired silhouette of his boy hobbling down the road. And what does he do? Does he sit there with folded arms and a scowl on his face and say, "Well, let's see if this foolish boy can make it all the way up to the bunkhouse. Then I'll give him a piece of my mind"? Not on your life! The father leaps off the veranda and runs to his son, embraces him, covers his dirty, pigsty face with kisses, and treats him to a homecoming party, complete with the best fresh beef in the county.

As I sat in a Bible class one day, studying this parable, I suddenly realized that the real story is not so much the prodigal, but the *father* of the prodigal. Jesus was portraying *God* as the prodigal's father! Our Lord wanted us to realize that his Father, God Almighty, was just like the merciful father in this story.

And for the first time I grasped the gracious, loving nature of God.

At that moment the lightbulb went off in my head. At once I understood that God isn't sitting up in heaven, arms crossed, trying to prevent people from entering. Instead, he stands with arms wide open, trying in all conceivable ways to usher as many people *into* heaven as possible.

The Bible insists that when any of us makes it to heaven, we do so only because *God* has made it possible (Matt. 18:14; John 6:37, 39–40, 44; 1 Tim. 2:3–4; 2 Pet. 3:9). If he can discover any way for us to make it safely through heaven's gates, he'll see that it happens. *This* is the truth about our gracious God. He reaches out to bring us to his side, where he has stockpiled "pleasures forevermore" at his right hand (Ps. 16:11).

That's the truth about God! Our Lord is a loving Father. And believe it or not, Bible prophecy reveals God's kind nature as almost nothing else can. So deeply do I believe this, that I've dedicated the rest of my life to helping others grasp this breathtaking truth.

Prophecy Shows God's Amazing Love

People are interested in prophecy today as never before. I can't adequately express how thrilled I am at the way God is blessing the *Left Behind* fiction series that Jerry B. Jenkins and I are writing. I have to pinch myself. People all over the country ask me how and why the series took off the way it did. The truth is, I don't know. All I can say is that God loves to honor his prophetic Word. When we began, I certainly had no idea of what was to come. Initially, I envisioned only one book.

I got the original idea seventeen years ago while sitting on an airplane, and it burned in my soul from that day on. Although I was a successful nonfiction author with forty titles in print, I had never written fiction. At first I thought, *You know, I should try on my own to write a story based on prophecy.* At the time, three of my nonfiction-writing friends wrote novels. I picked up their books, thinking, *Hey, if they can do it, so can I.* But then I actually read what they had written. And I quickly realized the truth: *None of us can write good fiction.*

I profited by that experience and asked the Lord to hook me up with an experienced author of fiction. I did some looking, found a promising candidate, and together we wrote a book.

I paid him to throw it away.

It cost me a fortune to toss a 550-page book in the trash, but the final product just didn't have the quality I demanded. It didn't feel like *my* book; it didn't speak to my heart.

Then I met Jerry B. Jenkins—and the rest, as they say, is history. At the time of this writing, more than fifty million books from the series are in print worldwide. We estimate that at least one hundred thousand readers have so far made a decision to receive Christ as their Savior through the influence of these novels.

Now can you see why I have a deep passion to declare the mercy and love of God through the medium of Bible prophecy? I want to counter the false notion that only gloom, doom, and despair await this troubled world. Much to the contrary, the Bible proclaims that God has a magnificent plan for our future, a plan that reveals his mercy. When properly understood, prophecy shows us the astonishing steps God will take to help a maximum number of people enjoy a spectacular eternity with him.

We should all stand amazed at how many future events God has revealed, primarily in order to show us his love and mercy. Even now he is carefully and relentlessly at work, superintending the course of world events in order to bring about the glorious future he has foretold. Some important prophetic events appear to be unfolding even now, in our own day.

God *does* love this world! Bible prophecy proves it! And this great message of divine love has become the passion of my heart. I'm in my mid-seventies, and I feel a strong compulsion to do whatever I can in the time I have left to encourage men and women to earnestly study Bible prophecy.

One of the most important books of prophecy, Revelation, says, "Blessed [or happy] is he who reads and those who hear the words of this prophecy, and keep those things which are written in it; because the time is near" (1:3).

Do you want to enjoy the greatest possible happiness? Then you *must* strive to understand Bible prophecy. God promises in his Word to give a special blessing of happiness to all those who seek to grasp what he has revealed about the future. Those who neglect the prophetic plan of God lack something essential in their lives, particularly in relation to their understanding and appreciation of Jesus. It may be that you have little desire to understand Bible prophecy—but do you want to know Jesus better? If so, then you must invest some time in God's prophetic word. Don't forget that the Book of Revelation does not merely disclose future events, but is particularly "the Revelation of Jesus Christ" (Rev. 1:1). If you want to know Jesus as he truly is, you cannot afford to bypass Bible prophecy.

Amazing treasures await those who plunge into the world of Bible prophecy. For there we learn that if the Scriptures teach us anything about God, it's that he is *for* us. He is not against us! He calls us to obey him, not because he needs our puny efforts, but because he wants to bless our lives. And as we will discover, the key to opening the door to God's blessing is to say, "Here's my life, Lord. Do with it whatever you see fit."

Love from Cover to Cover

Still, you may wonder, *But how does Bible prophecy reveal to us the mercy of God?* That's what this book is all about. We'll see how he has used prophecy in the past to communicate his amazing grace, how prophecy can help us right now to experience his abundant love, and how prophecy will continue to convince men and women of God's gracious intentions, right up to the very end of history. All of that is to come in the following pages.

But we can say, right off the top, that from cover to cover, Bible prophecy powerfully proclaims the grace, mercy, and love of God to those who believe in him.

Find that hard to believe? Then I suggest you turn to the very first book of the Bible, Genesis. There you will discover that God was thinking prophetically as soon as the first humans sinned. Only moments after Adam and Eve took a bite out of the forbidden fruit, God declared to the evil one who had enticed them to sin, "I will put enmity between you and the woman, and between your seed and her Seed; He shall bruise your head, and you shall bruise His heel" (3:15). That's an amazingly gracious prophecy—at least, for the man and the woman! Even at this darkest of hours, our merciful God prophesied that he would send the Christ (the Seed of the woman) to defeat Satan ("he shall bruise your head") by dying on the cross ("you shall bruise His heel").

Imagine! Even before his special creatures had sinned, God already had designed a remedy, a potent solution for their estrangement from him—in fact, the only solution. For only God himself, in the person of his Son, Jesus Christ, could die for the sins of the whole world.

How hard could it be to love a God like that?

What's more, God has woven this gracious thread of prophecy all the way through the Bible. The word *grace* first appears in Scripture in Genesis 6:8, when we read that, "Noah found grace in the eyes of the LORD." The last book in Scripture, Revelation, opens with a reference to God's grace (1:4) and closes the same way (22:21). The middle of the book reminds us of the greatest act of grace in history, that Jesus Christ was "slain from the foundation of the world" (13:8).

Why this concentrated focus on grace? To give us courage, strength, and hope, particularly in uncertain times like these. Prophecy tells us that from the very beginning of history to its last gasp, God shows himself to be merciful, gracious, and loving beyond all imagination. And from the first book of the Bible to the last, prophecy declares that God has crafted an astonishing plan to bless untold millions of redeemed human beings with eternal life, eternal significance, and eternal joy.

I say it again: No one has to be afraid of the God of prophecy!

In fact, there is only one kind of god we *do* have to fear: the one who doesn't exist, the one who rubs his hands together and grins each time we fail, thereby earning his angry judgment. *That* is a god to fear.

Happily, that is not the God of the Bible. That is not the God of prophecy. The God of Scripture is *for* us. He is always available to us, always attentive to our needs. And prophecy assures us that his ears are always attuned to our cry.

Just the other day I saw a bumper sticker that made me both smile and reflect. Its message featured just two lines, but they say a lot about our times:

> Where are we going?
> And why am I in this hand basket?

Bible prophecy shouts loud and clear, "You *can* know where you're going; you don't have to remain in the dark. And you *do not* have to stay in a place that takes you exactly where you don't want to be!"

I love Bible prophecy because it reveals a kindhearted God who is merciful and gracious beyond all expectation. But perhaps most marvelous of all is the open invitation he gives to each one of us: *Come and see!* (Ps. 66:5; Isa. 66:18).

I say, let's take him up on his offer.

2

The God of the Prophets

Where would we be without the Old Testament prophets? For one thing, without them, we'd also be without some of the greatest spiritual leaders the English-speaking world has ever produced.

Consider two such leaders—one American, one British, and both named Charles. Charles G. Finney (1792–1875) and Charles H. Spurgeon (1834–1892) helped millions of seeking men and women in their day to connect deeply with God. Yet neither might have burst upon the scene apart from the influence of the ancient prophets of God.

Finney describes how he spent several difficult days anguishing over the state of his soul. He knew the gospel intellectually, but it had never made much of a difference in his life. As he grew increasingly aware of his need for divine mercy, he grew progressively more agitated. He wrote in his memoirs:

> Just at that point, this passage of Scripture seemed to drop into my mind with a flood of light: "Then shall ye go and pray unto me, and I will hearken unto you. Then ye shall seek me and find me, when ye shall search for me with all your heart." I instantly seized hold of this with my heart. I had intellectually believed the Bible before; but never had the truth been in my mind that

faith was a voluntary trust instead of an intellectual state . . . I knew that it was God's word, and God's voice, as it were, that spoke to me.[1]

The word Finney heard came from the prophet Jeremiah (29:12–13 KJV).

On the spot Finney declared that he would take God at his word, that God could not lie, that therefore he was sure the Almighty had heard his prayer and that he would certainly find the God he sought.

God heard Finney's petition and soon afterward the future revivalist found the mercy he had so earnestly sought. He wrote:

> The repose of my mind was unspeakably great. I never can describe it in words. The thought of God was sweet to my mind, and the most profound spiritual tranquility had taken full possession of me . . . No words can express the wonderful love that was shed abroad in my heart. I wept aloud with joy and love; and I do not know but I should say, I literally bellowed out the unutterable gushings of my heart. These waves came over me, and over me, and over me, one after the other, until I recollect I cried out, "I shall die if these waves continue to pass over me." I said, "Lord, I cannot bear any more"; yet I had no fear of death.[2]

The next morning Finney described how God's mercy had rescued him: "He then cleared the subject up so much to my mind that it was in fact impossible for me to doubt that the Spirit of God had taken possession of my soul."[3]

Many have called Charles H. Spurgeon the "Prince of Preachers." At the height of his popularity he spoke twice a week in the six-thousand-seat Metropolitan Tabernacle in London. Yet he wrote, "I sometimes think I might have been in darkness and despair until now had it not been for the goodness of God in sending a snowstorm, one Sunday morning, while I was going to a certain place of worship." Forced by the weather to enter a Primitive Methodist Chapel, Spurgeon joined about a dozen people in worship, and although "they sang so loudly that they made people's heads ache," he didn't mind, for "I wanted to know how I might be saved, and if they could tell me that, I did not care how much they made my head ache."[4]

When the regular minister did not show up, a member of the congregation began to preach. Spurgeon described the impromptu preacher as "a very thin-looking man, a shoemaker, or tailor, or something of that sort . . . really stupid," and said the man "was obliged to stick to his text, for the simple reason that he had little else to say."[5] The preacher chose the text, "Look unto me, and be ye saved, all the ends of the earth"—a verse from the prophet Isaiah (45:22 KJV). The man didn't have much of an idea about how to preach Isaiah, but he spoke what he knew. Spurgeon's description of what happened that morning is still priceless:

> He did not even pronounce the words rightly, but that did not matter. There was, I thought, a glimpse of hope for me in that text. The preacher began thus:—"My dear friends, this is a very simple text indeed. It says, 'Look.' Now lookin' don't take a deal of pains. It ain't liftin' your foot or your finger; it is just, 'Look.' Well, a man needn't go to College to learn to look. You may be the biggest fool, and yet you can look. A man needn't be worth a thousand a year to be able to look. Anyone can look; even a child can look. But then the text says, 'Look unto *Me.*' Ay!" said he, in broad Essex, "many on ye are lookin' to yourselves, but it's no use lookin' there. You'll never find any comfort in yourselves. Some look to God the Father. No, look to Him by-and-by. Jesus Christ says, 'Look unto *Me.*' Some on ye say, 'We must wait for the Spirit's workin'.' You have no business with that just now. Look to *Christ.* The text says, 'Look unto *Me.*'"[6]

The man went on like this for about ten minutes, until he reached "the end of his tether," according to Spurgeon.

> Then he looked at me under the gallery, and I daresay, with so few present, he knew me to be a stranger. Just fixing his eyes on me, as if he knew all my heart, he said, "Young man, you look

very miserable." Well, I did; but I had not been accustomed to have remarks made from the pulpit on my personal appearance before. However, it was a good blow, struck right home. He continued, "and you always will be miserable—miserable in life, and miserable in death,—if you don't obey my text; but if you obey now, this moment, you will be saved." Then, lifting up his hands, he shouted, as only a Primitive Methodist could do, "Young man, look to Jesus Christ. Look! Look! Look! You have nothin' to do but to look and live."[7]

At once Spurgeon said he saw:

. . . the way of salvation. I had been waiting to do fifty things, but when I heard that word, "Look!" what a charming word it seemed to me! Oh! I looked until I could almost have looked my eyes away. There and then the cloud was gone, the darkness had rolled away, and that moment I saw the sun; and I could have risen that instant, and sung with the most enthusiastic of them, of the precious blood of Christ, and the simple faith which looks alone to Him. Oh, that somebody had told me this before, "Trust Christ, and you shall be saved."[8]

So did two of the most influential and revered spiritual leaders in the English-speaking world find the mercy and grace of God. And how did they find it? Through the words of two of the most honored prophets in the Old Testament.

So what was it about these prophets that cause their words to live on yet today? Let's take a look.

The Best God Had

I believe the testimony of the prophets on the nature of God is crucial because these remarkable servants really were the best God had. No wonder the apostle Peter called them "holy men of God"! (2 Pet. 1:21).

It's tough to name a godly king or judge in the Old Testament who wasn't a prophet as well. And when we list the great heroes of the Old Testament, whom do we most often discuss?

Samuel, Elijah, Elisha, Daniel, Isaiah, Jeremiah, Ezekiel, David, and Moses. Not only were all these men the special servants of God for their generation, all of them were also prophets. In their time they knew the Lord better than anyone else. They had a special insight into the nature and character of God.

Do you really want to know who God is? Then understand him from the prophets. If we listen to their testimony regarding the nature of God, we will see the light burning at the end of our own tunnels. Everyone has problems and we all look to God for solutions. How much better to call upon the God whom the prophets knew so well!

Jonah, the Rebellious Prophet

Have you heard of Jonah, a rebellious prophet who took the first submarine ride in history? Oddly enough, this man ended up surfing undersea currents in the belly of great fish precisely *because* he knew God to be gracious and merciful. But that takes a little explanation.

Jonah lived sometime around the eighth century B.C., when Assyria dominated the affairs of the ancient Near East. From about 900–600 B.C., Assyria overran Mesopotamia through its powerful and vicious armies. Historical accounts of the time tell us it was not uncommon for the Assyrians to take the heads of its conquered foes and pile them up in huge heaps as a not-so-subtle warning to others.

Nineveh, the capital of Assyria, had become the greatest city in the world. A wall almost eight miles around enveloped the city, while a population of at least 120,000 lived within its walls.[9] A much larger administrative district surrounded the walled city; the whole complex was often referred to as "Nineveh." The huge site amounted to an enormous metropolis.

God told Jonah to go to that teeming city and proclaim, "Yet forty days, and Nineveh shall be overthrown!" (Jon. 3:4). Assyria had long posed a threat to Israel, and since Jonah was a

Hebrew prophet, perhaps he could see that one day this powerful Gentile nation would destroy Israel (an event which did in fact occur in 722 B.C.). So when God told Jonah to call the Ninevites to repent, he feared that they really *might*. Therefore, instead of heading to Nineveh, he fled in the opposite direction, to the seaport town of Joppa. There he booked passage to the even more distant region of Tarshish.

The familiar Bible story describes how the seas grew rough and stormy and threatened to sink his vessel. Jonah counseled the sailors to throw him overboard, and reluctantly, they did. We're told "a great fish" immediately swallowed the disgruntled prophet. After three days and nights spent in the depths of the sea, even the fish couldn't stomach that rebel, so the beast ejected the prophet onto the beach.

This time, when God instructed Jonah to preach in Nineveh, he complied—and the city responded with what may be the biggest revival in history. The Bible says the entire population of Nineveh—from the king to the lowliest of servants—put on sackcloth, began to fast, and repented. God saw their change of heart and relented from sending destruction. And so the Book of Jonah reminds us what kind of God we serve. He is the sort of Lord who loves to show mercy!

Still, while the repentance of the Ninevites greatly pleased God, it didn't please Jonah at all.

"Ah Lord," the prophet prayed, "was not this what I said when I was still in my country? Therefore I fled previously to Tarshish; for I know that You are a gracious and merciful God, slow to anger and abundant in lovingkindness, One who relents from doing harm" (Jon. 4:2).

Can you imagine? A prophet used by God to spark the greatest revival in history—and he bitterly complained about it! He didn't like this turn of events, because from his perspective the recipients of God's grace hailed from the "wrong" nation. Jonah wanted God to wipe the filthy Assyrians off the face of the earth—and instead he *spared* them!

Don't miss what happened. The prophet ran from God, not because he feared a God eager to hurl down bolts of judgment, but because he knew God to be gracious, merciful, and deeply loving. This was too much for Jonah to handle.

True to form, however, God wasn't through with this prophet.

Jonah lingered for a few days outside Nineveh, hoping that God would change his mind and obliterate the city. It's hot in this part of the world, and Jonah felt overjoyed when overnight the Lord caused a vine to grow over his head to give him a measure of relief from the blazing sun. But early the next day, God sent a worm to wither the vine. And that made Jonah even more furious.

"Is it right for you to be angry about the plant?" God asked his prophet.

"It is right for me to be angry," Jonah replied, "even to death!"

That's when Jonah learned a second lesson about God's kindhearted and merciful nature.

"You had pity on the plant for which you have not labored, nor made it grow, which came up in a night and perished in a night," God said. "And should I not pity Nineveh, that great city, in which are more than one hundred and twenty thousand persons who cannot discern between their right hand and their left—and much livestock?" (Jon. 4:10–11).

Jonah felt compassion for a plant that helped him feel comfortable; God felt compassion toward a people that for many years had scorned and blasphemed him.

Despite himself, Jonah tells us a great deal about the nature of God. Jonah wanted judgment; God wanted mercy. Jonah rooted for death; God championed life.

Thank the Lord, God won!

And I thank the Lord, too, that Jonah didn't originate this idea of God as merciful, gracious, slow to anger, and abounding in love. He learned it from yet another prophet.

Of Locusts and Repentance and Love

About a century or so before the time of Jonah, another Hebrew prophet named Joel ministered to the people of Judah. In his days, the nation enjoyed unparalleled prosperity—but affluence led many to forget that they enjoyed their wealth only through the blessing of God. Joel, whose name means "Yahweh is God," could not allow this sad state of affairs to continue unchallenged.

A terrible locust plague had engulfed his nation, and Joel used the calamity to encourage his countrymen to turn back to the Lord. He declared that if they refused to repent, a plague even greater than mighty locust armies would devastate the nation on the great and terrible "day of the LORD" (Joel 2:11).

Joel's short book reveals that he knew intimately the temple and its ministry, and that he firmly grasped the geography and history of his land. As a spiritually mature man, he pled with his nation to turn away from their rebellion and return with their whole hearts to the God of their fathers.

I had never paid enough attention to the message of this "minor prophet" until I discovered him anew in my devotions. His book covers only three short chapters and it's easy to miss him among the myriad Old Testament prophets. But there, in the second chapter of his book, I saw it. Joel, a great saint of God, wanted to teach me about his good Lord. Read carefully what he had to say:

> "Now, therefore," says the LORD,
>   "Turn to Me with all your heart,
> With fasting, with weeping,
>   and with mourning."
> So rend your heart, and not your garments;
>   Return to the LORD your God,
> For He is gracious and merciful,
>   Slow to anger, and of great kindness;
> And He relents from doing harm.
>
> (Joel 2:12–13)

Did you catch Joel's stunning picture of God? Certainly the prophet didn't shrink from warning his people that God would soon judge their sin. He used graphic pictures and arresting images to encourage God's people to leave their false gods and their sinful ways of life and to return to the Lord. He urged them to come to God with their whole hearts, not merely with some religious show.

But what ultimate reason did Joel give to his countrymen for returning to God? What was his ace in the hole? What truth did he most lean on to encourage them to "return to the LORD your God"? Make sure you don't miss it: "For He is gracious and merciful, slow to anger, and of great kindness; and He relents from doing harm."

Doesn't that sound familiar? It should! It sounds just like the message of Jonah, who lived about a century after Joel. No doubt Jonah had been reading Joel's little book!

This idea of a merciful God must have flourished in ancient Israel, for both Amos and Malachi (two minor prophets who lived near the end of Old Testament history) referred to their merciful God as "gracious," and both major prophets, Isaiah and Jeremiah, referred to him as "merciful." God described himself to Jeremiah in these words: "'I am merciful,' says the LORD; 'I will not remain angry forever. Only acknowledge your iniquity'" (Jer. 3:12–13).

What comfort this is to sinners in any age, to know that they can find "mercy" when they admit their sin to God. God himself said so! There is no better guarantee of forgiveness than that given by God himself.

Do you want to believe in a God like that? I know I do, for that is the kind of God I need, one who understands the thoughts and intents of my heart—and who yet, because of his mercy, wants to bless me anyway.

These prophets weren't alone in "getting" the message. The truth is, the good news about God's love goes even deeper and further back, long before their time.

The Clock Turns Still Further Back

That God is merciful should take none of us by surprise. Consider the Book of 2 Kings. Several times this sacred record of Israel's history mentions what it calls "the sons of the prophets" (2:3, 5, 7, 15; 4:1, 38; 5:22; 6:1; 9:1). I have a hunch that the great prophet Elijah founded a school of prophets through which he helped his followers to understand that our merciful God is gracious, slow to anger, and abundant in lovingkindness.

No doubt it was the effective ministry of this school of prophets that prompted King Hezekiah to write a letter to his people in which he reminded them, "the Lord your God is gracious and merciful, and will not turn His face from you if you return to Him" (2 Chron. 30:9).

Happily, we cannot say that Elijah—even though he founded the school of the prophets to formally teach young prophets the ways and nature of God—originated this delightful concept. Long before his time, the greatest king in Israel's history—and a prophet in his own right—penned the following words: "But You, O Lord, are a God full of compassion, and gracious, longsuffering and abundant in mercy and truth" (Ps. 86:15).

No wonder David could say, after such a great confession, "Oh, turn to me, and have mercy on me!" (v. 16) The nature of God continued to inspire him when he wrote:

> The Lord is merciful and gracious,
> Slow to anger, and abounding in mercy.
> He will not always strive with us,
> Nor will He keep His anger forever.
> He has not dealt with us according to our sins,
> Nor punished us according to our iniquities.
> For as high as the heavens are high above the earth,
> So great is His mercy toward those who fear Him.
> As far as the east is from the west,
> So far has He removed our transgressions from us.
> (Ps. 103:8–12)

David, who seemed to know God as well as anyone in the Old Testament, mentioned the mercy of God no fewer than fourteen times in his writings—and that's not counting Psalm 136, where twenty-six times he declared that God's "mercy endures forever."

Long before Jonah; long before Joel; long before even Elijah, King David extolled the infinite mercy, grace, and love of the Lord. The "sweet psalmist of Israel" could never get over the boundless mercy of his God, and he eagerly set to music his joyful understanding of God's love.

But do you want to know something? Not even David originated this idea. It predated even him . . . by a long, long time.

The Lawgiver Himself Speaks

What part of the Old Testament did David, Elijah, and his fellow prophets study to become so convinced of the mercy and grace of God? Where in Scripture did they turn? No doubt they opened their scrolls of Torah to learn from Moses, the lawgiver himself.

When did Moses live and minister? No one can say for sure, but many conservative scholars date the Exodus sometime around 1446 B.C., an estimate that fits well with other biblical data. If this date is accurate, we can calculate that approximately seven hundred years separated Moses from Jonah. Yet their testimony about the loving nature of God does not vary in the slightest.

In Exodus 33, Moses gave us a remarkable account of his unique interaction with God. By this point in the narrative, the Israelites already had left Egypt, camped at Sinai, received (and broken) the Ten Commandments, and suffered their first deadly bout with idolatry. Moses had angrily shattered the first set of tablets containing the commandments, and God had summoned him once more to the mountaintop to receive a new set.

Oh, and one more thing. Moses had a tiny request of God: "Please, show me Your glory" (Exod. 33:18).

Wow!

What did Moses mean when he asked God to "show me Your glory"? He wanted to see God as he truly is. He wanted to know him intimately. He wanted to receive a revelation of the heart of God. What is the Lord *really* like? How would God describe himself? How would he communicate his nature, his character, his deepest self?

What a gargantuan request Moses made of the Lord! But more astonishing still, God gladly honored the request.

God told Moses to stand on a certain part of the mountain. When the Lord would make his "glory" pass by, he promised to put Moses in a cleft in the rock and cover him. Note how the Bible describes this amazing event: "And the LORD passed before him and proclaimed, 'The LORD, the LORD God, merciful and gracious, longsuffering, and abounding in goodness and truth, keeping mercy for thousands, forgiving iniquity and transgression and sin'" (Exod. 34:6–7).

There it is again—an amazing picture of God, painted by the Lord himself for one of his chief prophets. About Moses, God had said, "you have found grace in My sight, and I know you by name" (Exod. 33:17). And *this* man—a prophet who knew God "face to face" (Exod. 33:11), a man whom God called by name (Exod. 3:4)—testified that God's nature overflows with mercy and grace, love and faithfulness.

This makes it obvious that neither Jonah nor Joel, nor any of the other prophets mentioned, originated the idea that God was merciful. This truth came from God himself when he called Moses into his service. "The LORD your God is a merciful God," he declared (Deut. 4:31).

Let's Get the Right Idea

Too many men and women suffer under the mistaken notion that our God is a God of judgment. It is true that he will judge people for their sin—but only as a last resort (see chapter 6). Yet because he is a God abundant in love, he longs to deliver us from judgment by calling us to repentance and faith. This was the unchanging message of the prophets over a period of fifteen hundred years before Christ, eight hundred years before Christ, and seven hundred years before Christ.

What does this tell us? It reveals that the most spiritual people throughout history understood that God delights in doing good to his people.

Despite what you might have thought, despite what you may have been told, if you accept the message of God's prophets—those godly servants whom Peter called "holy men of God [who] spoke as they were moved by the Holy Spirit" (2 Pet. 1:21)—then you can come to God without fear. You can realize that he is gracious, merciful, slow to anger, long-suffering, abundant in loving-kindness, and rich in goodness and truth. And he relents from doing harm.

Consider this carefully. God loves us and wants the best for us. He has shown us in countless ways that he is for us. Our God looks to us with merciful eyes and a heart full of grace and long-suffering.

The Real Problem

Many people do not experience the mercy and kindness of God because they refuse to do his will. God freely offers his mercy to all mankind, but always upon the condition that they obey him. If they choose to disobey him, he cannot guarantee them his blessing.

History shows that those individuals and nations who disobeyed him either received his judgment or failed to receive the mercy and blessings they could have enjoyed. Such people often regard God as cruel or mean-spirited. They seem unable to understand that they cannot do their own thing—disregarding his will and plan for their lives—and still receive his mercy.

God challenges both Israel and us like this: "In mercy I give you a choice: Obey me and I will bless you; disobey me and I will judge you." Those who disobey his will and his commandments (as provided in the Bible for our good) look up to God and say, "He is a God of judgment." Those who obey him look up to him and say, "He is a God of mercy." Your view of God depends on where you stand, in obedience or disobedience to him.

We clearly see God's mercy in his offer of forgiveness to all who have sinned and come "short of the glory [or will] of God" (Rom. 3:23 KJV). From Adam and Eve to King David, from the thief on the cross to Saul of Tarsus (who became the apostle Paul), and to you and me—he makes this matchless offer: "In love and mercy I sent my only Son to die for your sins. I raised him from the dead so that you would know I accepted his sacrifice. All you have to do is call upon me for forgiveness and salvation, and I will give you eternal life."

Nothing could be more gracious than that.

In the final analysis, God leaves the decision up to you. He—and his prophets—declared his mercy, and now you can accept it or reject it. He tells us in Deuteronomy 30:19: "I call heaven and earth as witnesses today against you, that I have set before you life and death, blessing and cursing; therefore choose life, that both you and your descendants may live."

How do you see God? Do you see him as merciful, gracious, and forgiving? Or do you see him as judgmental, angry, and mean? The Bible is clear—the choice is yours.

The best part of his mercy is that we can reach out to him any time we need him. When we sin, when we need direction or help—or when we just want to praise and thank him for his goodness and mercy—he is as near as our prayer.

I can love and serve a God like that. And I think you can, too.

When you are in distress, and all these things come upon you in the latter days, when you turn to the LORD your God and obey His voice (for the LORD your God is a merciful God), He will not forsake you nor destroy you, nor forget the covenant of your fathers which He swore to them. (Deut. 4:30–31)

3

The God Who Reveals Secrets

Many years ago my good friend, Dr. D. James Kennedy—the pastor of Coral Ridge Presbyterian Church in Fort Lauderdale, Florida—was walking out of a grocery store with his wife when he saw a tabloid advertising something like "50 Prophecies of Ten Leading Psychics for the Next Year!" *That might be interesting*, he thought. So he grabbed a copy, paid the cashier, took home the magazine, clipped out the article, and gave it to his secretary to file.

Ten years went by. One day he decided to preach a series on prophecy. He retrieved his folder on prophecy and found this old clipping. He read it and wondered, *How many of these prophecies really took place?* So he checked.

Not a single prophecy had been fulfilled. A perfect record, but not one to boast about!

Dr. Kennedy's experiment so intrigued me that I recently decided to duplicate his test. A couple of weeks ago I bought a copy of the *Sun*, which touts itself as "America's Best-Loved Weekly." The lead article, "101 Predictions & Prophecies for You and Your Loved Ones from World's Leading Seers and Psychics," shared space with such scintillating fare as "Professor

Turns Stripper—Her Own Amazing True Story" and "Cloned Sheep Dolly Leads Scientists to Fountain of Youth"![1]

I intended to leave the prophecy article in my own files for a few years, then take it out and see how many of its predictions had panned out. But after the terrorist attacks at the World Trade Center and the Pentagon, as well as the crash of a fourth hijacked airliner in Pennsylvania, I decided to retrieve the article and see who might have foretold—or even alluded to—such earth shattering events.

If these psychics could really see the future, I reasoned, at least *one* of them should have hinted at the disaster. Beyond all doubt, the attack was the biggest domestic story in decades. Time after time we heard news commentators compare the assault to the bombing of Pearl Harbor on December 7, 1941, when Imperial Japanese forces carried out a sneak attack and plunged America into World War II. The 9/11 calamity should have created a huge blip on any true modern prophet's radar screen. So how many of these "leading seers and psychics" even hinted at it?

Not one.

Oh, they did warn that a UFO would appear over the White House, prompting an immediate doubling of Social Security benefits; that a fifty-foot-tall vision of a weeping Virgin Mary would appear over the Dome of the Rock in Jerusalem; that a Bigfoot-like primate would kill twelve shoppers at a San Francisco mall; and that Hawaii would secede from America and become a territory of New Zealand.

But not a single "seer" even vaguely suggested the disaster inflicted on the United States by a well-organized group of terrorists (unless you count the "Church of England theologian the Very Reverend Horace Bartholomew," psychic advisor to the royal family, who predicted that "Palestinian separatists" would send "life-like robots on suicide bombing missions"[2]).

Would you be willing to bet your life on such "prophecies"? I sure wouldn't. And yet many individuals consider such "seers" to be great prognosticators of the future!

But if you really want to know what the future holds, why go to men and women with such atrocious track records? Why not go to somebody who *really* knows the future, someone who has publicly uttered no fewer than a thousand predictions . . . *with an accuracy rate to date of 100 percent?*

He Knows the End from the Beginning

Do you realize that 28 percent of the Bible was prophetic at the time it was written? Dr. John Walvoord, who has dedicated more than sixty years of his life to studying Bible prophecy, has identified more than one thousand prophecies in the Bible, five hundred of which already have been fulfilled.[3] The others are yet to come.

So if that's true—if God already has fulfilled five hundred prophecies, with another five hundred yet to unfold—can we trust him when he tells us about days yet to come?

No mere human could forecast the future with the detail and accuracy that God has demonstrated. So far as God is concerned, prophecy is little more than history written in advance. Only God knows the future. I can't picture what lies ahead or foretell what's about to happen. But God is able to accurately tell us "things to come." No wonder he describes himself with words like these: "I am God, and there is no other; I am God, and there is none like Me, declaring the end from the beginning, and from ancient times things that are not yet done, saying, 'My counsel shall stand, and I will do all My pleasure'" (Isa. 46:9–10).

Beginning in ages past, God has seen fit to forecast the future—and everything always happens just the way he said it would. In fact, that is one way we know he exists and that he cares for us. From the very first, God has told us how history will wind up. Who can do that, but God alone? Certainly not mere human beings. And surely, not any false gods of wood or stone. And yet, somehow, men and women throughout history choose to abandon the sure Word of God and cling to the fantasies and lies of lesser authorities. Even ancient Israel made this tragic error.

The chosen people of God had no reason to disbelieve in the living, almighty God—but time after time, they abandoned him to follow idols. By Ezekiel's day, they had sunk especially low. "In visions of God" the Lord took the exiled prophet on a tour of the Jerusalem temple. There, near the entrance to the north gate of the inner court, he saw an "idol that provokes to jealousy" (Ezek. 8:3, 5). He was instructed to look through a hole in the wall of the temple. There, in an inner room, he saw seventy leaders of Israel worshiping detestable idols (8:10–11). He also saw Israelite women weeping for Tammuz, the Babylonian god of spring vegetation whose death was thought to bring on the scorching days of summer (8:14). And there, between the altar and the portico, he saw twenty-five men with their backs to the temple and their faces bowed in worship to the sun (8:16).

So even in the city of God, in the holy place where God wanted to communicate his message to mankind, the Israelites had adopted the faith of Babylon, Satan's religion. There seems to be something in all of us that urges us down this catastrophic track. If we don't have much faith on the inside, we create religion on the outside. So the ancient people of God made their own gods and asked them to protect and prosper them. And how did the living God respond? Listen to his challenge:

> Let now the astrologers, the stargazers, and the monthly prognosticators stand up and save you from what shall come upon you.
>
> Behold, they shall be as stubble, the fire shall burn them; they shall not deliver themselves from the power of the flame; it shall not be a coal to be warmed by, nor a fire to sit before!
>
> Thus shall they be to you with whom you have labored, your merchants from your youth; they shall wander each one to his quarter, no one shall save you. (Isa. 47:13–15)

Despite God's many entreaties, the Israelites continued to turn to their silly seers and pitiful prophets. Rather than going to God for counsel—"In all your ways acknowledge Him, and He shall direct your paths" (Prov. 3:6)—the ancient Hebrews instead chose to acknowledge their idols. So God sadly observed, "All the counsel you have received has only worn you out!" (Isa. 47:13 NIV).

How unutterably sad. Man-made idols and man-made predictions can't save anyone. Only the living God can do that.

For decade after decade, God warned his people that disaster would strike if they continued to turn their backs to him. Yet for the most part, they ignored his warnings and grew ever more infatuated with their false gods and prophets. Eventually the Lord sent invaders from Assyria to destroy the northern kingdom of Israel. He permitted the southern kingdom of Judah to survive, but over the decades it also became increasingly corrupt. At last, after all of God's warnings went unheeded, Judah too fell to invaders, this time from Babylon.

And for many years this single fact of history really bothered me.

Why Babylon?

Why did Israel's Babylonian exile so perplex me? It confounded me because I couldn't think of any good answer to a very troubling question: *Why would God judge the children of Israel for idolatry by taking them from Jerusalem, the city of God, and sending them to Babylon, the source of all idolatry?*

One couldn't find a more pagan place in the ancient world than Babylon, a city that exported its idolatry all over the globe. So why would God send his holy people *there* for the sin of idol worship? It seemed to make no sense.

After pondering the question for many years, I finally came up with what may be the main reason. I think God wanted, once and for all, to show his superiority over the false gods of paganism. He knew that one of the best ways to prove his superiority would be to contrast his brand of prophecy with that of the most gifted magicians, enchanters, sorcerers, and astrologers that Babylon had to offer (much as he did in the great contest between Elijah and the false prophets of Baal).

Who *really* knew what lay ahead? God, or the false gods of Babylon? Why not pit the best the pagan world had to offer against a true prophet of God?

Enter the young man Daniel.

A True Prophet of God

Babylonian invaders probably took Daniel captive after an attack on Jerusalem by Nebuchadnezzar in 605–604 B.C. At that time the king carried off some of the temple articles, as well as a number of boys from the Hebrew royal family and the nobility—"young men in whom there was no blemish, but good-looking, gifted in all wisdom, possessing knowledge and quick to understand, who had ability to serve in the king's palace" (Dan. 1:4). These he trained in the Babylonian way of life.

While most of these young captives abandoned much of their religious heritage, Daniel and at least three of his friends determined to honor the God of their fathers, even in this hostile new land. After thriving through a stiff initial challenge (Dan. 1), Daniel and his friends soon faced an even bigger threat.

Perhaps we could feel the tension more deeply if we tried to imagine that we ourselves landed back in ancient Babylon with Daniel and his friends. Just for a moment, let's put ourselves in the place of Arioch, commander of the king's guard, and see how this story played out.

❦

Rarely have I seen the king so upset. I have served him now for many years and have come to expect bursts of violent temper— but this was beyond anything I'd ever seen. He told us that a troubling dream had made him anxious. And when *he* gets anxious, we *all* get anxious!

The king ordered the empire's best seers and prophets to appear before him and demanded that they interpret his dream for them—nothing so unusual about that. But this time he threw in an unexpected twist. He insisted that these poor wretches recount to him his dream *before* they interpreted it! Can you imagine?

He figured that if he first described his dream, they could make up anything they pleased and call it the "right interpretation." (To be frank, I think these "prophets" have a long history of such deceit. But that's just my opinion.) This unsettling dream felt unique and special to King Nebuchadnezzar and had cost him some sleep. So he required his seers first to describe the dream in order to prove they had the power to accurately interpret it. True to form, he backed up his demand by declaring that if they could not do what he ordered, he would cut them into pieces and turn their houses into piles of rubble.

Let me tell you, on that day I was glad to be a soldier and not numbered among the royal soothsayers!

Every one of these petrified men reacted just as you might expect, sputtering and spewing and quivering and protesting, "But O king, there is not a man on earth who can do what the king asks! No king, however great and mighty, has ever asked such a thing of any magician or enchanter or astrologer. What the king asks is too difficult. No one can reveal it to the king except the gods, and they do not live among men."

How stupid can you get? That was exactly the wrong thing to say (even if true). I shouldn't have to tell you that the king exploded. His face grew bright red, the veins bulged out of his neck, he leaped from his throne, and he screamed that all the wise men in Babylon should immediately be put to death.

As commander of the king's guard, that bloody task fell to me. "Guards!" I shouted. "Gather these worthless traitors and throw them behind bars until his majesty decides the most fitting way to rid the earth of them!"

Then I bowed low before the king and hurriedly left his presence, assuring him that I would speedily carry out his decree. It does not pay to disappoint the king!

Because not all of the royal seers had appeared before the king, it was up to me to round up the rest of these vermin and deliver them into my lord's hands. When I found one of them, a foreigner named Belteshazzar (in his native tongue he is called Daniel), and informed him of his fate, he asked with greatest respect, "Why did the king issue such a harsh decree?" When I explained what had happened, he asked to be taken to see the king. I did not expect this, but immediately I sent him to the palace in custody of several trusted soldiers. Meanwhile, I carried on my urgent work of rounding up the city's seers.

I do not know what this man said to his royal majesty, but my officers told me that soon afterward, he came hustling out of the throne room with a look on his face unlike any they had ever seen. He should have appeared terrified, worried, out of his mind with fear and despair. Instead, they reported he had the look of a man who knew something the rest of us did not.

"He seemed concerned, but not frightened," reported Baladan, one of my most trusted men. "I don't know how else to explain it—and forgive me for my poor words—but he had the look of someone preparing to appear before a king even greater than Nebuchadnezzar."

Early the next morning, this man sought me out and boldly said, "Do not execute the wise men of Babylon. Take me to the king, and I will interpret his dream for him."

I felt so astonished I could hardly speak, but I saw in him what my men had observed the previous day. He did not appear at all frightened, and even his look of concern had vanished. I did not know this man or much about his background, but I felt that, somehow, he really *could* meet the king's dreadful demands!

I suppose that is why I introduced him as I did. The king meets many men, day after day, and often he does not remember who has appeared before his throne, even though their visit took place the day before. Confident that this Belteshazzar had some magic powerful enough to tell the king his dream and give the correct interpretation, I boasted that I was responsible for finding him.

"I have found a man among the exiles from Judah who can tell the king what his dream means," I announced. I admit it; I craved the enormous reward that I knew the king would give for such unexpected success. Who can blame me?

As soon as Belteshazzar opened his mouth, however, I regretted my decision. I expected him to brag how he alone among the wise men of Babylon could meet the king's demand, how he had magic powerful beyond anyone living, how no mystery under heaven could stay hidden from him.

But he said no such thing. When the king asked whether he could describe the dream and tell him what it meant, this man said, without flinching, "No wise man, enchanter, magician, or diviner can explain to the king the mystery he has asked about."

What did he just say? Immediately I saw my life flash before my eyes. Had I not declared that this man could recount the king's dream? Had I not claimed he could accurately interpret it? Had I not announced that *I* was the one who had found him among the exiles of Judah? What would the king do to *me* if this Belteshazzar proved as inept as all the other royal seers?

I felt myself reaching for my sword to strike down this charlatan, when I heard him continue: "But there is a God in heaven who reveals secrets, and he has made known to King Nebuchadnezzar what will happen in days to come."

And then this man—the one *I* found, the one *I* had the sense not to execute—gave the king not only an accurate description of his dream, but an interpretation that left all of us open-mouthed and astonished.

I am a military man, not a prophet or a politician, so I admit I didn't grasp all that Belteshazzar told the king that day. All I remember is a sweeping vision of the future, full of grand and terrible kingdoms that will one day crumble before a final, mighty King who is to reign forever.

King Nebuchadnezzar must have understood more of it than

I, for he did something I have never seen him do—no, not even close to it—in all my long years of service. He actually *fell prostrate* before this foreigner, before this Hebrew prophet, and ordered that incense be presented to him. "Surely," he said to him, "your God is the God of gods and the Lord of kings and a revealer of mysteries, for you were able to reveal this secret!"

Who could have expected such a turn of events? How glad I am that my vast experience enabled me to locate this amazing prophet of God.

❧

And how glad *I* am that "there is a God in heaven who reveals secrets"! (Dan. 2:28). God allowed his holy people to be taken captive to Babylon, the center of world idolatry, in order to show that all of that pagan kingdom's priests and advisors were impotent compared with God. The most powerful sorcerers and magicians in the empire could not recall or interpret Nebuchadnezzar's dream. But Daniel could, because he loved and served the true God, the only one who knows the secrets "of the future." As I have said, to God, prophecy is merely history written in advance.

This single prophecy in Daniel 2 should be enough, by itself, to prove the supernatural character of Bible prophecy and the true nature of the God who reveals it. Some 2,600 years ago, this Hebrew prophet sketched out the broad outlines of world history from his lifetime to the end of time. Jesus called this same period "the times of the Gentiles" (Luke 21:24)—meaning the era when the Gentiles would rule the world. And it was all prophesied ahead of time in a dream that God put into the mind of an ancient despot named Nebuchadnezzar.

What, exactly, did Nebuchadnezzar dream? He had a vision of a large statue: head of gold, chest and arms of silver, belly and thighs of bronze, legs of iron, and feet partly of iron and partly of clay. A rock supernaturally cut out of stone struck the statue on its feet, reducing it to fine dust that the wind blew away. Then the rock grew into a huge mountain that filled the earth.

And what did the dream mean? Daniel explained that the vision concerned the future governments of the world. He described four major world empires that would arise before the end of history. First among them was the Babylonian Empire (the head of gold); then would come the Medo-Persian Empire (the chest and arms of silver); then the Greek Empire under Alexander the Great (the belly and thighs of bronze); and finally, the Roman Empire, brutal and strong as iron (represented by the two legs and feet).

It is an interesting fact of history that, during the reign of Constantine, the Roman Empire divided into two halves: East and West, half ruled from Rome and the other half from Constantinople. In the final days of world history this last empire will reconstitute itself through a ten-part confederacy. Yet it will be "partly strong and partly brittle," for its "people will be a mixture and will not remain united, any more than iron mixes with clay" (Dan. 2:42–43 NIV). Out of that group of ten, one man will arise to become the last secular world leader—but only for a short time. In those days, Daniel says, "the God of heaven will set up a kingdom which shall never be destroyed; and the kingdom shall not be left to other people; it shall break in pieces and consume all these kingdoms, and it shall stand forever" (v. 44).

Daniel gave this prophecy 2,600 years ago. Why didn't the prophet say there would be five world kingdoms? Why not six? Why just four? Ghengis Khan tried and failed to rule the world. Napoleon tried. Kaiser Wilhelm tried. Hitler tried. None succeeded. Why have there been only four world empires since Daniel's day?

Because God said there would be only four.

Today's greatest intellects are encouraging us to move toward a ten-ruler council based out of the UN, representing ten geographical areas of the world. Daniel says that something like this will surely happen, only to be smashed by Jesus Christ when the King of kings and Lord of lords returns to earth to set up his everlasting kingdom. We're on the threshold of seeing Jesus establish his millennial kingdom!

When I started preaching on prophecy fifty years ago, I had to prove to skeptics that the world was heading toward a one-world government. I needed to provide copious notes and relevant quotations. I don't have to bother anymore. I have only to mention that the world has an obsession with a one-world government, and people nod their heads. They know it's coming.

Our world is rapidly going global. Every time I get on an American Airlines flight I hear a flight attendant say, "Welcome to the One World Alliance." The one-world government is no longer a question of *if,* but of *how soon?* With almost three thousand innocent people murdered by evil men on September 11, 2001, it is only natural to ask ourselves, "Is this what the Hebrew prophets and Jesus himself warned would happen someday?" In his Word, the God of prophecy has recorded events of the future—and they could happen in our generation.

With the invention of neutron bombs, biological warfare agents, and the appearance of well-armed terrorists bent on the destruction of the West, humankind is coming to the conclusion that the only solution is to bring everyone together under one ruler. But can you imagine the dangers in such a plan? The world would still have one depraved human being ruling over *everything!* Yet in days to come, the world surely will submit to a Nebuchadnezzar-type despot, whom we call the Antichrist.

Isn't that incredible? We see these things happening in our own time. We're witnessing the dream of Nebuchadnezzar come to fulfillment before our very eyes.

He Wants Us to Get Ready

Amazing as all of this is, none of it should surprise us. Why not? Because God said it would happen, and the prophecies in his Word always come true.

The God who reveals secrets has spoken clearly in his Word regarding the future, and we do not need to run to any other source to find instruction or comfort in these last days. "Knowing this first," wrote the apostle Peter, "that no prophecy of Scripture is of any private interpretation, for prophecy never came by the will of man, but holy men of God spoke as they were moved by the Holy Spirit" (2 Pet. 1:20–21).

Because God is a revealer of secrets who has chosen to outline many of the major events of history before they happen, we should naturally expect Bible prophecy to be unlike any other prophecy. And it is! *Five hundred* prophecies without a miss strongly suggest that we can trust the next five hundred. They will all be fulfilled right on time, just as Scripture indicates.

God's prophecies remain infinitely superior to those in the *Sun* or the *Enquirer* or to the predictions of any merely human psychic, seer, medium, astrologer, fortune-teller, tarot card reader, or any other false prophet.

We should take none of this for granted. Remember, God is not obligated to tell us *anything* about the future. Only his heart of love compels him to give us a big "heads up" concerning events coming down the pike. He wants us to be prepared, to get ready for the paradise to come, and to avoid a severe judgment we needn't suffer. The prophet Amos understood this clearly, and so declared, "Surely the LORD God does nothing, unless He reveals His secret to His servants the prophets" (Amos 3:7).

But *why* should God feel so intent about revealing his plans ahead of time? What is it about his nature that prompts him to describe for us certain things to come? We'll look at that next.

4

Why Prophecy?

Dad, I don't know if I'm ready for this."

Jim Greene paced back and forth, leaving behind a trail of worry in the thick, blue carpet of his parents' living room. Later that day he planned to wedge himself into his overpacked old car and drive halfway across the country to begin college at his father's alma mater. He had picked this school himself—his dad had tried hard not to pressure him—but now, on the cusp of his new adventure, Jim wavered.

"What if I get there and I hate it?" Jim wondered out loud, still pacing. "What if I can't find any decent friends? Californians are a lot different from midwesterners—what if they don't want anything to do with me? And the classes! You said it yourself, Dad, this school is academically demanding. What if I can't cut it?"

Bob Greene let his anxious son voice his concerns, one by one, until the tide of worries seemed to ebb. Then he rose from the couch, put both of his strong hands on Jim's unsteady shoulders, and asked him to sit for a while and just listen. Jim flopped onto the couch.

"Son," Bob began, "I know a little how you feel. I remember feeling like that myself, almost a quarter of a century ago. But I have to tell you, most of your concern will evaporate soon after you arrive and settle in. May I tell you why?"

When Jim nodded wearily, Bob began telling his son (not for the first time!) about what to expect once he set foot on campus. He described the grounds, how the college had won countless awards for both beauty and student safety. He mentioned a few of the student groups on campus that had helped him feel at home so long ago. He raved about the faculty and reminded his son that the size of the school made it possible for its professors to interact more personally with their students than was possible at most other universities. He waxed eloquent about Homecoming, about the annual Halloween and costume bash, about scores of other highlights during the school year.

As Jim listened and saw the enthusiasm his dad so easily expressed for his old school, a familiar gleam began to reappear in his eyes. But he still had some misgivings.

"I appreciate knowing all of that," Jim said, "but Dad, how can you *guarantee* me that I won't flame out? I don't want to come running home with my tail between my legs!"

Bob took one look at his uneasy son, shifting his slight frame from side to side, and couldn't resist giving him a quick hug. He loved his boy, and while he knew he would miss him terribly, he believed Jim had made exactly the right decision. He knew Jim well enough to know that his son wouldn't let a bout of nerves keep him from following through on his carefully considered plan. He just needed some reassurance.

"Jim," he said softly, "I can't guarantee that you won't face some tough times. College isn't high school, and the challenges there are a good deal more . . . well, challenging. And I've cautioned you already about some of the things to avoid. You'll probably hear about all the 'excitement' available in Kurtz Park after dark; but if you're smart, you'll stay away. We've already gone over all of this. The bottom line is this: there's a great future waiting for you at a great school in California, and you wouldn't be the sharp young man I know you to be if you let some very natural anxiety keep you from enjoying it."

With that, Bob once more gave a quick hug to his now-grinning son and added, "Now, let's make sure you're all ready to go. Okay?"

"Okay," Jim replied, and then both men, still filled with conflicting emotions, headed outside to the sagging automobile that would soon carry Jim to a new adventure and into a new life.

A Loving "Heads Up"

Just as Bob wanted to assure his son that he had made a good decision about where to attend college, so God wants to assure his own children about the fabulous future awaiting them. In one sense, that's all prophecy is—a "heads up" about what is to come.

Because our Lord loves us and wants the very best for us, in his Word he has laid out both enticements and warnings regarding the future. Through prophecy, he encourages us to make wise decisions, to choose what is wonderful and nourishing and life giving and to avoid what is horrific and ghastly and self-destructive. Through prophecy, he wants to reduce our anxiety about the future even as he whets our appetite for the staggering surprises to come. This is why the apostle Paul could exult, "Eye has not seen, nor ear heard, nor have entered into the heart of man the things which God has prepared for those who love him" (1 Cor. 2:9).

Still, I expect that many thoughtful readers may have a question. "If God loves us so much," they say, "and biblical prophecy demonstrates his love, then why does so much of prophecy sound so negative? Why does so much of it seem to detail doom and gloom and coming judgment? Why doesn't it tell us more about the positive?"

It's a good question. In reply, I'd argue that, first, the Bible *does* tell us a great deal about the unbelievable blessings waiting for us in days to come—far more than many people think (see chapter 13). What God already has revealed about his plans for blessing and honoring his children ought to send chills running up and down our spines. What a glorious future awaits us!

At the same time, however, it is true that a great deal of Bible prophecy describes coming judgment. The question is, why should this be? I think there's a good answer. In my view, both elements of biblical prophecy—blessing *and* judgment—demonstrate God's unfathomable love for his creatures.

Our loving Lord describes enough of the wonders to come to entice us into making a decision to experience these wonders for ourselves. Yet he does not reveal the best; this he saves for later. But why should this surprise us? Our God, among all his other attributes, is also a master marketer. He knows better than to give away the best parts of his coming extravaganza by revealing them in an ad campaign. He doesn't want you and me to get so enthralled with his advertisements for coming attractions that we miss the real thing. Therefore he reveals only enough of his future delights to make us want to experience them for ourselves.

And what, then, should we make of the Bible's focus on future judgment? Why should the Lord give us so many details of a frightening and horrible time to come? How does *this* show us God's relentless love?

It does so in the same way a loving father or mother shows genuine love for his or her children. All loving parents want the best for their children—and that includes warning them away from danger. Just as Bob warned his son, Jim, against visiting Kurtz Park after dark, so God warns us against landing in a place of terrible judgment. Bob did not tell Jim about Kurtz Park simply to scare him or because he enjoyed seeing his son squirm. He told him about the dangers to keep him safe.

The same is true of God. He tells us frightening details about the judgment to come, not to scare us or to see us squirm, but to keep us far away from that judgment. We do *not* have to suffer the awful judgments that prophecy describes, any more than

Jim had to suffer the injuries awaiting him in Kurtz Park. The only question is, will we heed the Bible's prophetic warnings?

God has given us the awesome power of choice. When he created Adam, he wanted a creature with the ability to choose whether he would obey God. God wanted someone with whom he could share the wonders of eternity, but he did not want to populate eternity with robots. That is why all of us have a free will. God gives us the choice during this life to decide whether we will obey God or do our own thing. God leaves that choice to us.

God gives us so many explicit descriptions of future judgment because he'd rather have us *read* about judgment than *experience* it. Did you know that Jesus Christ spoke of hell about four times as often as he spoke about heaven? He wants to bless us, not judge us, so he moves in all possible ways to encourage us to choose peace and safety rather than wrath and punishment. He gives us a lot of information about coming judgment in order to keep us from falling into it, while he tells us only enough about coming glory to lure us into enjoying it for ourselves.

Prophecy Reveals the Supernatural Hand of God

God uses prophecy not only to warn people away from judgment and to draw them into a joyful life with him, but also to reassure the world that he does in fact exist and that he remains active in the affairs of this troubled planet.

If he wanted to, God could continually demonstrate his presence and power by unveiling one awesome miracle after another—making the ocean stand up in a heap, causing the sun to travel backward in the sky, stationing a brigade of armed angels above the Kremlin—but for his own reasons, he chooses not to do so. No wonder the great prophet Isaiah said of him, "Truly you are a God who hides himself" (45:15 NIV).

Through Bible prophecy, however, God has left an everlasting witness of his reality and activity. Prophecy is the clarion example of the supernatural hand of God in the Bible. If the

Bible really is God's revelation to humankind, then it ought to have some sign of the supernatural. It does—and we call it prophecy.

All prophecy communicates the unfolding plan of God, and it does so in order to show the world that there is a God in heaven who reveals secrets. Listen to Isaiah once more:

Thus says the LORD, the King of Israel, and his Redeemer, the LORD of hosts: "I am the First and I am the Last; besides Me there is no God.

"And who can proclaim as I do? Then let him declare it and set it in order for Me, since I appointed the ancient people. And the things that are coming and shall come, let them show these to them.

"Do not fear, nor be afraid; have I not told you from that time, and declared it? You are My witnesses. Is there a God besides Me? Indeed there is no other Rock; I know not one." (Isa. 44:6–8)

God reveals himself throughout Scripture in passages just like this. The Bible is not really a single book, but a library of sixty-six books, written over fifteen hundred years by at least forty different authors, all of whom had varying levels of education and unique backgrounds. And yet it is a composite whole. That in itself is a miracle.

Not only that, but intelligent college graduates and scholars with advanced degrees continue to discuss this book, even though its most recent section was written more than nineteen hundred years ago. Its most ancient parts were written some thirty-five hundred years ago. There's a timeless magic about the Word of God that reveals the hand of God. And we see his supernatural hand especially in prophecy.

Prophecy Answers the Urgent Questions of Life

Why does God bother with prophecy? Through prophecy, God answers our most urgent questions. No matter where we live or how we grew up, everybody on earth seems to ask some version of five key questions: *Who am I? Where did I come from? Why am I here? Where am I going? How do I get there?*

I find it interesting that we don't learn the answers to these crucial questions in public school. We don't learn them in college or graduate school. But we do learn the answers to all five questions in the prophetic Word of God. Consider briefly what Bible prophecy has to say about these questions.

1. Who Am I?

Scripture tells me that I am a child of God, the special object of God's eternal love. How do I know for sure? Bible prophecy tells me so, and it backs up its promise by supplying example after example of fulfilled predictions.

God says through the prophet that all those who commit their lives to him through faith are "called by My name." He says he created us "for My glory" (Isa. 43:7). He aims to lavish his love on his children for all eternity, as David prophesied so long ago: "For I have said, 'Mercy shall be built up forever; Your faithfulness You shall establish in the very heavens'" (Ps. 89:2).

The gift of God's only Son for our salvation, in fulfillment of prophecy, proves forever that we human beings are important to God and that we have eternal worth.

2. Where Did I Come From?

All of us naturally wonder where we come from. Several states recently have opened up their formerly closed adoption records, and floods of citizens are taking advantage of unsealed court documents to discover their biological parentage. We all want to know our origins, even beyond the identity of our mother and father. Do our lives have meaning? Do we have a rich ancestry? Or are we mere cosmic accidents, the result of some random biological process that happened millions of years ago in some primordial ooze?

The Word of God answers with a loud and unequivocal "in the image of God has God made man" (Gen. 9:6 NIV). In the

Bible we learn that God himself said, "Let Us make man in Our image, according to Our likeness; let them have dominion over the fish of the sea, over the birds of the air, and over the cattle, over all the earth and over every creeping thing that creeps on the earth" (Gen. 1:26). We are men and women created for dignity and honor and even glory! Our Creator loves us, and in mercy he sent his Son to die for our sins, so that we might live with him for eternity. That, in a nutshell, is the Christian message—the greatest message on earth.

3. Why Am I Here?

God makes it very clear that we are the special objects of his love. A famous verse that continues to pop up at ball games around the country reminds us, "For God so loved the world that He gave his only begotten Son, that whoever believes in Him should not perish but have everlasting life" (John 3:16). We are here to be loved and to love in return.

God made this purpose so central to his plans that he announced, long before it happened, that he would send his Son to pave the way for our journey to heaven. He loves us so much that he gave the most precious thing he had. He didn't send some magnificent, glorified angel to save us; he sent his only begotten Son.

A dear friend of mine, Art Peters, served as my associate pastor for many years. Before that, he and I were college roommates. I never would have graduated were it not for Art. He is one person for whom I would give my life. I wouldn't volunteer for the job, but I'd do it if necessary.

God gave Bev and me two boys and two girls. One day I was driving to work, thinking of my appreciation and affection for Art, and I thought, *I would give my life for this man. But I would not give the lives of either of my two sons or daughters! My life is expendable, but not the lives of my children.*

Yet God looked at all of us ingrates, and still loved us so much that he gave his only Son for us. He hinted at this amazing love centuries before Christ came when he told his people:

"Since you were precious in My sight, you have been honored, and I have loved you; therefore I will give men for you, and people for your life" (Isa. 43:4). We are on this planet to be loved by God and to share his love with others.

4. *Where Am I Going?*

When the apostle Paul stood trial before the Roman governor Felix because of his faith in Christ, he said to this powerful man:

> But this I confess to you, that according to the Way which they call a sect, so I worship the God of my fathers, believing all things which are written in the Law and in the Prophets.
>
> I have hope in God, which they themselves also accept, that there will be a resurrection of the dead, both of the just and the unjust.
>
> This being so, I myself always strive to have a conscience without offense toward God and men. (Acts 24:14–16)

Because Paul believed everything the prophets had written, he looked forward with expectation and confidence to the resurrection. He believed that because his Lord had risen from the dead, so would he one day rise from the dead. His words only restated what Jesus had told his disciples at more length a few years earlier.

Jesus declared in Matthew 25 that when the day arrives for him to return to earth "in His glory," he will gather all the nations before him and will separate the people one from another, "as a shepherd divides his sheep from the goats" (vv. 31–32). Those who have submitted their lives to him he will place on his right, the honored place of his "sheep," while those who have rejected him he will treat as "goats" and place at his left. "And these [the goats] will go away into everlasting punishment," he said, "but the righteous [the sheep] into eternal life" (v. 46). Make no mistake, Jesus says, you *can* know where you are going. You simply have to make sure you're a "sheep" and not a "goat."

So how does one become a "sheep" and not a "goat"? How

can one become "righteous"? That inquiry leads right to the last major question.

5. How Do I Get There?

"For Christ also suffered once for sins, the just for the unjust, that He might bring us to God," wrote the apostle Peter (1 Pet. 3:18). That means that, while in our natural state we remain un-righteous—"goats," in Jesus' terminology—through faith in the risen Christ, we become righteous and the sheep of his pasture.

All of us begin life as "goats," insisted Paul: "For we ourselves were also once foolish, disobedient, deceived, serving various lusts and pleasures, living in malice and envy, hateful and hating one another." That's what a goat looks like, and it isn't pretty. Yet the story doesn't have to stay that way. "But when the kindness and the love of God our Savior toward man appeared," Paul continued, "not by works of righteousness which we have done, but according to His mercy He saved us, through the washing of regeneration and renewing of the Holy Spirit, whom He poured out on us abundantly through Jesus Christ our Savior, that hav-ing been justified by His grace we should become heirs accord-ing to the hope of eternal life" (Titus 3:3–7).

Does the hope of eternal life burn within *you*? It can! As Paul said, "there is laid up for me the crown of righteousness, which the Lord, the righteous Judge, will give to me on that Day, and not to me only but also to all who have loved his appearing" (2 Tim. 4:8).

In a marvelous way, prophecy answers the five major ques-tions of life.

Prophecy Demonstrates God's Love

Prophecy uniquely demonstrates to us the boundless love of God. It not only sketches out the marvelous era that's coming, but also gives us a peek into what we might expect even before then. Bible prophecy supplies such sneak peaks to at least three different groups.

1. To Godly Believers:
To Warn About Rough Waters Ahead

Bible prophecy warns believers that they may well have to endure a bumpy ride on earth before they reach their final destination in heaven. It does so in order to keep them from feeling surprised or angry at God when life turns suddenly sour.

Jesus himself told his followers:

> But beware of men, for they will deliver you up to councils and scourge you in their synagogues. You will be brought before governors and kings for My sake, as a testimony to them and to the Gentiles . . . Now brother will deliver up brother to death, and a father his child; and children will rise up against parents and cause them to be put to death. And you will be hated by all for My name's sake. But he who endures to the end will be saved. (Matt. 10:17–18, 21–22)

"Yes, and all who desire to live godly in Christ Jesus will suffer persecution," added the apostle Paul. "But evil men and impostors will grow worse and worse, deceiving and being deceived" (2 Tim. 3:12–13; similar warnings can be found in Daniel 7:25; Matt. 24:24; John 21:17–19; Acts 9:15–16, 14:21–22, 20:29–31; 1 Thess. 3:1–4; 2 Tim. 3:1–5; and 1 Peter 4:12–19). God wants his dearly loved children to know about the treacherous rapids ahead, so that they can continue to plunge forward in faith regardless of their circumstances. So Jesus tells us, "These things I have spoken to you, that in Me you may have peace. In the world you will have tribulation; but be of good cheer, I have overcome the world" (John 16:33).

2. To Wayward Believers:
To Encourage Them to Get Back on the Path to Life

God loves everyone, the wayward as well as those who please him by their godly choices and lifestyles. Nevertheless, the Lord does not take disobedience lightly; he will never simply turn his back on sin. He desires that all of us turn to him in faith and receive the benefits reserved for the obedient alone.

God delivers some special words of prophecy to those who know the right way, but who have somehow wandered away from it. Jesus says to the drifting members of the church at ancient Ephesus, "Remember therefore from where you have fallen; repent and do the first works, or else I will come to you quickly and remove your lampstand from its place—unless you repent" (Rev. 2:5). To the members of the church at Thyatira, he speaks even more strongly by declaring that he intends to cast them "into a sickbed" and that he "will kill her children with death, and all the churches shall know that I am He who searches the minds and hearts. And I will give to each one of you according to your works" (Rev. 2:22–23).

It is no small thing to know the Lord yet turn away from him in conscious rebellion! God's Word offers many similar prophetic warnings to believers who fail to live out their faith (see Deut. 30:1–6; Rom. 14:9–13; 1 Cor. 4:5, 6:1–15, 10:1–11; Eph. 5:3–7; Heb. 10:26–31, 13:4; 1 Pet. 4:1–7).

Still, God gives these warnings, not because he can't wait to lower the boom, but because he wants his people to rediscover the life and joy and fulfillment available only in him. As the prophet Hosea counseled his own wandering people:

> Come, and let us return to the LORD; for He has torn, but He will heal us; He has stricken, but He will bind us up.
>
> After two days He will revive us; on the third day He will raise us up, that we may live in His sight. (Hos. 6:1–2)

3. To Seekers:
To Help Them Find the Source of Life

It may be that you consider yourself neither a growing believer in Christ nor a Christian who has turned aside to do his or her own thing. Perhaps you are a "seeker," someone who is honestly trying to discover spiritual reality and a relationship with the God who made you. Talk show host Larry King has described himself on national television as an agnostic, but he is also a seeker. If that description fits you, I have good news: God has some prophetic words just for you.

God originally delivered part of his message to you through the apostle Paul, who one day found himself addressing a crowd of ancient seekers in Athens, the philosophical capital of the ancient world. Paul quoted some of their own Greek poets to prove that they too were God's offspring, and proclaimed:

> Therefore, since we are the offspring of God, we ought not to think that the Divine Nature is like gold or silver or stone, something shaped by art and man's devising.
>
> Truly, these times of ignorance God overlooked, but now commands all men everywhere to repent, because He has appointed a day on which He will judge the world in righteousness by the Man whom He has ordained. He has given assurance of this to all by raising Him from the dead. (Acts 17:29–31)

Paul had just preached the resurrection of Jesus Christ, telling his listeners that God was even then working within history "so that they should seek the Lord, in the hope that they might grope for Him and find Him, though He is not far from each one of us" (v. 27).

Then, as now, God wants his prophetic Word to touch you, to bring you to the place where you will see his supernatural hand and accept his offer of life through his Son, Jesus Christ. Jesus himself spoke prophetically of this when he said, "'Now is the judgment of this world; now the ruler of this world will be cast out. And I, if I am lifted up from the earth, will draw all peoples to Myself.' This He said, signifying by what death He would die" (John 12:31–33).

Jesus died alone on a Roman cross to make it possible for you to live with him in a heavenly city. Even now he continues to speak words of prophecy to you through the Bible, in order to draw you into his amazing love (see 2 Pet. 3:3–9).

How powerfully does Bible prophecy declare the astonishing mercy and grace of God!

A Welcome "Heads Up"

Two weeks after he arrived at college, Jim finally found time to sit down and write a note to his parents. He knew that he should have sent *some* word home before this, but, well, the time had just flown by.

The truth was, he was having too good of a time to write any letters!

He wrote:

Dear Mom and Dad,

I'm sorry I haven't written before now. No excuses, really. But the good news is, *you were right!* Dad, THANK YOU so *much* for giving me a "heads up" on what to expect here. The day after I arrived, I got in touch with a representative from one of the groups you recommended, and already I've made a lot of *great* friends through it. Amazing! And I know you said the campus was beautiful, but I couldn't have imagined how gorgeous until I actually got here. The brochures don't come close! And you'll be interested to know that I've already met with one of my professors (physics—*arghh*!). I thought he'd dismiss me as some annoying little freshman, but he actually invited me into his office for a "chat." And he made me believe I can really *do* this!

Dad, thanks again for reassuring me about my future here. You were *so* right! (And by the way, just yesterday we heard that somebody from the college was attacked in Kurtz Park around midnight. It turned out it was the same guy who invited me last week to join him for a little late-night "fun." Boy, am I glad you warned me about *that!* I might have actually been interested in going!)

I love you both! And Mom, don't worry about whether I'll have enough clean clothes. My roommate gave me a big duffel bag, and I'm stuffing my dirty clothes in there until I come home for Christmas!

Love, Jim

P.S. I'm kidding about the duffel bag. But I really could use some extra $$$ for an expanded wardrobe. California *rocks!*

(Just as the "prophecy" of Jim's dad came true regarding a good life at college, so too will the fulfillment of God's prophecies regarding the wonderful future he has in store for all of us. Be sure of this: None of us will regret accepting God's offer of salvation when we actually get to heaven and begin to experience the fabulous plan he has for our eternity. Particularly when we consider the alternative!)

5

Just as He Said He Would

Have you ever been called an unflattering name? I have. It's happened many times, and often in print. Consider one recent example.

A few weeks ago, in a monthly magazine dedicated to news about the Bible, a British New Testament scholar essentially called me a "pseudo-theologian" for championing the idea that, whenever possible, Bible prophecy should be interpreted literally. He believes that texts such as 1 Thessalonians 4:16–17—a passage that describes what is usually called the "Rapture" of the church (see chapter 11)—ought to be interpreted metaphorically or symbolically, not literally.

This man calls my interpretation of this passage "distorted" and considers the popularity of my fiction series, *Left Behind*, "puzzling, even bizarre." He suggests that my "pseudo-theological version of *Home Alone* has reportedly frightened many children into some kind of (distorted) faith" and instructs his readers that "Paul's mixed metaphors of trumps blowing and the living being snatched into heaven to meet the Lord are not to be understood as literal truth, as the *Left Behind* series suggests, but as a vivid and biblically allusive description of the great transformation of the present world."[1]

It should not surprise anyone, then, that even as this man scorns the idea of a "literal 'rapture' in which believers will be snatched up to heaven," he feels compelled to give his own imaginative version of what Paul's words ought to mean for us today. While the apostle explicitly says that he wrote these words to comfort bereaved Christians, this scholar hopes that we will "reuse" Paul's potent images in order to "subvert the political imagery of the dominant and dehumanizing empires of our world."[2]

Apparently, we needn't feel too concerned about what Paul actually wrote or about how the apostle himself intended his words to be used and understood. Why not? Because, declares the scholar, "Understanding what will happen requires a far more sophisticated cosmology than the one in which 'heaven' is somewhere up there in our universe, rather than in a different dimension, a different space-time, altogether."[3]

In other words, this academician wants to jettison what he considers an ancient "mythology" for a more contemporary one. After all, how could the ancients possibly be expected to comprehend such profound mysteries? They didn't have today's scholars to guide them!

As you might imagine, I firmly reject any such modern conceit. I do not believe that we need to "reuse" the images and words of Bible prophecy to properly understand and benefit from them. Of course, when biblical writers intentionally use metaphors and symbols, we must try to understand what they meant to convey through these images. But when they speak plainly—when they employ nonpoetic language in a straightforward way—what right have we to pronounce their words "metaphorical" or their ideas merely "symbolic"? How can we usurp the authority to give their words whatever interpretation suits us? Certainly, we may disbelieve their message if we so choose. But we have no justification to claim that they meant "Z" when their own words declare they meant "A."

He Means What He Says

Before we go any further, let me set your mind at ease. This chapter is not going to be a long and boring technical discussion of hermeneutics, the science of biblical interpretation. Excellent works exist on that important topic, and interested readers would greatly profit from reading one or more of them.[4]

Instead, I intend to *show* why we ought to interpret prophecy literally, whenever the passage in question suggests such an approach. And I want to accomplish my goal by showing how several prophecies of the past were actually fulfilled in their own day. If we see that God most often fulfilled past prophecies in a literal way, shouldn't that suggest how we ought to interpret prophecies that pertain to the future?

I don't believe that God gave us prophecy to keep us confused about what lies ahead. Modern "prophets" may speak in riddles, mumbling one vague sentence after another, but the God of prophecy speaks in order to be understood, believed, and obeyed. We can have confidence that he means what he says, for always in the past his prophecies have come to fulfillment *exactly as he foretold they would.*

We would do well to remember the words of Jeremiah the prophet, who explained to his erring people why God had brought the Babylonians against them: "And now the LORD has brought it about; he has done just as he said he would" (Jer. 40:3 NIV).

He always does.

The Cost of Rebuilding Jericho

Let's start with a simple example. Way back in the days of the conquest of Canaan, the Lord gave a straightforward prophecy about a certain pagan city. Following the plan of God, Joshua and his countrymen attacked and destroyed Jericho, situated about seventeen miles northeast of present-day Jerusalem. Note what happened next:

> Then Joshua charged them at that time, saying, "Cursed be the man before the LORD who rises up and builds this city Jericho; he shall lay its foundation with his firstborn, and with his youngest he shall set up its gates." (Josh. 6:26)

Many years went by while this prophecy lay dormant. But then in the ninth century B.C., some four centuries after Joshua, the Bible says: "In Ahab's time, Hiel of Bethel rebuilt Jericho. He laid its foundations at the cost of his firstborn son Abiram, and he set up its gates at the cost of his youngest son Segub, in accordance with the word of the LORD spoken by Joshua son of Nun" (1 Kings 16:34 NIV).

I admit that one prophecy does not a pattern make, but this is an important test case. How was this prophecy fulfilled? Without question, it came to pass literally, just as the words were given, exactly as Joshua uttered the curse four hundred years before. We do not need to reinterpret the general's words metaphorically or symbolically. We do not need to find some deeper meaning in the text. The Lord fulfilled this prophecy precisely as Joshua had predicted.

"And now the LORD has brought it about; he has done just as he said he would."

David's House and the Sword

Beyond all doubt, one of the greatest heroes of the Bible is King David, who learned to trust God while shepherding his father's flocks. Even though he was the youngest in his family, God chose him to become king and "shepherd My people Israel" (2 Sam. 5:2). To this day, we look to David's psalms for comfort, instruction, and encouragement.

Yet like all of us, David had his faults. Hero or not, he could act very foolishly. His most infamous sin concerns his adultery with a woman named Bathsheba. David got her pregnant, then arranged for her husband to die in battle so he could have her for himself.

Despite God's love for David, the Lord could not look with favor on what his disobedient servant had done. With characteristic bluntness, the Bible says simply, "But the thing that David had done displeased the LORD" (2 Sam. 11:27).

In a memorable confrontation with Nathan, a faithful prophet of God, the Lord exposed David's sin and pronounced a stinging judgment on him. David would never forget the frightful words spoken against his terrible sin:

> Thus says the LORD, the God of Israel: I anointed you king over Israel, and I delivered you from the hand of Saul.
>
> I gave you your master's house and your master's wives into your keeping, and gave you the house of Israel and Judah. And if that had been too little, I also would have given you much more!
>
> Why have you despised the commandment of the LORD, to do evil in His sight? You have killed Uriah the Hittite with the sword; you have taken his wife to be your wife, and have killed him with the sword of the people of Ammon.
>
> Now therefore, the sword shall never depart from your house, because you have despised Me, and have taken the wife of Uriah the Hittite to be your wife. (2 Sam. 12:7–10)

The sword shall never depart from your house. Even in his own day, David saw this prophecy kick literally into action. His own son, Absalom, began an armed rebellion against his father, forcing David to flee for his life. Eventually, Absalom died at the hands of David's own soldiers.

The subsequent history of the royal line reads like an account written in blood. David's son and heir, Solomon, executed with the sword many of his enemies, including his own brother, Adonijah (1 Kings 2:22–25). Solomon's son, Rehoboam, suffered through continual warfare throughout his reign (1 Kings 14:30). Assassins murdered more than one of David's descendants (2 Kings 12:19–21, 14:19–20). At one point, an evil queen wiped out nearly the entire Davidic line, leaving only one survivor (2 Kings 11:1–3). And the final king of Judah, Zedekiah, was forced to watch as the invading Babylonians "killed the sons of Zedekiah before his eyes" (2 Kings 25:7).

And the fulfillment of the prophecy didn't stop there. Why would it? God had told David, "The sword shall *never* depart from your house." True to his word, the Lord did not sheath the sword . . . even when it came to his own Son, Jesus Christ, "the son of David." Some authorities estimate that King Herod killed as many as two thousand baby boys from Bethlehem in his mad attempt to eliminate the newborn "King of the Jews" (Matt. 2:13–18). And a little more than three decades later, angry men wielding swords and clubs arrested Jesus in the Garden of Gethsemane, heavily armed Roman soldiers nailed him to a cross, and there our Lord died—in fulfillment of prophecy.

Today, so far as we know, no living descendants remain of the line of David. When Jesus cried out, "It is finished" (John 19:30), he not only announced that he had paid the penalty for human sin, but also that the prophecy leveled against David's house had found its final fulfillment in him. And so once again, the Lord kept his word.

"And now the LORD has brought it about; he has done just as he said he would."

The Demise of Ahab and Jezebel

In contrast to David, the Bible fingers Ahab as one of the worst kings of Israel. This perverse man "did evil in the sight of the LORD, more than all who were before him," the Bible says, and "did more to provoke the LORD God of Israel to anger than all the kings of Israel who were before him" (1 Kings 16:30, 33).

Yet if it were possible, Ahab married someone even more depraved than he. The name of his wicked wife, Jezebel, has gone down in history as a synonym for everything wayward and corrupt.

In his mercy and grace, God allowed even these two loathsome characters to continue to live and rule—until they tried his patience once too often. When Ahab sulked that a man named Naboth refused to sell him a vineyard, Jezebel conspired to kill the man so that her husband could claim the dead owner's property. By hatching this scheme, the malevolent couple reached the point of no return and God quickly pronounced judgment on both through the mouth of the prophet Elijah. To Ahab, Elijah said, "In the place where dogs licked the blood of Naboth, dogs shall lick your blood, even yours." And of Jezebel he declared, "The dogs shall eat Jezebel by the wall of Jezreel" (1 Kings 21:19, 23).

Three years later, another prophet, Micaiah, proclaimed that Ahab's time for judgment had come; the king would die in battle. Trying to avoid detection by his foes, Ahab disguised himself before riding out to the front lines. But Scripture says, "Now a certain man drew a bow at random, and struck the king of Israel between the joints of his armor." Within hours Ahab was dead. His men brought his corpse back to Samaria and buried it there, then washed his bloody chariot at a pool—"and the dogs licked up his blood while the harlots bathed, according to the word of the LORD which He had spoken" (1 Kings 22:34, 38).

So much for Ahab. What about Jezebel? She continued to live for several years, never repenting of her many sins. Finally the Lord appointed a man named Jehu to wipe out Ahab's family and to rule in his stead. When Jezebel heard that Jehu had come to Jezreel,

> she put paint on her eyes and adorned her head, and looked through a window.
>
> Then, as Jehu entered at the gate, she said, "Is it peace, Zimri, murderer of your master?"
>
> And he looked up at the window, and said, "Who is on my side? Who?" So two or three eunuchs looked out at him.
>
> Then he said, "Throw her down." So they threw her down, and some of her blood spattered on the wall and on the horses; and he trampled her underfoot. (2 Kings 9:30–33)

Jehu then went on his way to celebrate his bloody achievements. Some time later, he gave the order to retrieve Jezebel's body and give it a proper burial, since she had been born into royalty. But when his men looked for her corpse, "they found no more of her than the skull, and the feet and the plams of her hands." They returned to Jehu to report their findings, and he replied, "This is the word of the LORD, which He spoke by His servant Elijah the Tishbite, saying, 'On the plot of ground at Jezreel dogs shall eat the flesh of Jezebel'" (2 Kings 9:35–36).

Let's recap. Elijah had said that dogs would lick up Ahab's blood at the spot where Naboth had died—and that is exactly what happened. Elijah had said that dogs would eat Jezebel's flesh in Jezreel—and that is exactly what happened.

Notice, there are no metaphorical meanings here. No symbolic interpretations. Just the literal fulfillment of the prophet's plainly spoken words.

"And now the LORD has brought it about; he has done just as he said he would."

The Varying Fortunes of Tyre and Sidon

Ezekiel's predictions concerning the separate destinies of Tyre and Sidon, two sister cities of ancient Phoenicia, have to rank among the most remarkable of all fulfilled Bible prophecies.

The key prophecy about Tyre can be found in Ezekiel 26:3–14, while a corresponding prophecy about Sidon appears in Ezekiel 28:20–23. The two passages predict very different futures for these cities.

Ezekiel lived and prophesied in the sixth century B.C. At that time in history, Tyre had achieved a position of stunning wealth and power. While Sidon appears to be the older city, Tyre's merchant fleets had brought her vast riches, allowing her to accumulate luxury items coveted throughout the region.

While her proud ships freely sailed the Mediterranean in search of even greater affluence, the prophet Ezekiel looked down the corridors of time and revealed that Tyre's favored position would not last forever. He made at least six startling prophecies, all of which were fulfilled literally. Consider each of them:

1. Nebuchadnezzar of Babylon Would Destroy the Mainland City of Tyre (26:8).

After besieging the city for thirteen years, Nebuchadnezzar broke down its gates . . . and found almost no one there. He discovered the former inhabitants had fled to an island about half a mile off the coast, where they had built another fortified city. While the Babylonians destroyed mainland Tyre in 573 B.C., the island fortress remained a significant power for hundreds of years.

2. Tyre Would Be Scraped Bare by Her Enemies, to Flat Bedrock (26:4).

After Alexander the Great defeated the Persians in 333 B.C., he marched toward Egypt and demanded that the Phoenician cities receive him and deny their ports to the Persians. The island fortress of Tyre refused, so Alexander took the rubble of mainland Tyre and used it to build a causeway to the island. He literally scraped the ancient site bare to build his road into the sea. His remarkable engineering feat still remains today.

3. Conquerors Would Throw the City's Stones, Timber, and Rubble into the Sea (26:12).

Alexander could find no nearer material to build his causeway than the ruins of the original city of Tyre, so his armies threw the ancient city's stones, timber, and rubble into the water. The Tyrians resisted him energetically, but eventually Alexander battered down their fortress walls and sacked the island city. Even so, in subsequent years the city repeatedly rebuilt itself.

4. Many Nations Would Attack Tyre (26:3).

Through the centuries after the attacks by Babylon and Greece, many other nations fought against Tyre. Invading

Greeks under Antigonus attacked the city; the Romans occupied it; the Crusaders took it; and Islamic forces wiped it off the map. Until its final demise, it never wanted for invaders.

5. Tyre Would Never Be Rebuilt (26:14).

The long history of Tyre as a major city finally came to an end in A.D. 1291, when Islamic troops obliterated it and either killed its people or sold them into slavery. Never again did a metropolis emerge from its ruins, even though a freshwater spring with a flow estimated at ten million gallons a day continues to pour forth at the mainland site of ancient Tyre.[5] This would appear to be an excellent spot for a modern city—but God said it would never rise again, and it hasn't.

6. Fishermen would spread their nets over the site (26:5).

Today, small fishing boats anchor near the ancient site of Tyre. A small fishing village lies nearby, and its residents use the place to dry their nets in the sun—just as God had said.

The specific nature of Ezekiel's prophecies against Tyre appear even more startling when contrasted with his predictions regarding Sidon, just twenty-five miles to the north. Through Ezekiel, God declared:

> Behold, I am against you, O Sidon; I will be glorified in your midst; and they shall know that I am the LORD, when I execute judgments in her and am hallowed in her.
>
> For I will send pestilence upon her, and blood in her streets; the wounded shall be judged in her midst by the sword against her on every side; then they shall know that I am the LORD. (Ezek. 28:22–23)

While this surely does not amount to a happy prediction, neither does it call for the city's destruction, as in the case of Tyre. The prophecy foretells terrible times and predicts that many will die violently in Sidon, but never says the city would be scraped bare like a rock or have its ruins tossed into the sea.

In fact, the city has been plundered and its citizens butchered time after time, but even today Sidon remains the third largest city in Lebanon, after Beirut and Tripoli. A website dedicated to the modern city calls it "a busy commercial center with the pleasant, conservative atmosphere of a small town. Since Persian times this was known as the city of gardens, and even today it is surrounded by citrus and banana plantations."[6]

That's a far cry from the situation in 351 B.C., when forty thousand Sidonians chose to lock their gates and set fire to their city rather than surrender to the forces of Artaxerxes III. In subsequent years, the city fell to the Romans, to the Byzantine empire, to the Crusaders, to the Franks, and finally to the Mamlukes. Because of its location in southern Lebanon, the city has been shelled in modern times by Israeli forces.

True to Ezekiel's prediction, blood has flowed in the streets of Sidon, with the sword on every side. Yet this ancient city continues to exist. Just as the prophet had predicted.

"And now the LORD has brought it about; he has done just as he said he would."

Israel a Nation Again

The eyes of the world once more have fastened on Israel, a tiny Jewish nation in the Middle East that didn't even exist before the last century. Why should such a small country command such global attention? Doesn't the world offer more alluring places than Palestine?

Perhaps. But Israel's global importance is hardly accidental. It has landed at the very center of the world stage, precisely as God said it would, so long ago.

In scores of places throughout the Old Testament, the Lord announced that he would one day regather his chosen people back to their ancient homeland, and there bless them beyond anything they had ever known (see Ezek. 36–37; Jer. 23:3, 24:6, 32:36–41, 33:14–26; Zech. 8:8). Yet he also warned them that before the delightful times would roll, a horrific period would rock them to the very limit (see chapter 10).

These texts all say that in the last days, Israel would be

brought back into the Holy Land and Jerusalem would once more rise to become a city of worldwide importance and controversy. "I am going to make Jerusalem a cup that sends all the surrounding peoples reeling," God declared in Zechariah 12:2 (NIV).

Today we probably do not read these prophecies with the respect they deserve, since Israel became a state more than half a century ago. But do we remember how long the Jewish people had lacked a homeland in Palestine?

In ancient times, the Jews had caused their Roman conquerors such fits for so long, that in A.D. 135, after the Bar Kokhba uprising, the emperor Hadrian banned all Jews from Jerusalem and declared that any Jew found left alive in the city could be killed. He renamed Jerusalem *Aeolia Capitolina* and prohibited circumcision and public instruction in the Torah. As a result, most Jews fled their homeland and scattered throughout the world. And that remained the situation for seventeen hundred years.

History shows us that *no* nation has ever come together again after losing its homeland for more than three centuries. Beyond that, no national group has ever been able to sustain its ethnic distinctiveness after three hundred years of forced exile. Have you ever met a Babylonian? A Hittite? An Assyrian or a Phoenician or a Trojan (and I don't mean someone from USC)? Of course not. As distinct people groups, they all sank beneath the sands of time.

But what about the Jews? How is it that, for seventeen hundred years after the Israelites lost their homeland, they still exist as a people? What makes the Jews so different from every other ethnic group? Only one answer suffices: God has committed himself to fulfilling every promise he gave to Abraham and Moses and David and Jesus.

So it was that in 1948, Israel again became a nation. Today, about five million Jewish men and women have made their home in the Holy Land, with more arriving every year.[7] And it's all happening because God said that in the end times, he was going to bring his people back to the land.

Regardless of what you think of the politics involved; regardless of what you think of the sociological forces involved; regardless of what you think of the strength of the human spirit—the fact is that the modern nation of Israel has been brought back from the land of nothingness. *No* other people has *ever* experienced anything like it. In fact, for centuries, many readers of Bible prophecy thought they had to read passages about the Jews returning to their homeland as symbolic, as metaphors for something else. How could such a thing *literally* come true, they reasoned?

Well, the Lord is now at work bringing his ancient people back to their ancestral homeland. Just as he said he would.

"And now the LORD has brought it about; he has done just as he said he would."

The Danger of Nonliteral Interpretation

When we don't understand how some Bible predictions could possibly come true, when our minds refuse to accept that some prophesied event could really take place as described, we tend to look for a way out. We jettison the literal approach and seek a more "natural," a more "human," a more "rational" interpretation.

Of course, this is nothing new. Abraham, the man the Bible holds up as a prime example of faith, along with his wife, Sarah, did the same thing. And the world has suffered for their interpretive error ever since.

Perhaps you remember the story. God promised Abraham that he would not die childless, but that in his old age he would father a son. Abraham received the promise for the first time when he was already seventy-five years old. He accepted the news with gladness, and then waited.

And waited.

And waited some more.

The years dragged by, and still no son had arrived. Finally, after a decade of continued barrenness, Sarah suggested to her husband that, just perhaps, they had misunderstood God's promise. Maybe it was not meant to be taken literally. After all, custom allowed for a maidservant to bear a child for a childless wife. Perhaps God intended to fulfill his promise through Hagar, Sarah's Egyptian slave girl. That certainly made more sense, humanly speaking.

So it was that Abraham listened to his wife and impregnated Hagar. Nine months later, she gave birth to a son, whom she named Ishmael. An angel prophesied that Hagar's son would be a:

> wild donkey of a man;
>   his hand will be against everyone
> and everyone's hand against him,
>   and he will live in hostility
> toward all his brothers.
> (Gen. 16:12 NIV)

Abraham knew this, yet longed for this son to become the fulfillment of God's promise. But the Lord refused. "No, Sarah your wife shall bear you a son, and you shall call his name Isaac; I will establish My covenant with him for an everlasting covenant, and with his descendants after him" (Gen. 17:19). The following year—true to God's word and a full quarter century after God had first spoken the promise—Isaac was indeed born to Abraham and Sarah.

A time for celebration! And yet, so were planted the roots of today's Middle East turmoil. Why? The Jews trace their ancestry back to Isaac, while the Arabs count Ishmael as their father. And the hostility predicted so long ago continues to boil.

The deadliest terrorist attack in modern history occurred on September 11, 2001, when nineteen "sons of Ishmael" snuffed out the lives of almost three thousand guiltless victims. Their associates have declared war on the West and are using the most advanced means possible to try to force the world to submit to their hate. Even now, striving to equip themselves with modern weapons of mass destruction, these religious fanatics think they please God by killing all who stand in their path of world conquest. Their evil touches even the most innocent among us.

I felt deeply moved when I saw the troubled eyes of a little three-year-old girl on the front page of *USA Today*, looking longingly for the answer to her most important question: "Where's Mommie?" I read that she, like one thousand other children, had lost at least one parent in the attacks. In her case, it was her *only* parent. I kept that picture with me for a week and prayed for that little tyke each day, asking God to take care of her in a special way. I know what it is like to have lost a parent while still a child—but to have lost one's *only* parent—I can only imagine the crushing feelings of loss.

I wonder—what might have happened had Abraham and Sarah taken God at his word? How might things be different today had they decided against interpreting the Lord's prophecy in any way other than literally?

At the least, their experience ought to teach us to proceed very, very slowly before we ever decide that, in order to avoid a "ridiculous" scenario, we must interpret Bible prophecy symbolically or metaphorically.

A hundred-year-old man and a ninety-year-old woman, having a baby together? Sounds pretty ridiculous to me. Yet it's just what God had in mind, all along.

We're Living in Prophetic Times

Why do I insist on a literal fulfillment of prophecy? Because about five hundred prophecies already have been fulfilled in just that way. It is therefore logical to assume that the remaining prophecies also will be fulfilled literally.

Make no mistake, we are living in prophetic times. Our generation has more reason to believe that Jesus could come in our lifetime than did any generation before us.[8] I'm not saying he *will* return in the next few years, but I am convinced we have more reason to believe that he could come today than did any other generation in history. The signs of the times are everywhere. Just look around—they're right in front of you.

Of course, no one knows the day or the hour of Christ's return (Matt. 24:36)—but this sure looks as if it may be the season. For one thing, it just so happens that travel and information have exploded, just as Daniel predicted for the end of the age (Dan. 12:4).

Isn't it interesting that Daniel, some 2,600 years ago, made that prediction? Why would he select travel and knowledge? Human speed of travel remained basically constant for millennia. Humankind could travel no faster than horseback until about 120 years ago. Only with the advent of railroads did speed of travel begin to escalate.

Today, astronauts can travel in modern spacecraft at speeds of more than 24,000 miles per hour. All of these great velocities are made possible by breathtaking leaps in knowledge. Without such an expanding storehouse of information, we never could have so vastly accelerated our speed of travel.

And yet here is Daniel, some 2,600 years ago, prophesying that knowledge and travel would enormously increase as history wound to a close. What he predicted so long ago is now coming true—literally.

God intends that his prophecies give us hope, direction, and confidence for today. He tells us of the future so that we might trust him at this very moment. When we refuse to take him at his Word—when instead we substitute our own, more "sophisticated" ramblings—we are the ones who lose.

The Excitement Builds

I never grow tired of reading Paul's prophetic writings. I see in them the apostle's boundless enthusiasm for what God is going to do in and with this old world. As you read his letters, you can't help but detect an excitement, a trembling expectation, an electric anticipation that God is about to thrill his creation with a divine show never before seen by men or angels. If Paul were alive on earth today, I get the feeling that he wouldn't need a megaphone to declare his living hope in the soon return of Christ. He'd shout himself hoarse declaring the word!

Now, compare Paul to the scholar we met at the beginning of this chapter, the man who feels compelled to interpret Paul metaphorically, to "reuse" his words in a fashion more in keeping with modern sensibilities. "I don't deny," the scholar admits, "that I believe some future event will result in the personal presence of Jesus within God's new creation."[9] Well, at least that's something.

But I wonder—where is the giddy excitement that Paul so obviously felt? Where is the breathless anticipation? Where is the passionate spirit that drove the apostle to the four corners of the known world, proclaiming everywhere the glorious return of the King of kings and Lord of lords?

If it's there, I can't spot it.

As for me, I'll stick with my literal interpretation of Bible prophecy. I'd rather face God one day and hear him ask, "Tim, why didn't you seek a 'deeper meaning,' a more sophisticated understanding of the words in my Book?" than to hear him sadly wonder, "Tim, why didn't you simply believe what I told you?"

No. Every new morning that God gives me, I grow more thrilled about what the Lord has in store for his beloved children. And there's no reason why you can't share that same excitement.

Today, as in the past, he does just what he says he will!

6

No Pleasure in Wrath

A little book written by a longtime friend of mine has spent several months tearing up the nation's best-seller lists. Its phenomenal success has caused many in the media and publishing worlds to scratch their heads in wonder over an obscure Old Testament character named Jabez.

The Prayer of Jabez, by Bruce Wilkinson, has introduced millions of readers to an unfamiliar (but very ancient) way of praying that reacquaints us with a God who wants to bless us more than we want to bless ourselves. In his slim volume, Bruce clearly describes for us the gracious nature of God.

Have you ever pondered the fact that God *wants* to bless his creation? It's his nature to give lavishly, to provide extravagantly, to supply abundantly.

But I can already hear the questions. "Fine," someone says, "but then why *doesn't* he bless us?"

Do you want to know why? Most often, it's because we don't obey him.

God's Tough Love

I have to be honest with you. You must understand one thing about God: if you disobey him, he is going to lovingly discipline you. "Do not be deceived," the apostle Paul reminded us, "God is not mocked; for whatever a man sows, that also he will reap. For he who sows to his flesh will of the flesh reap corruption" (Gal. 6:7–8).

God is love, but he is also holy. God wants the best for us, but he also knows that sin will keep us from the best. Therefore he will send our way whatever discipline may be necessary in order to move us back onto the road to life.

Of course, I realize as well as anyone that God's discipline doesn't, at the time, *feel* like love. But as every parent knows, "tough love" is often the only way to train defiant children. For that reason:

> "For whom the LORD loves He chastens, and scourges every son whom He receives" . . .
>
> We have had human fathers who corrected us, and we paid them respect. Shall we not much more readily be in subjection to the Father of spirits and live?
>
> For they indeed for a few days chastened us as seemed best to them, but He for our profit, that we may be partakers of His holiness.
>
> Now no chastening seems to be joyful for the present, but painful; nevertheless, afterward it yields the peaceable fruit of righteousness to those who have been trained by it. (Heb. 12:6, 9–11)

God really *does* want to bless us with "the peaceable fruit of righteousness." He really does want the best for us. How sad, then, that sometimes, the only way we learn is the hard way.

How God wishes that it were otherwise!

But don't take my word for it. The real question is, what does God himself say? What does he teach in his Word? You might be surprised to discover the truth.

God Doesn't Want to Punish Anyone

The Bible makes it clear that God takes no pleasure in causing anyone pain. He never rubs his hands together in glee at the thought of dispensing divine judgment. If you have pictured God as some kind of celestial cop, eagerly waiting to ticket hapless motorists who violate his cleverly concealed speed traps, then you desperately need a different picture of the Lord!

The prophets certainly did not see God as someone who delighted in doling out punishment. While they never minimized sin, they always reminded their people of the merciful, loving nature of the Lord they served.

Through the prophet Jeremiah, for example, God declared,

> I myself said,
> "How gladly would I treat you like sons
>   and give you a desirable land,
>   the most beautiful inheritance of any nation."
> I thought you would call me "Father"
>   and not turn away from following me . . .
> Return, faithless people;
>   I will cure you of backsliding.
> (Jer. 3:19, 22 NIV)

Jeremiah knew that the heart of God beat strong for the welfare and the blessing of his beloved people. Therefore he reminded his countrymen that although God "causes grief, yet He will show compassion according to the multitude of His mercies. For He does not afflict willingly, nor grieve the children of men" (Lam. 3:32–33).

Did you catch that? *He does not willingly bring affliction or grief to the children of men.*

The prophet Ezekiel labored to convey the same message to his contemporaries in exile. At least twice in his own book, Ezekiel reveals the Lord pleading with the Israelites to turn away from their sin. "Cast away from you all the transgressons which you have committed, and get yourselves a new heart and a new spirit," implores the Lord. "'For why should you die, O house of Israel? For I have no pleasure in the death of one who dies,' declares the LORD God. 'Therefore turn and live!'"

(Ezek. 18:31–32). Just in case his urgent message failed to get through, God repeats himself a little later: "'As I live,' says the LORD God, 'I have no pleasure in the death of the wicked, but that the wicked turn from his way and live. Turn, turn from your evil ways! For why should you die, O house of Israel?'" (Ezek. 33:11).

It's a good question. Why would any of us choose death when God offers us life? Why would any of us choose judgment when we could enjoy God's blessing?

The truth is, even though our sin deserves divine punishment, God loves to dispense mercy and grace. The psalmist understood this perfectly. In recalling the sorry spiritual record of his people during their rebellion in the wilderness, he marveled that, even so, God was "full of compassion, forgave their iniquity, and did not destroy them. Yes, many a time He turned His anger away, and did not stir up all His wrath" (Ps. 78:38).

Why does God restrain his anger? Why does he not stir up his full wrath? Only because he is a merciful God who loves us and hates the very thought of ever having to judge us.

God Laments What Must Be Done

While God takes no pleasure in punishing rebels, he will, as a last resort, reluctantly bring down his hand of judgment. Yet even then, he laments what must be done.

The Book of Hosea preserves a moving and poignant scene from the emotional life of God. The Lord knew that his people Israel had crossed a point of no return when they continued to serve and worship dead idols, despite many warnings. Their stubbornness broke his heart. "I drew them with gentle cords, with bands of love," he remembered, "and I was to them as those who take the yoke from their neck. I stooped and fed them" (Hos. 11:4)—and yet they rejected all his passionate appeals. Judgment at last had become inevitable . . . and this, the Lord could hardly bear:

(How can I give you up, Ephraim? How can I hand you over, Israel? How can I make you like Admah? How can I set you like Zeboiim? My heart churns within Me; My sympathy is stirred. (Hos. 11:8))

One can almost hear the Lord's heart breaking. When I read a heartrending lament like this one, deep from the very soul of God, it's almost impossible not to recall a similar wail that pierced the Judean air many centuries later. One day as Jesus Christ stood under the shadow of Jerusalem's walls and foresaw the devastation coming upon the city for its refusal to believe and obey God, he cried out, "O Jerusalem, Jerusalem, the one who kills the prophets and stones those sent to her! How often I wanted to gather your children together, as a hen gathers her chicks under her wings, but you were not willing!" (Matt. 23:37).

Discipline must follow an unrepentant heart, but that doesn't mean God likes handing out the necessary punishment. Over the years I've heard many jokes and stories about loving parents who tell their disobedient children, right before a spanking, "This is going to hurt me a lot more than it's going to hurt you." But there's no joking about such a sentiment when it comes from God. Sometimes, he has no option left but to discipline those he loves—yet such a harsh course of action always wounds his tender heart.

We Bring Disaster on Ourselves

Probably the hardest thing for God to take in all this is that we bring such trouble on ourselves. Who knows how much of the pain and suffering we endure could have been avoided had we turned our faces, and not our backs, toward God?

As the Lord looked into the future of ancient Judah and saw the devastation coming upon her because of her infatuation with idols, he described burned and deserted towns, a wasted landscape, and foreigners cruelly enslaving whatever Israelites had escaped the slaughter. And then he asked a crucial question:

> Have you not brought this on yourself, in that you have forsaken the LORD your God when He led you in the way?
> And now why take the road to Egypt, to drink the waters of Sihor? Or why take the road to Assyria, to drink the waters of the River?
> Your own wickedness will correct you, and your backslidings will rebuke you. Know therefore and see that it is an evil and bitter thing that you have forsaken the LORD your God, and the fear of Me is not in you. (Jer. 2:17–19)

Despite this rebuke, the people refused to listen. They gave no reply at all, except to continue in their detestable practices. So the Lord asked his question again, this time to a remnant of the nation that fled to Egypt:

> Why do you commit this great evil against yourselves, to cut off from you man and woman, child and infant, out of Judah, leaving none to remain, in that you provoke Me to wrath with the works of your hands, burning incense to other gods in the land of Egypt where you have gone to dwell, that you may cut yourselves off and be a curse and a reproach among all the nations of the earth? (Jer. 44:7–8)

God's questions to Judah suggest one for us. When will we learn that it is up to *us* whether we suffer under God's awesome hand of judgment? He has given us the power to decide our own fate. What he said to Jeremiah remains true today: "The instant I speak concerning a nation and concerning a kingdom, to pluck up, to pull down, and to destroy it, if that nation against whom I have spoken turns from its evil, I will relent of the disaster that I thought to bring upon it" (Jer. 18:7–8).

The same choice is left to each of us as individuals. If judgment comes upon us, it does so only because we have chosen it.

God Wants True Repentance,
Not Nice Words

So how can we avert suffering for even one instant under the wrath of God? How can we remove ourselves from his awful judgment? A pair of two-word phrases gives us the biblical answer: "Turn from" and "Turn to."

Let's allow Ezekiel to explain the first phrase: "'Therefore I will judge you, O house of Israel, every one according to his ways,' says the LORD God. 'Repent, and turn from all your transgressions, so that iniquity will not be your ruin'" (Ezek. 18:30).

God asks us to repent, to turn from our sin and our offenses. But it is not enough merely to stop doing what will only cause our own downfall. We also need to take a positive step, to turn *to* God. So the Lord tells us, "Turn to me and be saved, all you ends of the earth; for I am God, and there is no other" (Isa. 45:22 NIV).

It's a simple spiritual formula, but the only one that works. "Let the wicked forsake his way, and the unrighteous man his thoughts," said Isaiah, "let him turn to the LORD, and He will have mercy on him; and to our God, for He will abundantly pardon" (Isa. 55:7).

It sounds simple enough, but too often we run into a nasty problem. See if you can detect the difficulty in the phrases below:

- "I am innocent; he is not angry with me."
- "I have not sinned."
- "My Father, my friend from my youth, will you always be angry? Will your wrath continue forever?"

According to the prophet Jeremiah, the people of Israel used these very phrases to rationalize their behavior just before divine judgment fell. Some accused God of being the problem (2:29). Some sanctimoniously proclaimed that they remained on good terms with God (3:4). And some brazenly denied their guilt (2:35). When trouble came, however, they shouted, "Arise and save us" (2:27).

But God is never hoodwinked. "This is how you talk," he declared, "but you do all the evil you can" (Jer. 3:5 NIV).

The Lord knows we all have a tendency to substitute phony repentance for the genuine article. The psalmist admitted that his people would flatter God "with their mouth, and they lied to Him with their tongue; for their heart was not steadfast with Him, nor were they faithful in His covenant" (Ps. 78:36–37). None of this ever fools God.

"Nevertheless the solid foundation of God stands," Paul wrote, "having this seal: 'The Lord knows those who are His,' and, 'Let everyone who names the name of Christ depart from iniquity'" (2 Tim. 2:19). True repentance cannot help but display itself in the new life of the one who genuinely turns away from sin and turns to God. That is why Paul said, "I preached that they should repent and turn to God and prove their repentance by their deeds" (Acts 26:20, NIV). And it's also why he taught, "To the pure all things are pure, but to those who are defiled and unbelieving nothing is pure; but even their mind and conscience are defiled. They profess to know God, but in works they deny Him, being abominable, disobedient, and disqualified for every good work" (Titus 1:15–16). It's completely up to us whether we will feel God's hand of love on our shoulders or his hand of judgment on our backs.

God Repeatedly Sends Word

God doesn't, however, merely give us the choice and then retire to a corner until we make our decision. He loves us too much to act so passively. Instead, he sends us repeated encouragements and warnings to heed his Word and to accept his gracious offer of life.

"Again and again I sent my servants the prophets, who said, 'Do not do this detestable thing that I hate!'" said the Lord to his wandering people. "But they did not listen or pay attention;

they did not turn from their wickedness or stop burning incense to other gods. Therefore, my fierce anger was poured out; it raged against the towns of Judah and the streets of Jerusalem and made them the desolate ruins they are today" (Jer. 44:4–6 NIV).

Our own situation does not have to turn out so grim. Today, we have not only the words of the prophets to remind us how to avoid God's righteous judgment, but also living men and women to whom the Lord has committed "the ministry of reconciliation." As the apostle Paul said, "we are ambassadors for Christ, as though God were pleading through us; we implore you on Christ's behalf, be reconciled to God" (2 Cor. 5:19–20).

Sometimes God speaks to us through a friend or a business associate. Perhaps he uses a neighbor, a relative, or someone sitting next to us on a plane or train or ferry. Maybe he sends a magazine article our way, or a book like this one. He has his methods, and his couriers! We can't begin to imagine all the complex ways God manages to get his message to our ears.

But we can understand *why* he goes to all of this trouble. He does so because he loves us and he wants us to escape the judgment that will surely overtake those who insist on going their own stubborn way.

God Employs Escalating Judgments

Even when God decides that the time for judgment has come, he doesn't unload all of his wrath at once. Even in judgment, he shows mercy. His goal is never to inflict as much suffering as possible, but as little.

Therefore, the Lord normally employs escalating judgments in order to get our attention and persuade us to change our life course. He increases the intensity of his discipline in proportion to the stubbornness of our hearts. He takes no pleasure in causing us distress, but he takes less pleasure in allowing us to walk blindly into oblivion.

A passage in the book of the prophet Amos illustrates how

our merciful God slowly turns up the heat in order to keep us from marching into eternal fire. Notice how each succeeding judgment increases in intensity—and note, too, how at each level God hopes that we will grasp our perilous situation and turn to him.

Level 1:

"I gave you empty stomachs in every city
    and lack of bread in every town,
yet you have not returned to me,"
    declares the LORD.

Level 2:
"I also withheld rain from you
    when the harvest was still three months away.
I sent rain on one town,
    but withheld it from another.
One field had rain;
    another had none and dried up.
People staggered from town to town for water
    but did not get enough to drink,
yet you have not returned to me,"
    declares the LORD.

Level 3:
"Many times I struck your gardens and vineyards,
    I struck them with blight and mildew.
Locusts devoured your fig and olive trees,
    yet you have not returned to me,"
declares the LORD.

Level 4:
"I sent plagues among you
    as I did to Egypt.
I killed your young men with the sword,
    along with your captured horses.
I filled your nostrils with the stench of your camps,

> yet you have not returned to me,"
> declares the LORD.

Level 5:

> "I overthrew some of you
>   as I overthrew Sodom and Gomorrah.
> You were like a burning stick
>   snatched from the fire,
> yet you have not returned to me,"
>   declares the LORD.

Level 6:

> Therefore this is what I will do to you, Israel,
>   and because I will do this to you,
> prepare to meet your God, O Israel.
>
>   (Amos 4:6–12 NIV)

May I ask a personal question? Is there a chance you see anything like this happening in your own life, right now? Has one disaster struck after another, until you reel from the blows? If so, could it be that God is trying to get your attention? Could it be that he wants to use these hardships to turn your heart toward him in repentance and faith?

I'm no prophet; I can't say for sure what God may be trying to do in your life. But I do know that his Word counsels us to "endure hardship as discipline; God is treating you as sons. For what son is not disciplined by his father?" (Heb. 12:7 NIV). And I have learned:

> But let none of you suffer as a murderer, a thief, an evildoer, or as a busybody in other people's matters.
>
> Yet if anyone suffers as a Christian, let him not be ashamed, but let him glorify God in this matter.
>
> For the time has come for judgment to begin at the house of God; and if it begins with us first, what will be the end of those who do not obey the gospel of God? (1 Peter 4:15–17)

If you believe that God may be trying to get your attention through a "Level 1" kind of difficulty, then I urge you to stop where you are, take inventory of your spiritual condition, repent of your stubbornness, and turn to God. Believe me, you don't ever want to find out what his "Level 6" looks like.

God Wants Us to Understand

Whenever God sends judgment into someone's life, he wants that person to understand what is happening. Pain for the sake of pain accomplishes nothing. Therefore, when we find ourselves under the disciplining hand of God, we ought to learn what God wants from us.

God sends judgment so that we might understand our spiritual danger and turn from our sin. He shows us his mercy in countless ways, not the least of which is his deep yearning for us to grasp and take to heart the discipline he carefully measures out.

God Will Judge Severely Those Who Refuse to Repent

God does everything he can to prevent us from reaching Amos's "Level 6"—but those who ultimately reject God's mercy and blessing will surely receive his judgment and wrath.

"But in accordance with your hardness and your impenitent heart," wrote the apostle Paul, "you are treasuring up for yourself wrath in the day of wrath and revelation of the righteous judgment of God, who 'will render to each one according to his deeds': Eternal life to those who by patient continuance in doing good seek for glory, honor, and immortality; but to those who are self-seeking and do not obey the truth, but obey unrighteousness—indignation and wrath, tribulation and anguish, on every soul of man who does evil" (Rom. 2:5–8).

We don't have to guess about this. We can name many historical examples that demonstrate God's unbending commitment to both grace and justice. Let's briefly consider just two of them.

Sodom and Gomorrah, the two wicked cities Amos mentioned, provide a good example of how God balances his mercy with his justice. The Lord told Abraham that he was about to destroy these two ancient pits of evil. Abraham, because he was a prophet of God (Gen. 20:7), knew of God's merciful and righteous character. So he asked:

> Would You also destroy the righteous with the wicked? Suppose there were fifty righteous within the city; would You also destroy the place and not spare it for the fifty righteous that were in it? Far be it from You to do such a thing as this, to slay the righteous with the wicked, so that the righteous should be as the wicked; far be it from You! Shall not the Judge of all the earth do right? (Gen. 18:23–25)

As Abraham well knew, we can always trust God to do what is right. So the Lord agreed to Abraham's plea. Then Abraham began a series of further appeals, which ended with God agreeing to spare the cities if only ten righteous people could be found living within them. Such is the great mercy of our great God!

Sadly, however, not even ten righteous citizens could be located in Sodom and Gomorrah. Not even *ten*, in a population of thousands. And so the hand of divine judgment fell swiftly and severely on the doomed cities. Today, archaeologists believe the remains of Sodom and Gomorrah may be found far beneath the salty waters of the Dead Sea. And there they have remained, silently testifying to the awesome justice of God.

Another ancient city provides yet another glimpse into both the love and holiness of God. Remember the city of Nineveh, the Assyrian capital, mentioned in chapter 2? God told Jonah to go there and preach repentance, and much to the prophet's dismay, the people repented. True to his nature, God then refrained from dealing out the judgment they had earned.

A few decades later, however, the Ninevites reverted to their former barbarism and God *did* send judgment on them—so severely that for many centuries, skeptics denied that Nineveh had even existed. Because archaeologists had not yet discovered a shred of evidence for the city, critics of the Bible ridiculed its awesome descriptions of Assyria's capital.

How thorough was the destruction of this city? Even by 401 B.C., when the Greek mercenary Xenophon passed by the area during his retreat from an ill-fated expedition to Persia, no visible trace of Nineveh remained. About 150 years ago, however, some British archeologists noticed a big mound of dirt near Mosul, Iraq. They got to digging around this tell, and soon they found not only some ancient ruins, but the great city of Nineveh, exactly as the Bible had described it.[1]

God is patient, but he will not withhold his hand of judgment forever. "It is a fearful thing to fall into the hands of the living God," warned the writer to the Hebrews (10:31).

Perhaps the most fearful thing of all, however, is that judgment never need fall in the first place.

God Judges,
but He Also Restores

Have you ever tried in one sitting to read through the Book of Jeremiah? It's not easy. Jeremiah has to be one of the darkest books in the Bible, featuring page upon page of one divine judgment after another. No wonder Jeremiah is known as "the weeping prophet." He wept at the disobedience of his people and he wept over their coming judgment.

Yet even in this book, so full of terrifying pronouncements of doom, we repeatedly get bright glimpses of God's loving heart. Although Jeremiah prophesied that his rebellious people would be shattered, slaughtered, or sent into exile, he also predicted a better day would come. So the Lord said through his prophet:

> I have surely heard Ephraim bemoaning himself:
> "You have chastised, and I was chastised,
> Like an untrained bull;
> Restore me, and I will return,
> For You are the LORD my God.
> Surely, after my turning,
> I repented;
> And after I was instructed,
>   I struck myself on the thigh;
> I was ashamed, yes, even humiliated,
> Because I bore the reproach of my youth."
> Is Ephraim My dear son?
> Is he a pleasant child?
> For though I spoke against him,
> I earnestly remember him still;
> Therefore my heart yearns for him;
> I will surely have mercy on him, says the LORD.
>   (Jer. 31:18–20)

Yes, God would judge his people. Yes, they would suffer greatly. Yes, terror would grip each surviving heart. And yet God has a tremendous word in his vocabulary that ought to give us great hope:

Nevertheless!

Nevertheless, I will bring health and healing to [Jerusalem]; I will heal my people and will let them enjoy abundant peace and security. I will bring Judah and Israel back from captivity and will rebuild them as they were before. I will cleanse them from all the sin they have committed against me and will forgive all their sins of rebellion against me. Then this city will bring me renown, joy, praise and honor before all nations on earth that hear of all the good things I do for it; and they will be in awe and will tremble at the abundant prosperity and peace I provide for it. (Jer. 33:6–9 NIV)

Despite our sin, despite our arrogance, despite our stubbornness and rebellion and immorality, God longs to reach down and exchange our hearts of stone for hearts of flesh. He wants to turn us into trophies of his grace, rather than examples of his judgment. A new day is coming for the nation Israel. And a new day can come for you, too.

Forgiveness Is Available

God wants us to look to him in the midst of our despair. You may be in such bad shape that you feel as though you're sinking in quicksand. You admit that you've done shameful things. And you think, *Oh, God, could I ever be forgiven?*

I have good news for you. You *can* be forgiven, for we have a merciful God. And when he forgives, he cleanses us from all unrighteousness and removes our sin from us as far as the east is from the west (1 John 1:9; Ps. 103:12). In fact, he remembers our sin no more (Isa. 43:25).

Recall the story of David and Bathsheba. David committed a series of gross sins, but when Nathan confronted him with his guilt, he immediately confessed his evil and repented of it. The beauty of David's story is this: as God looked back over the king's life—all eighty years of it, not just his "pre-Bathsheba" days—he didn't even see the sin. David rejoiced in this, so much so that in his last words he declared:

> Is not my house right with God?
> Has he not made with me an everlasting covenant,
>   arranged and secured in every part?
> Will he not bring to fruition my salvation
>   and grant me my every desire?
>
> (2 Sam. 23:5 NIV)

It's as if David's sin had been thrown down a ravine. If you were standing with God and looking at David's life, you'd see right over the chasm to the "good stuff" on the other side. And you'd see that David was still a man after God's own heart.

The skeptic might say, "How could God see someone that despicable and still say he was a man after God's own heart?" He could say it because once we confess our sin to God and turn from it, God so completely removes it from us that he no longer even sees it. As God looked back over David's life, all he saw was the "green" part of his life, the part dedicated to him.

Of course, this God of mercy, this God of love, is also a God of justice. He will come at the end of time, bringing judgment on unrepentant mankind. Everyone, during his or her lifetime, has the opportunity to obtain either the mercy and grace and long-suffering of God, or his judgment.

I urge you, don't be like the American satirist and cartoonist Jules Feiffer, who once said, "Christ died for our sins. Dare we make his martyrdom meaningless by not committing them?"[2]

And don't be like the ancient Israelites, either, who so provoked God that in 587 B.C. he sent the Babylonians to destroy Jerusalem, the temple, and the whole Hebrew way of life. Some of the saddest words in the Bible appear near the end of 2 Chronicles. The author looked back over his people's history and wrote:

> The LORD, the God of their fathers, sent word to them through his messengers again and again, because he had pity on his people and on his dwelling place. But they mocked God's messengers, despised his words and scoffed at his prophets until the wrath of the LORD was aroused against his people and there was no remedy. (2 Chron. 36:15–16 NIV)

Thank God, there is yet a remedy for us. Make sure you don't despise it.

The coming of Christ will bring an era of blessing, a peerless time of hope for the believer. But for the nonbeliever, it will be a time of disaster. For the believer, this world is as bad as it gets. For the nonbeliever, this world is as good as it gets.

The day is soon coming when the Lord will return to rectify

all things. And at that moment, it will be too late to make a decision about God. As Paul wrote, "Behold, now is the accepted time; now is the day of salvation" (2 Cor. 6:2).)

If you haven't done so already, make today the best day of your life (so far) by personally inviting Jesus Christ into your life. And discover for yourself what God's favor feels like.

PART TWO

JESUS, THE SPIRIT OF PROPHECY

7

Jesus:
The Essence of Prophecy

Back in 1995, when Bev and I visited Beijing, China, we saw something that gave us goose bumps. We were strolling across the Great Wall, along with our communist entourage and our Christian guide (although the others didn't know of his faith), when we heard a siren.

We all turned to see an ambulance speed by. As it passed us, I saw a red cross emblazoned on its door. And I thought, *That's interesting—a red cross even in communist China!* I found it all the more remarkable because the country had been a communist state for more than fifty years.

When we returned to our hotel, I found a young waiter with whom we had become quite friendly and asked him, "Why do you have a red cross on the door of the ambulances here?"

"Oh, don't you know?" he replied. "All over the world, the red cross is a symbol of humanitarianism."

I thought I might get such an answer, so I had another question ready for him. "And why is it red?"

He looked at me, thought for a moment, and finally admitted, "I don't know."

His puzzlement gave me the perfect opportunity to explain what the Bible says about the blood of Jesus Christ, God's Son, and how it cleanses us from all sin. I told our young waiter that Jesus died on a blood-stained cross in order to give life-saving, spiritual aid to everyone who would commit his or her life to him in faith.

No one can deny the pervasive, worldwide influence of Jesus Christ. A red cross, even in communist China, still points directly back to Jesus!

Head and Shoulders Above Everyone Else

Jesus Christ so changed the world that his influence has spread even to nooks and crannies that one might never expect. For example, on a recent trip to Israel, I noticed scores of tourist buses, most of them bursting with evangelical Christians from America. *What do the Israelis think when all these men and women visit Israel to remember Jesus Christ?* I wondered. So I asked our guide, a major in the Israeli armed forces and a teacher with a master's degree.

"Oh, we think that Jesus Christ was the greatest Jew who ever lived," he replied, looking me straight in the face.

His answer floored me. Even a well-educated major in the Israeli army would consider Jesus "the greatest Jew who ever lived"! Most Israelis don't believe that Jesus is the Messiah, of course—that's the step I believe they will take during the Tribulation (see chapter 10)—but even now, many declare Jesus Christ to be the greatest Jew who ever lived.

With the success of the *Left Behind* series, my coauthor Jerry B. Jenkins and I have been interviewed on several nationally broadcast programs. Recently we appeared on the *Larry King Live* show. During a break Larry said to us, "You know, I'm a Jew. I consider myself an agnostic. But I believe Jesus Christ is the most influential person who ever lived." Later I was told he gave a very similar quote to *Time* magazine.

Think about this for a moment. Why should even "secular" people respect Jesus Christ so deeply? Leave contemporary witnesses for a moment and consider that staid old reference tool, the *Encyclopedia Britannica*. Did you know that it dedicates about twenty thousand words to Jesus Christ? That's more ink than it gives to Albert Einstein, Joan of Arc, Karl Marx, George Washington, Madame Curie, Vladimir Lenin, Abraham Lincoln, Mother Teresa, or to *any* other person in history. Why should that be so?

Or consider the testimony of H. G. Wells, a popular author and skeptic of the nineteenth century who hated Jesus Christ. When he finished writing *The Outline of History*, his five-volume history of the world, he discovered that he had dedicated more pages to Jesus Christ than to anyone else, by far.

Now, why is that? About six billion people inhabit the earth at this moment, and most scholars estimate that number to represent about one-sixth of all those who have ever lived.[1] If they're right, about thirty-six billion human beings have populated earth. Isn't it interesting that, among all those billions, one person stands head and shoulders above everybody else?

And then consider this: most other world leaders had a lifetime to make their impact, while Jesus Christ made his mark in less than four years of public ministry. Imagine! By popular consent, Jesus Christ has influenced this world more than anyone else. He has no rivals. And he did it all *in three and one-half years!*

Jesus, the Spirit of Prophecy

Now can you see why it should be no surprise that Bible prophecy centers on Jesus Christ? Jesus is both the goal and the subject of Bible prophecy. All things find their focus in him. For that reason, Revelation 19:10 says, "the testimony of Jesus is the spirit of prophecy." We could legitimately reverse that phrase and say that the spirit of prophecy is the testimony of Jesus.

In essence, most prophecy testifies to Jesus. That's one of the reasons I get so wound up about the idea of prophecy. I love studying prophecy because it communicates Christ; except for a few passages that concern pagan nations like Egypt and Edom, you can hardly read a prophetic passage where Jesus doesn't come into play. Jesus is the one who makes the future possible for the rest of us.

And don't think for a minute I'm exaggerating! Jesus is not only the most influential person in history; he's also the subject of more Bible prophecy than anyone else. At least 129 times, the Old Testament prophets predicted that Jesus would come—and in his first coming he fulfilled every one of those prophecies. (For a list of these prophecies, see the *Tim LaHaye Prophecy Study Bible.*)

The possibility of *any* other person fulfilling these prophecies is so tiny it can't be imagined. Experts in probability have determined that the chance of one man accidentally fulfilling *just eight* of these prophecies is one in 10^{17}—an astronomically small probability. If we were to increase the number of prophecies to forty-eight, the chance of accidentally fulfilling all forty-eight falls to one in 10^{157}—a tiny number beyond human comprehension.[2]

And yet Jesus fulfilled *all 129* Old Testament prophecies!

Can you imagine what it might have felt like to have lived in the days of Elijah, Elisha, and the major prophets, when they prophesied about the Messiah to come? The apostle Peter said, "The prophets, who spoke of the grace that was to come to you, searched intently and with the greatest care, trying to find out the time and circumstances to which the Spirit of Christ in them was pointing when he predicted the sufferings of Christ and the glories that would follow" (1 Pet. 1:10–11 NIV). The prophets predicted both Jesus' sufferings and his glory. Consider just a few of their amazing predictions.

Jesus Fulfilled Messianic Prophecy

1. The Messiah Would Be Born in Bethlehem.

About five hundred years before the birth of Jesus, the prophet Micah predicted that the Messiah would be born in Bethlehem of Judea:

But you, Bethlehem Ephrathah, though you are little among the thousands of Judah, yet out of you shall come forth to Me the One to be Ruler in Israel, whose goings forth are from of old, from everlasting. (Micah 5:2)

Why should such a great hero be born in Bethlehem? That little town tended to get lost among the four hundred other villages in Israel; in Micah's day it probably had a population of no more than two hundred. And yet, since Joseph considered Bethlehem his ancestral home, that's where he had to return when the Roman Empire demanded that he register for the census (Luke 2:1–3). Joseph and Mary had to leave their home in Nazareth and head south to Bethlehem.

I've always found it interesting that the Scripture uses the phrase "great with child" to describe Mary at this momentous time (Luke 2:5 KJV). Late-term though she was, she climbed on a donkey, traveled about ninety rough miles, and delivered her child safely in Bethlehem. And I've often wondered: *How did she last until Bethlehem?*

Many years ago when I pastored a little Baptist church in Pumpkintown, South Carolina, Bev and I were expecting our first child. Our daughter was a little slow, like her father, and she didn't want to come on schedule. In fact, it took her a good nine-and-a-half months to decide to make her appearance in this world.

While we waited for our stubborn little doll to arrive, the doctor made a suggestion. "Why don't you take a long ride on a country road?" he said. Since we had nothing *but* mud roads where we lived, we regularly took the doctor's advice.

Can you imagine a young woman traveling ninety miles on a donkey, while she was "great with child"? Why wasn't that baby born in any one of a number of cities in Nazareth? Why wasn't that child born at Jerusalem, four miles from Bethlehem? Why didn't he make his appearance until Bethlehem?

He didn't because the prophet, speaking more than five hundred years before Jesus arrived, said that the Messiah would be born in Bethlehem. That's incredible—and that's only one of the 129 prophecies concerning the first advent of Messiah.

But let's jump ahead a bit. A full fifty of the Bible's messianic prophecies involve events connected to the Lord's death—and Jesus fulfilled them all. Consider just a few of them.

2. The Messiah Would Be Betrayed by a Close Friend.

You've probably never met a man named Judas, and for good reason. Nobody wants to name a son after the infamous disciple who betrayed Jesus with a kiss. Yet even this terrible act of treachery had been predicted: "Even my own familiar friend in whom I trusted, who ate my bread, has lifted up his heel against me" (Ps. 41:9).

It's interesting to note two details about this verse. First, the term translated "familiar friend" is more literally "a man of peace." Disciples customarily greeted their rabbis with a "kiss of peace." Therefore none of the other disciples would have known what Judas had planned when he kissed Jesus in the Garden of Gethsemane. None of them realized his kiss enabled the rabble to identify Jesus as the man to arrest.

Second, before Jesus celebrated the Lord's Supper with the rest of his disciples, he dismissed Judas with a bit of shared bread, according to John:

> When Jesus had said these things, He was troubled in spirit, and testified and said, "Most assuredly, I say to you, one of you will betray Me."
> Then the disciples looked at one another, perplexed about whom He spoke. Now there was leaning on Jesus' bosom one of His disciples, whom Jesus loved. Simon Peter therefore motioned to him to ask who it was of whom He spoke. Then, leaning back on Jesus' breast, he said to Him, "Lord, who is it?"
> Jesus answered, "It is he to whom I shall give a piece of bread when I have dipped it." And having dipped the bread, he gave it to Judas Iscariot, the son of Simon.

> Now after the piece of bread, Satan entered him. Then Jesus said to him, "What you do, do quickly." But no one at the table knew for what reason He said this to him. (John 13:21–28)

Just as it had been prophesied, Jesus' close friend, Judas, "lifted up his heel" against his Lord after sharing his bread.

3. The Messiah Would Be Betrayed for Thirty Pieces of Silver.

Zechariah prophesied some five hundred years before Christ that the Messiah would be betrayed for thirty silver coins (Zech. 11:12)—the price of a slave in ancient times (Ex. 21:32). By Zechariah's time, this sum had become a way of indicating a trifling amount, so the prophet adds the ironic note, "that princely price they set on me" (Zech. 11:13). Matthew 26:14–16 tells us that Judas agreed to hand Jesus over to the mob for a piddling thirty silver coins.

4. The Betrayal Money Would Be Used to Buy a Potter's Field.

Zechariah further prophesied that the money involved in the betrayal of the Messiah would be thrown into the temple to a potter: "And the LORD said to me, 'Throw it to the potter'— that princely price they set on me. So I took the thirty pieces of silver and threw them into the house of the LORD for the potter" (Zech. 11:13).

The Gospels tell us that when Judas realized the full implications of his action, he was "seized with remorse" and tried to return the betrayal money to the chief priests and the elders. When they rebuffed his attempt, he threw the money into the temple and left to hang himself. The chief priests picked up the money but refused to put it into the temple treasury, since they considered it "blood money." Therefore they used the funds to buy "the potter's field, to bury strangers in" (Matt. 27:3–8).

5. The Messiah Would Be Scorned by Crowds.

It feels almost eerie to read David's prophecy of the Messiah's unjust execution (Ps. 22). Many startling points of fulfillment can be seen in the crucifixion of Jesus. But consider just one—the reaction of the crowds to the Messiah's death:

> I am . . . scorned by men
> and despised by the people.
> All who see me mock me;
> they hurl insults, shaking their heads:
> "He trusts in the LORD;
> let the LORD rescue him.
> Let him deliver him,
> since he delights in him."
>
> (Ps. 22:6–8 NIV)

Compare these prophesied words to the ones actually shouted by the angry enemies of Jesus as he hung on the cross: "He trusts in God," they screamed. "Let God rescue him now if he wants him, for he said, 'I am the Son of God.'" Matthew also recorded that "those who passed by hurled insults at him, shaking their heads" (Matt. 27:43, 39 NIV).

6. The Messiah Would Be Pierced Through the Hands and Feet and in the Side.

Several of the prophets predicted that the Messiah would be "pierced" physically (Isa. 53:5; Zech. 12:10). David gave the most specific description, writing, "dogs have surrounded Me; the congregation of the wicked has enclosed Me. They pierced My hands and My feet" (Ps. 22:16). For many centuries this verse greatly puzzled Jewish commentators, for it seemed inconceivable that the Messiah should have his hands and feet pierced. How could it be? Hebrew culture never punished anyone this way; it executed criminals by stoning. The scholars finally "solved" the puzzle by supplying vowels for the verse different from those that had been supplied historically (in ancient Hebrew, only consonants were written down; much later in history, scribes added a system of "vowel pointing" to help readers understand the ancient text). With these new vowels, the text read, "like the lion, my hands and my feet"—a nonsensical phrase, but one which removed the problematic "piercing."

The Romans had no such scholarly difficulties, and when they crucified Jesus, they unwittingly fulfilled this prophecy to the letter. They nailed the Lord's hands and feet to the cross; and later, to test whether he had died, they thrust a spear into his side (John 19:34, 20:25–27; Acts 2:23).

Interestingly, only during a historical window of about 130 years did the Romans use crucifixion to execute criminals; they began using it about sixty years before Jesus was born. And shortly after Jesus' death, even the Romans judged crucifixion to be such an inhumane form of execution that they quit using it. Yet during this window, the man whom Scripture calls "the Lion of the tribe of Judah" (Rev. 5:5) was literally pierced for our transgressions, just as Isaiah had prophesied.

7. None of the Messiah's Bones Would Be Broken.

At least one prophecy concerning the death of the Messiah doesn't, on the surface, seem to carry much significance. Psalm 34:20 predicted that God would take such care of the Messiah that "He guards all his bones; not one of them is broken."

Some might think, *Hey, if he was going to die barbarically anyway, what difference did it make if none of his bones were broken?* Well, it makes a *big* difference if the one so killed is also God's fulfillment of the ancient Passover lamb.

Remember the old story? The Bible says God struck Egypt with ten awful plagues in order to persuade Pharaoh to release the Hebrews from slavery. The tenth and final plague killed all the firstborn of Egypt, both men and animals—unless a household had sacrificed a "Passover lamb" and applied the blood of the animal to the doorposts of the house. The Lord spared only those households; he promised to "pass over" them and not destroy their firstborn. God gave explicit instructions to his people that this lamb should be a male without defect—and that in killing it, they should take care to not "break one of its bones" (Exod. 12:46).

The New Testament calls Jesus Christ "our Passover lamb" (1 Cor. 5:7 NIV) and says that as the spotless Lamb of God, slain during Passover almost two thousand years ago, he was sacrificed so that we might enjoy peace with God. He died so that we might live—and in accordance with the Scripture, not one of his bones was broken (John 19:33).

Bible prophecy authenticates the identity and mission of the Messiah like almost nothing else, and all these prophecies point to only one man in history: Jesus Christ.

A Surprising Visitor

But how did Jesus himself interpret the Bible's messianic passages? Did he claim to be the Messiah, the Anointed One to come?

The Gospels leave no doubt that Jesus saw himself as the predicted Messiah.[3] One of the clearest examples of this can be found in Luke 4, where we are told he announced to surprised synagogue attendees from his hometown that he had come to fulfill messianic prophecy (v. 21).

Imagine that you had been in the audience that day. Suppose that you were a young Torah student, eager to hear a local rabbi's interpretation of God's holy Word. You learn that an itinerant teacher named Jesus has stopped off in Nazareth after preaching to excited crowds all over Galilee. And today you expect to hear him for yourself. You can hardly wait!

꧁꧂

Where is he? At times like this I especially regret how short my family tends to be. Uncle Zacchaeus tells me his lack of height doesn't keep him from doing good business, but we all question his use of the word *good.* As for me, when I sit down, I can't see much of anything. And right now, I really want to see *him*. Where is he?

Wait a moment . . . somebody seems to be standing up toward the front. Yes, he seems to be dressed like a rabbi, though I'm sure I've never seen him. That *must* be this Jesus fellow.

And look! Levi, the synagogue leader, is handing him the blessed scroll. I wonder what he will read for us? He's certainly taking his time. He must be scanning for something in particular—judging from where he appears to be in the scroll, I'd say he's going to choose something from one of the prophets. But wait! I think he's about to read:

> The Spirit of the Lord is upon Me, because He has anointed Me to preach the gospel to the poor; He has sent me to heal the broken-hearted, to proclaim liberty to the captives and recovery of sight to the blind, to set at liberty those who are oppressed; to proclaim the acceptable year of the LORD.

The prophet Isaiah! I *knew* it! But what is this? Is that *all* he's going to read? We just studied this passage in school last week, and I know the prophet goes on to say, "and the day of vengeance of our God." Why does this teacher not speak of the Lord's wrath against our enemies? How dare he cut short the reading? What sort of outrage is this? The synagogue ruler will not be pleased.

Ah, but I must wait for this visitor to speak. Perhaps he has an explanation; I ought to be patient. It appears he has returned the scroll to the attendant . . . now he is sitting down. I must listen carefully.

"Today this Scripture is fulfilled in your hearing."

What?! What did he just say? No, this cannot be. Could I have heard correctly? But I see from the looks on my classmates that I have not misunderstood. What under heaven can he mean, "Today this Scripture is fulfilled in your hearing"? He cannot mean that—no, I dare not even think it—that *he* is the Messiah? May God hold him accountable for his rash words!

It is true, we have heard reports that the Holy One of Israel wrought a few wonders in Capernaum through this man—but that does not make him the *Messiah*. What blasphemy! If he does not explain himself, and quickly, the elders will surely pick him up and throw him down the cliff. And I will help them, regardless of my size!

❦

As it happened, when Jesus finished speaking that day, the infuriated people of the synagogue ushered him to the brow of a hill on which the town was built, intending to throw him down. But Luke wrote simply, "Then passing through the midst of them, He went His way" (Luke 4:30).

Had anyone other than Jesus claimed to be the Messiah, of course, he *would* have been blaspheming. Yet Jesus, as the prophesied Messiah, came to fulfill all the prophecies written about him in God's Word. He not only preached the Good News to the poor and proclaimed freedom for the prisoners, he also accomplished what no prophet in Israel's history had ever done, not even Moses or Elijah or Isaiah. *He made blind people see* (Matt. 9:27–30, 12:22, 15:30, 20:30–34; John 9:1–7, 10:21, and so on). Who could doubt this was truly the Messiah?

But back to Nazareth. Why did Jesus stop his quotation of Isaiah 61 at the first half of verse 2? He did so because he had come the first time to "proclaim the acceptable year of the LORD," that is, the age of grace in which we're living. He did not come the first time to inaugurate "the day of vengeance of our God," something that is yet to occur (see chapter 10). That's why he stopped reading where he did.

The church has been preaching the gospel to the poor and sharing the truth of God with the world for the past two thousand years. During that time it is estimated that almost eight *billion* individuals have called on his name and received, through faith, the grace he came to offer.[4] Yet the time is drawing near when that same world will see "the day of vengeance of our God." Jesus came the first time to speak about the age of grace he was about to initiate, and to fulfill the Bible prophecies that pertained to that period of time. When he comes the second time, he will fulfill the remaining prophecies, exactly as they were given.

And that day is closer today than ever before.

The Culmination of Bible Prophecy

I have saved discussion of one messianic prophecy for last, because it overshadows all the others and gives them all eternal significance. While the cross no doubt is the most monumental event in history, it takes on meaning only because of the resurrection that followed it. Jesus rose from the dead, and in so doing he authenticated both his identity as the Son of God and his role as the Savior of the world.

Through the resurrection of Christ, God forever says to the world, "I am pleased with my Son's work on the cross." So the apostle Paul claimed that Jesus was "declared to be the Son of God with power according to the Spirit of holiness, by the resurrection from the dead" (Rom. 1:4). How do we know that Jesus could really forgive our sin, as he claimed? Because he rose from the dead, as predicted.

The Old Testament prophesied the resurrection of the Messiah in many ways and in many passages.[5] In one messianic psalm (16:10), David confessed to God that "You will not leave my soul in Sheol, nor will You allow Your Holy One to see corruption." David himself died, was buried, and his body decayed; so this passage could not refer to him, as Acts 2:29–32 makes clear. But Jesus literally fulfilled it when he rose from the dead on the third day after his crucifixion (Luke 24:45–47).

It is the resurrection of Christ that makes Christianity possible. If Jesus had not bodily risen from the dead, would anybody still be attending church? Would anyone consider the cross a positive symbol? The Romans crucified uncounted thousands, yet we don't commemorate the deaths of any other victim of the cross. The cross means only one thing to us today: Jesus. And his resurrection proves the truth of his message.

If Jesus of Nazareth—a natural, wonderful, but merely good man—had died on the cross, we would all still be in our sins. A mere man couldn't die for the sins of all humanity—but God could. God himself, in human flesh, is the only one who could present a sacrifice worthy of atoning for the sins of the world. This Jesus did, and this is the culmination of Bible prophecy.

See Jesus, See God

God best reveals himself in his risen Son. That's why it's important to focus on the prophecies of Jesus Christ and on his resurrection. According to the Bible, if you want to know what God is like, you need to study Jesus.

Do you want to know how God feels? Then study how Jesus felt, for he revealed God.

Do you want to know what God thinks about the future or the present or the past, about sin or marriage or sex? Then examine what Jesus taught about these things. Study the life of Jesus Christ, because he declares God.

"The Son is the radiance of God's glory and the exact representation of his being, sustaining all things by his powerful word," said the writer to the Hebrews (1:3 NIV). When we look at Jesus, Scripture insists, we see God in action. And when we see Jesus, we see love and mercy, not hatred and anger.

Do you want to know what God thinks about people who feel "weary and scattered, like sheep having no shepherd"? Jesus felt great mercy for them (Matt. 9:36).

And what about little children? For a long time in history, adults tolerated children as necessities for continuing the race, but considered them of little account until they came of age. Yet Jesus entered that child-degrading age and said, "Let the little children come to Me, and do not forbid them; for of such is the kingdom of God. Assuredly, I say to you, whoever does not receive the kingdom of God as a little child will by no means enter it" (Mark 10:14–15). To fit a lovely frame around that beautiful picture, Mark tells us that Jesus "took them up in His arms, laid His hands on them, and blessed them" (v. 16).

It is this Jesus who provides the focus of Bible prophecy. It is this Jesus whose resurrection from the dead culminates Bible prophecy. And it is this Jesus who is coming again to judge the living and the dead, to reign on the throne of David, and to present his kingdom to the Father "that God may be all in all" (1 Cor. 15:28).

We should never feel afraid of Bible prophecy, or of the God who gave it, for prophecy wonderfully expresses the Lord's mercy. Infinite love shines strong and bright in Jesus, in the heart of his Father, and in the core of Bible prophecy.

And it always will.

8

Jesus: *The* Prophet

Ⓘf you were asked to pick the greatest cartoon superhero of all time, whom would you nominate?

Superman? Batman? Wonder Woman?

If you were asked to name the greatest U.S. president, whom would you suggest?

Abraham Lincoln? George Washington? Franklin Delano Roosevelt?

If you were asked to name the greatest philanthropist in world history, whom would you identify?

Alfred Nobel? Andrew Carnegie? Mother Teresa?

How about the greatest American media mogul? *William Randolph Hearst? Ted Turner?* The best basketball player? *Michael Jordan? Oscar Robertson?* The most important scientist? *Sir Isaac Newton? Albert Einstein?* The most influential movie director? *Steven Spielberg? Cecil B. DeMille?*

It's hard to think of a single category of "greatest" anything and come up with the name of just one individual who indisputably reigns over everyone else. Fans of any of the celebrities mentioned above (and of many other celebrities who weren't mentioned) could make a good case that their particular hero should be considered "the best" or "the greatest" or "the most important." And no one could prove them wrong.

There is one category, however, in which a single name *does* rise to the top of the list. Beyond all question, he remains the greatest in his field. Neither before him nor after him did anyone arise who could challenge him for his title.

If I were to ask, "Who is the greatest biblical prophet of all?" how would you answer?

Moses? No. *Elijah?* Certainly not. *Isaiah?* Nope. *Daniel? Paul? Peter? John?*

If you guessed any of those men, you'd be wrong. None of them qualify; not by a long shot. Although all of them rank as great prophets, they pale alongside the greatest of them all. Only one man deserves the title "*The* Prophet," and we call that man . . .

Jesus.

What Else Would We Expect?

I admit, we don't normally think of Jesus as an unsurpassed prophet. Much more likely, we call him by other titles: Savior, Lord, Son of God, Good Shepherd. And he is all of those things, of course—but he's also the greatest prophet who ever walked the earth.

Did you know that Jesus prophesied more than anyone who has ever lived? It's true. Think of anyone in the Bible—Isaiah, Daniel, Jeremiah, John—you name the prophet, and Jesus prophesied more.

Not long ago I started going through the Gospels in my devotional times and wrote down the many Bible references regarding the prophecies of Jesus. Do you know what I discovered? Matthew alone records thirty-nine prophecies of Jesus. Mark lists forty; Luke describes thirty-five; and so far in John I've found more than sixty prophecies from the lips of Jesus. Many of these predictions are parallel accounts of the same prophecy, of course, but even these numbers should remind us that Jesus prophesied a great deal during his three-and-a-half years of public ministry.

But why should this surprise us? What else would we expect from the man Scripture calls "*The* Prophet"?

A Worthy Successor to Moses

In the weeks just before ancient Israel was to end its long wilderness wanderings and finally enter the Promised Land, the people had to make a number of final preparations. The Book of Deuteronomy records how the Hebrew nation got ready for its new life in Canaan. Moses reiterated for his people the holy laws of God and warned them repeatedly not to turn from the covenant they had made with the Lord.

In many ways, this must have been a tough time for Moses. After he had led Israel so faithfully out of Egypt and through forty difficult years in the wilderness, he himself would not be permitted to enter the Promised Land. Through one impetuous but very public act of sin (Num. 20:6–12), Moses earned God's rebuke and lost the opportunity to lead Israel into Canaan. Instead, that job would pass to Joshua.

I doubt the men and women of Israel slept very well, knowing that their revered leader of more than four decades would not accompany them into their new homeland. I can imagine their fears: *How will we ever replace Moses' experience? What if Joshua isn't ready for the job? Who will speak to God for us? How will we know what the Lord requires of us, if Moses isn't around to ask?*

Perhaps to quell those very fears, God gave Moses and the nation a comforting prophecy in Deuteronomy 18:17–19. In it he told them to expect the arrival of another prophet, like Moses, yet even greater. Moses himself had told his people, "The Lord your God will raise up for you a Prophet like me from your midst, from your brethren. Him you shall hear, according to all you desired of the Lord your God in Horeb in the day of the assembly, saying, 'Let me not hear again the voice of the LORD my God, nor see this great fire anymore, lest I die'" (Deut. 18:15–16). God heard the Israelites' request and so declared to Moses, "What they have spoken is good. I will raise up for them a Prophet like you from among their brethren, and will put My words in His mouth, and He shall speak to them all that I command Him. And it shall be that whoever will not hear My words, which He speaks in My name, I will require it of him" (vv. 17–19).

After Moses died, Joshua took over the reins of national leadership and led the Israelites into the Promised Land. But the predicted "Prophet" did not come.

In the succeeding years, Israel settled into her land and saw the miraculous hand of God at work among her people. When the time came for Joshua to pass off the scene, the old general called the elders of Israel to his deathbed and told them, "you know with all your hearts and in all your souls that not one thing has failed of all the good things which the LORD your God spoke concerning you. All have come to pass for you; not one word of them has failed" (Josh. 23:14). Centuries later, King Solomon repeated virtually the same statement to his own subjects (1 Kings 8:56).

And yet, one of God's promises had yet to be fulfilled. "The Prophet" had not come.

The centuries rolled on, and pagan invaders conquered the land. First Israel, the northern kingdom, fell to the Assyrians; then Judah, the southern kingdom, fell to the Babylonians. Great prophets appeared on the scene to warn the nation about coming judgment, prophets with the revered names of Samuel, Nathan, Elijah, Elisha, Isaiah, Jeremiah, Ezekiel, Daniel, Haggai.

But still, *the* Prophet did not come.

Some time around the fourth century B.C., a long epoch of prophetic silence fell on the nation. For hundreds of years, no true prophet of God arose to speak God's words to the people of Israel. Great leaders did appear, such as the Maccabees, who defeated the Syrians under Antiochus IV in about 164 B.C. and rededicated the temple in Jerusalem (the festival of Hanukkah dates to this time, a holiday mentioned in John 10:22).

Yet *the* Prophet remained absent. Would God ever fulfill his promise?

Then one day, a wild-looking man appeared in the Judean wilderness, publicly denouncing the people's sin and challenging them to repent and be baptized. The man wore camel's hair and a leather belt and ate locusts and wild honey, and the eager crowds swelled to hear him. A prophet at last! God had broken his long silence! And they wondered: *Could this be the one?* So they asked him: "Are you Elijah?"

"I am not," he replied.

No doubt they held their breath and sucked in their lips as they awaited the answer to a follow-up question: "Are you *the* Prophet?" But again they felt disappointment.

"No," he answered simply. Then who was he? "I am 'The voice of one crying in the wilderness: "Make straight the way of the LORD,"'" he declared (John 1:21–23).

Anyone who knew anything about the remaining promises of God understood from the man's answer that he saw himself as the forerunner to the Messiah. The prophet Isaiah had predicted that someone would appear to prepare God's people for the coming of the Lord (Isa. 40:3)—and this man claimed to be that "someone." So for whom did he prepare the way?

For Jesus.

At long last, in fulfillment of God's promise, *the* Prophet had arrived in the person of Jesus Christ. The people quickly recognized Jesus as this long-awaited one when he performed several remarkable miracles (John 6:14). Later, the apostles explicitly identified Jesus as *the* Prophet foretold by Moses (Acts 3:19–23).

The world has never seen anyone like Jesus. Not only is he the subject of more Bible prophecies than anyone else, but he himself came as the greatest Prophet of all. He saw things in advance unseen by anyone else. And because he caused many of his prophecies to be written down, we can study what he had to say about the future—events both future to his hearers and some still future to us.

Fulfilled Prophecies of Jesus

Did you know that of the approximately one hundred prophecies that Jesus gave, scores already have been fulfilled? Some were fulfilled within hours of his giving them; some came to pass within his lifetime; and others came to fulfillment years after his death. Let's briefly consider just five of Jesus' remarkable prophecies.

1. A Woman, Some Perfume, and a Worldwide Report

A beautiful scene unfolded one day in a town named Bethany at the home of a man named Simon. Only days before Jesus went to the cross, an unnamed woman approached him and poured a jar of expensive perfume on his head. Those present knew the value of this exotic fragrance, known as "pure nard," and they grumbled that it could have been sold for more than a year's wages and the money given to the poor. So they sharply rebuked the woman.

Can you imagine how intimidated the woman must have felt? She had come to the house because she felt powerfully moved by this Jesus and what he had done for her. Perhaps he had forgiven her of all her sins, as he had done with another woman who earlier had wet his feet with her tears, wiping them with her hair (Luke 7:36–48). So she brought this costly perfume, anointed Jesus' head with oil—and received a sharp rebuke.

Jesus would not stand for it. "Let her alone," he commanded. "Why do you trouble her? She has done a good work for Me. For you have the poor with you always, and whenever you wish you may do them good; but Me you do not have always. She has done what she could. She has come beforehand to anoint My body for burial" (Mark 14:6–8).

And then, to make sure no one in the room could miss the

significance of the woman's actions, he uttered a unique prophecy. "Assuredly, I say to you," he declared, "wherever this gospel is preached in the whole world, what this woman has done will also be told as a memorial to her" (Mark 14:9).

None of the Gospels were completed until at least thirty years after Jesus had ascended into heaven, yet when Matthew and Mark sat down to write, they both incorporated this story into their narratives. Wherever the gospel has gone since then, so has this story. And here we are, some two thousand years later, and Jesus' prophecy is still being literally fulfilled.

2. Peter Would Deny Jesus Three Times.

If you and I had been given the chance to guess beforehand who among the disciples might run out on Jesus when the going got tough, I doubt any of us would have picked Peter. He was the leader, the strong one, the outspoken one. More likely we would have chosen Thomas, the disciple who constantly fought his doubts, or Andrew, the quiet brother of Peter. Not even Peter thought Peter could possibly turn coward on his Master.

So it was on that fateful night that when Jesus predicted all his men would "be made to stumble" on account of him, Peter objected strenuously. "Even if all are made to stumble because of You, I will never be made to stumble," he boasted (Matt. 26:31, 33).

But Jesus knew better. He knew what was coming. I imagine him putting his hand on Peter's shoulder and softly but firmly saying, "Assuredly, I say to you that this night, before the rooster crows, you will deny Me three times" (v. 34).

Peter, of course, vigorously defended his own version of coming events. "Even if I have to die with You," he declared, "I will not deny You!" And there Jesus left it.

Just a few hours later a mob came to arrest Jesus and lead him away to an illegal trial before the Jewish council in the home of Caiaphas, the high priest. And there, in the courtyard, Peter three times hotly denied that he even knew Jesus. The third time, Matthew says he "began to curse and swear, saying, 'I do not know the Man!'" (Matt. 26:74).

At just that moment, the rooster crowed. Luke tells us that Jesus, still inside the house, turned and looked straight at Peter, who was still swearing in the courtyard. Immediately Peter remembered the Lord's prediction . . . and the gospel says, "Peter went out and wept bitterly" (Luke 22:62).

3. He Would Rise from the Dead on the Third Day.

Jesus prophesied more about his own arrest, torture, crucifixion, and resurrection than anything else. Multiple passages record his predictions that he would be executed and that he would rise from the dead on the third day.[1]

On that first Easter morning after the resurrection had taken place—but before it had become widely known—two bereaved women, both named Mary, walked to the grave of Jesus. No doubt they wondered how they were going to get a two-and-a-half-ton stone rolled away from the tomb entrance so they could anoint their Lord's body, in accordance with Jewish custom.

They needn't have worried. Matthew says that the arrival of an angel at the tomb caused a violent earthquake (and terrified some guards at the tomb, who "shook for fear of him, and became like dead men"). The angel rolled away the stone, sat on it, then turned to the women (while serenely disregarding the petrified guards) and said, "Do not be afraid, for I know that you seek Jesus who was crucified. He is not here; for He is risen, *as He said.* Come, see the place where the Lord lay. And go quickly and tell His disciples that He is risen from the dead, and indeed He is going before you into Galilee; there you will see Him. Behold, I have told you." (Matt. 28:5–7, italics added).

But Jesus had told them first.

4. The Differing Destinies of John and Peter

We ought to feel ecstatic that Jesus doesn't hold a grudge. I know Peter does.

You might think that, after the resurrection, Jesus would lambaste Peter for his triple-header denial. You might think that the cowardly disciple would get a sharp rebuke and a stinging, "I told you so."

But none of that happened. What did happen is that Jesus brought a repentant Peter back into the fold, reaffirming his role of leadership in the new church. "Feed My lambs," Jesus told Peter. "Tend My sheep. Feed My sheep" (John 21:15–17).

That done, the Lord prepared Peter for the hard times ahead by giving him a prophecy of his own death. "Most assuredly, I say to you," Jesus declared, "when you were younger, you girded yourself and walked where you wished; but when you are old, you will stretch out your hands, and another will gird you and carry you where you do not wish." John then added an explanatory note: "This He spoke, signifying by what death he [Peter] would glorify God" (John 21:18–19).

Tradition tells us that Peter was crucified about A.D. 68—upside down at his own request, since he did not feel worthy to die in the same manner as had his Lord. Despite Jesus' slightly veiled prophecy, Peter must have grasped how this prediction would be fulfilled, for he immediately looked around, saw his friend John, and asked, "But Lord, what about this man?"

In his usual straight-shooting way, Jesus replied, "If I will that he remain till I come, what is that to you? You follow me" (John 21:21–22).

Understandably, the rumor quickly spread that John would not die; but as John himself explained, Jesus did not say that he would cheat death, but that the Lord had his own plans for the apostle (v. 23). In fact, history tells us that John lived to a ripe old age and received the vision for the Book of Revelation probably around A.D. 95. And so Jesus' very different prophecies came to very literal fulfillment.

5. Capernaum, Bethsaida, and Chorazin Would Die.

Jesus spoke not only words of tenderness and affirmation, but also words of severe judgment. It was the latter that he pronounced on three ancient cities named Capernaum, Bethsaida, and Chorazin.

The Bible tells us that Jesus performed "most of His mighty works" in these cities, yet their residents did not repent (Matt. 11:20). So Jesus pronounced upon them a most chilling prophecy:

> Woe to you, Chorazin! Woe to you, Bethsaida! For if the mighty works which were done in you had been done in Tyre and Sidon, they would have repented long ago in sackcloth and ashes. But I say to you, it will be more tolerable for Tyre and Sidon in the day of judgment than for you.
>
> And you, Capernaum, who are exalted to heaven, will be brought down to Hades; for if the mighty works which were done in you had been done in Sodom, it would have remained to this day. But I say to you that it shall be more tolerable for the land of Sodom in the day of judgment than for you. (Matt. 11:21–24)

It is never good for a city to hear the Lord of Glory pronounce "woe" upon it, but these three had earned it. The Bible tells us that three of the disciples—Peter, Andrew, and Philip—counted Bethsaida as their hometown (John 1:44), and Jesus fed the five thousand somewhere near the city. Jesus himself had lived, taught, healed the masses, and paid taxes in Capernaum (Mark 1:21, 2:1–2; Matt. 8:5–13, 17:24). So while this trio of cities often had heard the gospel, none of them had responded.

What happened to the three bustling towns? Chorazin died out at least by the time of Eusebius, a fourth-century A.D. church historian. Capernaum, apparently the largest and most important of the three cities, so completely faded away that archaeologists to this day aren't sure whether its remains can be found at Tell Hum or Khan Minya (although most favor the former site). And Bethsaida? Bethsaida has so wholly vanished from history that no one is even sure where to look for its ruins.

A word to the wise: If Jesus has been speaking to you, don't ignore his message. The "woe" that follows carries too big a pricetag.

Prophecies Yet to Be Fulfilled

While Jesus predicted many things that came about either in his lifetime or shortly afterward, he also forecast a number of events that still pertain to our future. The greatest of these prophecies, without question, is what we call the Olivet Discourse.

Picture the Olivet Discourse as the prophetic clothesline on which every other Bible prophecy ought to be hung. This is the granddaddy of all prophecies. Only when we understand its teaching can we effectively come to grips with the rest of Bible prophecy.

The most complete record of the Olivet Discourse is found in Matthew 24 (Mark 13 and Luke 21 give more abbreviated accounts). Some interpreters believe the whole prophecy refers to events already past (the "preterist" viewpoint), but several features of the passage seem to make this impossible (see especially vv. 14, 29–31). Although this viewpoint continues to grow in some circles—among those who do not interpret prophecy literally—it is impossible to prove. Some suggest that Nero (who never once visited Jerusalem) was the Antichrist, but he did not desecrate the temple, as both Jesus and Daniel prophesied. In addition, *many* prophecies in Revelation have yet to be fulfilled. One of the most ridiculous preterist suggestions is that John wrote the Book of Revelation *before* the destruction of Jerusalem, and not in A.D. 95., as the early church believed. The idea that John didn't write the Apocalypse during his exile to Patmos would have surprised the early church, for not until the fourth century did anyone even propose that someone else besides John might have written the book!

I believe a more probable interpretation is that Jesus spoke of "the end of the age" with both near and distant events in mind. He predicted the soon destruction of Jerusalem and the temple (vv. 1–2), both as a validation of the rest of his prophecy and as a picture of the greater terrors to come, as John describes them in Revelation. And Jesus referred to the more distant future (vv. 3–35) in response to his disciples' question, "When will this happen, and what will be the sign of your coming and of the end of the age?" (v. 3)

While we do not have space in this chapter to study the whole Olivet Discourse, I would like to highlight two of its prophetic features—one already fulfilled, the other increasingly pertinent.

1. The Destruction of the Temple

Jesus gave the Olivet Discourse in response to his disciples' star-struck comments regarding the beauty of Herod's temple in Jerusalem. They wanted their Lord to admire the facility and its grounds as much as they did—but he responded with the curt words, "Do you not see all these things? Assuredly, I say to you, not one stone shall be left here upon another, that shall not be thrown down" (v. 2).

Try to imagine the disciples' shock at hearing such ominous words. King Herod began rebuilding the temple in the eighteenth year of his reign (20–19 B.C.). Forty-six years later it was still under construction, during the first year of Jesus' public ministry (John 2:20). Building would continue until A.D. 64. When finished at last, its gleaming white marble and porch faces covered with pure gold would have presented a brilliant spectacle from the Mount of Olives.

Yet Jesus said the whole thing would be trashed.

Fulfillment of his prophecy began in the spring of A.D. 70 at the hands of Roman troops under the command of Titus. Rome's legions had encircled Jerusalem to crush a four-year Jewish revolt. On August 29 of that year, against Titus's wishes, soldiers burned down the whole temple complex. Priests trying to defend the grounds removed bird-preventer spikes on the temple and threw them at the Roman troops. In the end, about six thousand Jews who had taken refuge in the temple died in the flames. Victorious Roman troops not only carried away several temple artifacts—the golden candelabrum, the table of showbread and other items, all depicted on the Arch of Titus in

Rome—but after the fires died out, they prowled through the rubble, dislodging stones and prying into the ruins for the gold that had melted in the intense heat.

In this way Jesus' words found literal fulfillment, while at the same time painting a ghastly picture of what still lay ahead.

2. Rampant Deception in the End Times

As we draw ever closer to the end of the age, the Bible predicts that spiritual deception will mushroom. Six times in Matthew 24, Jesus warns that false teachers and false prophets will multiply (vv. 4, 5, 11, 23, 24, 26). The world will have no lack of spiritual "options" from which to choose.

This is why I've given my life to teaching prophecy, so that men and women can avoid spiritual confusion and alarm (v. 6) as the world lurches toward the end of the age. Count on it: all kinds of isms and spasms and cults will burst on the scene the closer we get to the close of history. I want to urge people to keep their eyes on Jesus, the Spirit of prophecy. *He* is our focal point. Everything must be measured in relationship to him.

It isn't necessary to get confused by the competing claims of this or that prophet. The Bible furnishes at least three practical tests of a real prophet (Deut. 18:20–22). First, what he prophesies, happens—no exceptions. Second, what he prophesies never contradicts Scripture. Third, his prophecy never leads someone away from the living God and toward some other deity or commitment.

Spiritual deceivers always have walked among us, of course, but as we near the end, their numbers will sharply escalate. We would do well to remember the words of the apostle Paul: "For the time will come when they will not endure sound doctrine, but according to their own desires, because they have itching years, they will heap up for themselves teachers; and they will turn their ears away from the truth, and be turned aside to fables" (2 Tim. 4:3–4).

The time of confusion is coming, Jesus warned us; and in fact, it may already have arrived. We must be ready. I write books on prophecy so readers will not be deceived by the many false prophets and cult leaders of the last days.

As surely as the first part of Jesus' prophecy came true, so will every other part. In his grace and mercy and love he has told us ahead of time what will surely happen. Why? So that God's righteous judgments do not shatter us along with the unrepentant. He wants us to be ready when he comes.

Jesus, the Master Prophet

Jesus is the master prophet. Anybody can prophesy about the future, then walk away without any of it coming true. But who can prophesy scores of times and have every single prophecy come to pass? No one but an individual speaking the very words of God, who alone knows the end from the beginning. And that's why Jesus can be trusted so entirely.

Remember what God said when he promised Israel another prophet like Moses? "I . . . will put my words in His mouth," he declared of this Promised One, "and He shall speak to them all I command Him."

This was the very hallmark of Jesus' life and ministry. "My doctrine is not Mine," he told his followers, "but His who sent Me" (John 7:16). "The word which you hear is not Mine," he said once more, "but the Father's who sent Me" (John 14:24). "Whatever I speak, just as the Father has told Me, so I speak," he said yet again (John 12:50). And his words reveal his Father to be the merciful God of prophecy.

No wonder Jesus can be trusted as *the* Prophet in matters pertaining to the future! And no wonder he calls himself "the Alpha and the Omega, the Beginning and the End, the First and the Last" (Rev. 22:13). He came into this world not only to tell you and me many specifics about the life to come, but to encourage us to hear his words and heed them so that we might enjoy the life he wants to give us right here and now. So he says to us, with nearly his last words in the Bible: "And behold, I am coming quickly, and My reward is with Me, to give to every one according to his work . . . Blessed are those who do His commandments, that they may have the right to the tree of life, and may enter through the gates into the city" (Rev. 22:12, 14).

Jesus wants the very best for you. He speaks the very words of God to you so that you might spend eternity with him in heaven. As The Prophet, he invites you to join him forever in his Father's fabulous new creation.

Where else would you want to be?

9

Jesus' Greatest Prophecy: The Church

Most often when we speak of a fulfilled prophecy, we have in mind a specific time and location in which the prophecy came to fulfillment. It might take a year, fifty years, five hundred years, or even more for the prophesied event to occur—but when it makes its appearance, we can say, along with the Bible, "and so was fulfilled the word of the LORD."

At least one major prophecy from Jesus is not like that, however. Its fulfillment didn't occur at a single time or place. In fact, the power of this grand prophecy has continued to reverberate throughout the past two thousand years, changing forever the human landscape of our planet.

No one knows how long this prophecy will continue to be fulfilled. It may end its long run in the next second, or it may continue to shake the world for another two thousand years. Only God knows when he plans to "retire" this phenomenal prophecy.

In my opinion, its magnificent sweep through time and its enormous implications for the whole world make this the greatest prophecy Jesus ever uttered. And *you* can have a significant part in its ongoing fulfillment.

Who *Is* Jesus?

The prophecy came about one day while Jesus was walking along the road with his disciples near Caesarea Philippi, an ancient town about fifty miles southwest of Damascus. He knew that he had become the object of public discussion, rumor, and speculation, so he asked his disciples, "Who do men say that I, the Son of Man, am?" (Matt. 16:13).

The disciples immediately knew that Jesus used the term "Son of Man" to describe himself. Jesus often used this term—borrowed from a messianic passage in Daniel 7:13—to indicate his divine identity and special purpose. So one after another, Jesus' followers eagerly reported what they heard the people say about their charismatic leader.

"Some say you are John the Baptist," a few of them replied. This rumor apparently began in the palace of Herod the tetrarch, who earlier had executed John for his condemnation of Herod's illegal marriage to Herodias, the wife of his brother Philip (Matt. 14:1–12). When the tetrarch heard of the miracles Jesus was performing, the guilt-ridden man immediately thought John had somehow risen from the dead.

"Some say you are Elijah," other disciples suggested, clearly calling to mind the prophecy in Malachi 4:5, in which God promised to send the prophet Elijah to earth before the "great and dreadful day of the LORD."

"Others say you are Jeremiah or one of the prophets," called out several of the disciples, no doubt pleased that their Master had turned to them for news concerning his reputation in the community.

Jesus, however, wanted something more than reports of current events. "But what about *you?*" he asked. "Who do *you* say I am?"

And suddenly, all the disciples shut their mouths. Perhaps they hushed because they weren't sure what to say; maybe they intended to keep their theological options open. Whatever their reasons, all fell quickly silent—except for a single disciple whose booming voice broke the quiet. "You are the Christ, the Son of the living God," he declared.

In a unique moment of utter clarity, Simon Peter rocketed to greatness. He showed that *he* understood, even if no one else did. And Jesus warmly commended him for his supernatural insight.

"Blessed are you, Simon Bar-Jonah, for flesh and blood has not revealed this to you, but My Father who is in heaven," Jesus declared. "And I also say to you that you are Peter, and on this rock I will build My church, and the gates of Hades shall not prevail against it" (Matt. 16:17–18).

So Jesus gave the greatest prophecy that ever issued from his mouth—a prophecy concerning the church, a dynamic prediction that continues to find fulfillment even today, almost twenty centuries later.

On This Rock

Don't forget that when Jesus spoke this prophecy, the church did not yet exist. The Holy Spirit as yet indwelt none of the disciples, and one of them would soon betray Jesus and die in awful remorse. The church proper would not leap into being until Pentecost, fifty days after Jesus died and rose again. Only when the Holy Spirit came to indwell and fill all believers in Christ did the church first step onto the world scene.

This means that at the time Jesus spoke this prophecy, all that existed was a motley crew of ragtag disciples who spent much of their time debating who among them should be called "the greatest." Hardly much reason to inspire such a confident prophecy!

So what was it that prompted Jesus to speak these planet-transforming words? What moved him to give the prophecy? Certainly, it could not have been confidence in the unfaltering character of Peter. In just a little while, Jesus would rebuke Peter to his face, calling him "Satan" and telling him, "You are an offense to Me, for you are not mindful of the things of God, but the things of men" (Matt. 16:23). And just a short while after that, Jesus would predict (correctly) that Peter was but hours away from vehemently denying him three times.

No, it wasn't the stellar character of Peter that prompted this amazing prophecy. Jesus did not intend to build his Hades-defying church on the rock of Peter (in Greek, Peter means "little stone"), but on the solid rock of Peter's divinely revealed declaration: "You are the Christ, the Son of the living God."

"Christ" is the Greek form of the Hebrew word *Messiah,* which in turn means "anointed one." Peter saw that Jesus was the one "anointed" or chosen by God to fulfill all of the Scripture's prophecies of a coming Redeemer and Savior. When Peter called Jesus "the Son of the living God," he meant that Jesus alone, out of all of earth's billions, could be identified as the unique Son of the Father.

And Jesus declared that upon *this* rock, upon *this* declaration of divine truth, would he build his church.

I Will Build My Church

And what's so special about the church? Why should Jesus give such a remarkable prophecy about an institution that today receives so much bad press? Why should anyone care that "the gates of Hades" will not overcome the church?

Glad you asked!

When Jesus said that he was preparing to "build My church," he meant, "I'm going to start a new religion. I'm going to start Christianity. I'm going to start a new faith based on Peter's declaration, 'You are the Messiah, the Son of the Living God.'"

Jesus intended his prophecy as great, Good News. He wanted the world to know that he and his Father were about to create a living organism that would bless the whole planet. He wanted people everywhere to know that he and his Father had conspired together to bring joy, life, satisfaction, fulfillment, and hope to uncounted billions of men and women, girls and boys. And he wanted them to know that, no matter what dark times might momentarily obscure the light, *nothing* could stop him from blessing them through the worldwide ministry of the church.

Do you see why I call this Jesus' greatest prophecy?

The church is God's idea. He designed it from the very beginning to bring us courage and confidence. He created it as a place where new believers could come to spiritual maturity so that they could take the gospel to the entire world. I could name dozens of reasons why the church amounts to fabulous Good News, but consider just five:

1. You Needn't Be Born into the Church.

You don't have to be born physically into the church in order to enjoy its tremendous spiritual and community benefits. In fact, *no one* becomes part of the church through natural birth. Each of us is "adopted" into God's family, freely by faith, when we make the decision to repent of our self-will and personally receive Christ as our Savior and Lord. We do not become sons and daughters of God through natural, physical heritage. Anyone, anywhere on the globe, can choose at any moment to join God in what he is doing around the world through the church. Family background and genealogy have nothing to do with it; God invites every individual to come to him through faith in Jesus Christ, his Son (Rom. 10:9–10).

2. You Don't Have to Be from a Particular Race, Gender, or Nationality.

God wants his church to include believers from every tribe, nation, language, and racial group in the world. In his church, everyone enjoys equal standing, whether male or female, Jew or Gentile, lower class or upper class, black or white or red or yellow or brown. All are sons and daughters of God through faith in Jesus Christ (Gal. 3:26–28; Rev. 5:9).

3. You Don't Have to Wear Yourself Out, Trying to Become "Good Enough."

God does not require that we meet some level of "good behavior" before he'll let us into the church. He does not ask us to first make some difficult pilgrimage, accomplish some arduous task, or clean up our act through some painful act of penance. In fact, he tells us that it is impossible to earn a place among his people by working for it. So then, what *does* he require? He tells us to believe in his Son and to place our faith in him. That alone will gain us the spiritual blessings we seek (Eph. 2:8–9; Gal. 2:16).

4. You Don't Have to Be in Some Holy, Remote Place to Connect with God.

Because the Holy Spirit indwells his church, every place that a believer goes becomes a holy place. Jerusalem or Athens, Chicago or Beloit—all become holy places when God's people live there. Because of the church, we can "connect" with God wherever we are, whether in the lush, green mountains of New Zealand or the dry, brown sands of the Sahara (John 4:21–24; 1 Cor. 3:16).

5. You Don't Need Human Intermediaries to Connect with God.

In Old Testament days, men and women could make regular contact with God only through the mediation of divinely appointed priests. Guilty men and women had to offer regular sacrifices to God through these priests, and they had no way to directly "touch" God. That all changed in the coming of the church, when Christ died for our sins and gave the commission to his church: "Go into all the world and preach the gospel to every creature" (Mark 16:15). Now, each believer in Christ has direct access to God, without having to go through any human intermediary. All Christians are members of "a royal priesthood" (1 Pet. 2:9) and can confidently approach God without fear or worry (Heb. 4:16).

When Jesus gave his prophecy so long ago, he wanted to reassure us, two millennia later, that he would keep the blessings of his church flowing, regardless of the hard times that might come. At all times and in all places, the members of his church can always tap into Christ's "fullness" and the "treasures of wisdom and knowledge" to be found there (Col. 1:19, 2:3). That is why the apostle Paul could pray "that the eyes of your heart may be enlightened in order that you may know the hope to which he has called you, the riches of his glorious inheritance in the saints, and his incomparably great power for us who believe" (Eph. 1:18–19 NIV).

God wants his Son's church to be a tremendous blessing to *you!*

And the Gates of Hades

Jesus' prophecy not only declares a tremendous blessing, it also contains a not-so-veiled warning. While the Lord promised to sustain his church, he also predicted that "the gates of Hades" would oppose it.

What does this mean?

A quick look at world history makes his meaning painfully clear. Can you think of any other world religion that, for two thousand years, has been so universally opposed and persecuted by kings, dictators, malcontents, and religious leaders? For all of that time, somewhere in the world, Christian martyrs have shed their blood.

Do you realize that an estimated 69 *million* Christian martyrs have died since the foundation of the church?[1] What is all of this? It's a satanic attempt to stamp out the testimony of Jesus, the Spirit of prophecy. The gates of hell have raged against the church, trying to destroy it. Dictators and kings and false teachers and hostile religious leaders all have attacked it, seeking its obliteration. Yet despite intense persecution, the church has grown.

I think of John Wycliffe, often called the "Morning Star of

the Reformation," who died in 1384. Despite intense opposition from corrupt church leaders, he castigated ecclesiastics for their immorality and defied church tradition by translating the Bible into English so the common people could read it. About thirty years after his death, the Council of Constance declared Wycliffe a heretic and ordered his body disinterred and burned.

That same year, in 1415, a Bohemian religious reformer named John Huss—a man strongly influenced by Wycliffe—paid for his own dissent with his life. I consider Huss one of my favorite heroes.

Huss was such a great preacher that people came from far and near to hear him speak. He became so popular that the bishop of his area grew afraid of him. Huss vigorously condemned outrageous church abuses and claimed that Jesus, not some corrupt ecclesiastical official, was the true head of the church.

The bishop finally told Huss to stop his preaching, under threat of being burned at the stake. Huss refused and continued his work. When the Pope excommunicated him in 1410, riots broke out in Prague. Huss eventually was summoned to the Council of Constance to explain his beliefs, but when he arrived, his enemies arrested him and tried him for heresy. They attacked the doctrines he preached and demanded that he recant. When he refused, they condemned him to death.

And so the bishop who had for so long opposed Huss managed to send his enemy to the stake. In doing so he thought he had killed this troublesome, independent faith. "At last!" he said, "we have driven a spike through the heresy that plagues Hungary." And as the enemies of Huss (in Hungarian *huss* means "goose") lit the wood that consumed his flesh, this brave Christian martyr shouted out his last words: "Today you roast a goose, but one day a swan will come that you will not be able to cook."

Within a few years the bishop died and was buried. Typical for that time, they dug a grave in front of the cathedral where he had ruled, put a stone slab over it, and carved his name and dates on the marble.

About a century later, officials used the church to hold a ceremony for initiates into the Augustinian order. A young monk lay prostrate on the bishop's tombstone and there took his vows. The irony of this? The man's name was Martin Luther—the man through whom the Protestant Reformation would roar into life just a few years later.

I love that story, but for a long time I wondered if I'd gotten all the details right. Last September, my wife invited Lawrence Wright to speak at her great Concerned Women for America convention in Washington. Lawrence is a Lutheran minister and a great saint of God who shares our love for America, religious freedom, and the cause of Christ. I approached Lawrence after he had given a masterful message, quickly narrated the Huss story, and asked him, "Is this story true?"

He looked at me with a big smile and said, "Yes, that's exactly true. But I'll tell you something else about John Huss. Have you ever noticed the cross and the swan on the steeples of Lutheran churches?"

I had seen hundreds of Lutheran church steeples, but I never could identify the thing sticking out from it. He told me it was a swan and said, "The swan is there at the behest of Martin Luther."

What was Luther saying? The cross wordlessly testifies that Jesus Christ died for our sins, was buried, and rose again the third day. And the swan? The swan declares, as John Huss could say because of the resurrection of Christ, "I will live again." Indeed, the world had not heard the last of John Huss! Because Jesus lives, every believer in him too shall live.

Whole books have been written about the vast numbers of Christian martyrs who have given their lives for Christ. I recall Girolamo Savonarola, an Italian preacher and reformer who was hanged and his body burned in 1498. I think of William Tyndale, who opposed church corruption and published his own English language Bible; he was strangled to death and burned at the stake in 1536.

But don't think persecution died out centuries ago! More Christians died a martyr's death in the twentieth century than in all the centuries before it.[2] A 1997 U.S. State Department Report titled, "U.S. Policies in Support of Religious Freedom: Focus on Christians," lists no fewer than seventy-four nations in which persecution of Christians has mushroomed. In Egypt, Muslim converts to Christianity risk harassment, imprisonment, and torture. In Pakistan, Christians live outside the protection of the law and even a false accusation of blasphemy can lead to a death sentence. In China, Christians operating outside of the government-sponsored "official" church are constant targets of a government that sees them as a threat. In Burma, Christians fleeing persecution run to Thailand, where they continue to suffer for their faith. In Sudan, Christians have been enslaved, raped, and starved.[3]

Truly, "the gates of Hades" have done their best to stamp out the church of Jesus Christ. But will they succeed? *Never*, for our Lord has spoken!

Shall Not Prevail Against It

Despite the persecution, despite the unrelenting attacks of hell, the church of God marches on. Not only do a greater number of Christians live on planet earth than ever before, but they make up a greater percentage of the world's population than at any other time in history.

"I *will* build My church," Jesus said, "and the gates of Hades shall not prevail against it."

The keepers of the gates of Hades must have thought they had won a great victory when terrorists crashed two commercial airliners into the World Trade Center in New York City. But what they intended for evil, God used for good. He knows how to bring blessing even out of the worst horrors that humankind can conceive.

Countless men and women watched the tragedy unfold on their television sets and started asking themselves, "Would *I* have been ready to meet God today, had I been in one of those towers?" I've heard stories from all over the country, recounting how the disaster has changed for the better the spiritual course of thousands.

The message of the church is that you *can* be ready, right now. This was the very message of Jesus: that all can be saved, and saved now. He asked a crowd of listeners, "those eighteen on whom the tower in Siloam fell and killed them, do you think that they were worse sinners than all other men who dwelt in Jerusalem? I tell you, no; but unless you repent you will all likewise perish" (Luke 13:4–5).

We live in a fallen world where evil exists. Wicked men bent on destruction can cause awful devastation and disrupt the lives of innocent people. Yet the unchanging message of the church is this: "You intended to harm me, but God intended it for good, to accomplish what is now being done, the saving of many lives" (Gen. 50:20 NIV). So the apostle Paul can say, "We are hard pressed on every side, yet not crushed; we are perplexed, but not in despair; persecuted, but not forsaken; struck down, but not destroyed" (2 Cor. 4:8–9). How can he say such a thing? Because he can also say, "We know that the one who raised the Lord Jesus from the dead will also raise us with Jesus and present us with you in his presence. All this is for your benefit, so that the grace that is reaching more and more people may cause thanksgiving to overflow to the glory of God" (2 Cor. 4:14–15 NIV).

I learned recently that this thanks-producing grace last year reached a young defensive end for the Green Bay Packers named Kabeer Gbaja-Biamila. A fifth-round pick in the 2000 NFL draft, Gbaja-Biamila grew up a Muslim, but felt empty inside. He said he considered himself "a wicked person" because he was having premarital sex with two women.[4]

But when he met Gill Byrd, the former director of player programs for the Packers and a devout Christian, Gbaja-

Biamila saw something he wanted. Then one day while Gbaja-Biamila sat in Byrd's office, a man came in and started talking about Christ. When Gbaja-Biamila questioned him about some of the principal teachings of Christianity, the man respectfully and confidently answered all his queries. And on that day—September 26, 2000—the defensive end gave his life to Christ. He doesn't remember the man's name, but he thanks God for him. "He came in one day and then left," Gbaja-Biamila said. "He was like an angel."[5]

Soon afterward, an undistinguished young football career began to blossom. Through the first four games of the 2001 season, Gbaja-Biamila tied the NFL record for sacks, at nine. He credits his radical improvement to his conversion, even though he knows many reporters will roll their eyes at such a claim. "You ask me a question, I give you the answer," he says. "I can't make this up."[6]

Gbaja-Biamila illustrates for me how Jesus' prophecy about the church continues to plow ahead, even in the modern world. And I think the Packers' emerging young star would agree.

"I did it my way for 23 years; it brought me nothing," he admitted. "I was depressed, I was sad, I was trying to find my happiness in football, in people."[7]

And after he made Christ his Savior and became a part of the church Jesus died to create?

"It just shows me that God is good," he says. "I'm going to continue saying that: God is great."[8]

Living in the Church Age

The church age in which we're living didn't "just happen"; Jesus Christ himself predicted it. He proclaimed both its birth and its continued existence in Matthew 16 and, I believe, charted out its major life stages in Revelation 2 and 3.

At the time Jesus gave the prophecy, however, he hadn't even founded his church. Nor had he called it into being by the time he ascended into heaven. In fact, he didn't found the church for a full fifty days after his resurrection, when the Holy Spirit came at Pentecost.

And when the time came for the church to take its place in history, with whom did Jesus begin? He started with twelve uneducated men. I would *never* have used a group like that to found anything that I wanted to last forever. And yet it was this dubious group of fishermen and tax collectors and doubters who started a movement that has lasted for two thousand years—in fulfillment of Jesus' prophecy.

Did I just say, "lasted"? That doesn't begin to do justice to the truth. Not only has the church lasted, but this past Easter Sunday, I understand that upwards of *two billion* people all over the world entered a cathedral or a church or a home to commemorate the death, burial, and resurrection of Jesus Christ. Why?

"I will build my church," Jesus said, "and the gates of Hades will not overcome it."

If that isn't a great prophecy that shows the colossal love and mercy of God, I don't know what is.

10

Jesus' Scariest Prophecy: The Great Tribulation

Every time journalists from the secular press interview me, I marvel at the wildness of their ideas about the future. Their minds seem to snap, crackle, and pop with horrific images of catastrophe and chaos. They worry that the future will be a time of persecution, judgment, and utter disaster.

And in one way, they're right. The Bible does say that during the coming Tribulation, God will pour out his fierce wrath upon unrepentant humankind. Jesus himself said that the Tribulation will be unlike anything since the beginning of the world, or ever would be again. He declared that this most brutal seven years in human history will be so dreadful that "unless those days were shortened, no flesh would be saved" (Matt. 24:22).

While all that's true, we must be careful to put this terrifying period into perspective. The Bible does call this God's special time of wrath—but even in the midst of the Tribulation, our Lord plans to pour out his love.

I'm trying in these last days of my life to convince the world of the truth: God really is full of mercy and grace. Even in the coming age of unprecedented trouble and chaos—the worst period ever to engulf planet earth—he will amply demonstrate his long-suffering and grace and goodness.

So then, if we can see God's abundant mercy, grace, and love clearly displayed in the *worst* period of history, then what kind of amazing love must God be anxious to dispense at all other times?

I invite you now to step with me into the (perhaps) not-so-distant future, where we will witness a loving God at work, even in the midst of horror. We will see that God goes to extreme measures in order to reach people with the good news. I frankly hope that this short glimpse into days to come will whet your appetite to experience his amazing love for yourself.

The Purpose of the Tribulation

The Bible devotes more space to the seven-year Tribulation than it does to any other historical period. Most of the Book of Revelation describes the Tribulation, and the Old Testament contains scores of references to it.

The question is—*why?* Why concentrate so heavily on seven years of unparalleled anguish?

I believe the answer, surprisingly enough, is found in the love of God. Through the Tribulation, God plans to cause the earth to tremble and make men and women feel insecure about their eternal destiny, so that a maximum number of individuals will come to faith in Jesus Christ. God will pour out plague after plague and judgment after judgment, not to persecute anyone, but to shake people from their false sense of security. The Bible describes the Tribulation in such graphic detail because a huge population will exist at that time, and God wants to make sure that *everyone* has the opportunity to make a choice about where he or she will spend eternity. For immediately after the Tribulation, the Millennial Kingdom will begin—and after that, heaven!

Just ask yourself: *Why don't some of us come to faith right now?*

When we drive around in our big cars and live in our big houses and the lights work most of the time, we don't much concern ourselves with God. Things feel comfortable. When life deteriorates, however, we start to feel nervous. An incident from many years ago convinces me I'm right.

A dentist named Dr. Ron Jones used to attend the church I pastored in San Diego. After he found Christ, Ron became the most contagious witness for Jesus I've ever seen. As the outgoing president of the local Rotary Club, he wanted to get a Christian message to his brothers.

"Pastor," he said to me, "would you give the talk at our December meeting? That's the last program I can plan; I'm going out of office at the end of the year. I want you to give the gospel to these people at Christmastime."

I agreed, and the Rotarians put on an extravaganza. About 750 people showed up, including the mayor, the members of the city council, and all of the muckety-mucks of the community. As I stood facing the audience, preaching the gospel, the most bored faces I'd ever seen stared back. Men and women looked at me as if to say, "*What* is this madman saying?"

And then an earthquake struck.

As I watched, the water in the table glasses shook so violently that it spilled onto the tablecloths. The silverware bounced. The chandeliers swung back and forth and only slowly swayed to a halt.

Suddenly I had everyone's rapt attention.

That's what happens when our *terra firma* starts shaking. When an earthquake strikes, we cry out, "God, save me!" We feel helpless, vulnerable, fearful—and so we look up.

The Tribulation is designed to have exactly that effect. God has planned its harsh conditions to startle us wide awake: "In a little while I will once more shake the heavens and the earth, the sea and the dry land. I will shake all nations, and the desired of all nations will come," he declares (Hag. 2:6–7 NIV). And how will men respond to the shaking? Jesus gives the answer: "On the earth, nations will be in anguish and perplexity at the roaring and tossing of the sea. Men will faint from terror, apprehensive of what is coming on the world, for the heavenly bodies will be shaken" (Luke 21:25–26 NIV).

The purpose of the Tribulation is not to destroy us or torture us, but to get us to look to God, the long-suffering, merciful, gracious Lord of heaven. And when we look to him, the Lord promises to save whoever will approach him in repentance and faith.

God plans to use this dreadful seven-year period to bring a maximum number of people to faith. God *is* a God of judgment and he *will* pour out his wrath on the world, but prophecy shows how even the Tribulation proclaims God's loving nature. In the future he will manipulate the affairs of humankind to give everyone an opportunity to receive Christ.

Think of the Tribulation as a brief period designed to compress the decision-making process. Previous generations had a whole lifetime to decide what to do about God or Satan. Some of those alive during the Tribulation, however, will not have a full lifetime; they'll have only a short period to make their choice. During those terrible seven years, all hell will break loose in the battle between Satan and God for the souls of men and women. But I have good news—the Bible says that *millions* of individuals will come to faith in Christ during the Tribulation. It's going to be a titanic time.

Biblical Terms for the Tribulation

The name *Tribulation* comes from the term Jesus used when he said, "For then shall be great tribulation, such as was not since the beginning of the world to this time, no, nor ever shall be" (Matt. 24:21 KJV).

Long before Jesus gave this period its memorable name, however, the Bible spoke of its coming reality and fearsome nature. The "day of vengeance of our God"—the Tribulation—is taught some fifty times in the Old Testament. Consider just a few of the biblical terms for the Tribulation:

The time of Jacob's trouble (Jer. 30:7)
A time of trouble (Dan. 12:1)
The day of vengeance of our God (Isa. 61:2)
The day of the LORD (Isa. 13:6)
His (The Lord's) strange work (Isa. 28:21 KJV)

The New Testament calls this same period "the day of the Lord Jesus" (1 Cor. 5:5); "the day of wrath" (Rom. 2:5); "the wrath of God" (Col. 3:6); "the wrath of the Lamb" (Rev. 6:16); "the wrath to come" (1 Thess. 1:10); "the hour of trial" (Rev. 3:10); and "the hour of His judgment" (Rev. 14:7).

Even the terms that God uses to describe the Tribulation reveal its awesome character. No one could read these terrifying descriptions and still wish to personally experience "the day of God's wrath." And yet, when we look closely into what God tells us prophetically about this unique period, we discover new facets of his grace, mercy, and love.

Gracious Elements of the Tribulation

At some point just before the Tribulation begins, God will supernaturally take the church out of the world and bring her into the blessed presence of Christ, her Lord (see chapter 11). And yet God will never leave himself without a witness to the world (Acts 14:17). Even during the Tribulation, he will work vigorously to bring men and women to himself. Note the following six remarkable ways in which God will supernaturally intervene in the affairs of men in an attempt to make his message of invitation plain to all.

1. God Will Send His Spirit, as at Pentecost.

One Bible passage so sets my heart on fire that I carry it with me wherever I go. God promised through the prophet:

And it shall come to pass afterward that I will pour out My Spirit on all flesh; your sons and your daughters shall prophesy, your old men shall dream dreams, your young men shall see visions. And also on My menservants and on My maidservants I will pour out My Spirit in those days. (Joel 2:28–29)

The apostle Peter applied these verses to the day of Pentecost when the Holy Spirit led three thousand Jews to respond to the gospel (Acts 2:41). But what Joel said next did not happen on that Pentecost, so long ago:

And I will show wonders in the heavens and in the earth: blood and fire and pillars of smoke. The sun shall be turned into darkness, and the moon into blood, before the coming of the great and awesome day of the LORD. And it shall come to pass that whoever calls on the name of the LORD shall be saved. (Joel 2:30–32)

During the Tribulation, eyewitnesses will see Pentecost repeated, along with catastrophic signs in the heavens. This whole passage in Joel awaits consummation at the end of the Tribulation. At that time God will pour out his Spirit so that whoever calls upon the name of the Lord will be saved.

Don't think that just because the church is taken out of the picture through the Rapture, the Holy Spirit will vacate this world. He will remain alive and active on the earth, just as in the days of the Old Testament. He will not indwell believers as he does today, but he will continue to call men and women to faith in Christ.

The Tribulation will see a mighty outpouring of God's Spirit, as on the day of Pentecost two thousand years ago—only, just possibly, even greater. Evil forces will wax worse and worse, but God will also be active in power through his Holy Spirit.

2. God Will Commission 144,000 Spirit-Filled Evangelists.

My favorite verse in the Book of Revelation is found in chapter 7, verse 9: "After these things I looked, and behold, a great multitude which no one could number, of all nations, tribes, peoples, and tongues, standing before the throne and before the Lamb, clothed with white robes, with palm branches in their hands."

Who are these people? Verse 14 tells us: "These are the ones who come out of the great tribulation, and washed their robes and made them white in the blood of the Lamb."

Picture it—a multitude so vast that "no one could number" it! Since Revelation 9:16 mentions a figure of 200 million individuals, this number that no one could count must be still larger—a huge, mind-boggling figure. Yet that is how many men and women will come to faith during the Tribulation!

"Ah," someone says, "but how do so many persons commit their lives to Christ during such a hard time?" One major reason has to be the 144,000 "servants of our God" whom God commissions at the beginning of Revelation 7. Can you imagine what will happen when 144,000 Spirit-filled evangelists head to every corner of the world? When I think of powerful evangelists, I always think of the apostle Paul. He probably led more people to Christ and enjoyed a greater impact on Christianity than anyone who ever lived. But imagine what would happen if you could multiply him by 144,000—every man with a keen mind, resourceful spirit, and dedicated to getting the message out. My blood turns hot just thinking about it.

Who but a loving, gracious, merciful God could plan in advance to raise up 144,000 evangelists to go out in power and preach his message during that time of chaos? Yet in his infinitely kind way, God will reach out to gather a multitude that nobody can number. It will be the greatest soul harvest in history!

3. God Will Prepare Two Extraordinary Witnesses.

As if it weren't enough to prepare and send out 144,000 apostle Pauls, God also intends to give the world three-and-a-half years of Moses and Elijah.

"I will give power to my two witnesses, and they will prophesy one thousand two hundred and sixty days, clothed in sackcloth," he promised (Rev. 11:3). At the beginning of the Tribulation, God will commission two supernatural witnesses to call the world's attention to the choice every human must make. Not everyone, however, will greet their ministry with joy:

> And if anyone wants to harm them, fire proceeds from their mouth and devours their enemies. And if anyone wants to harm them, he must be killed in this manner. These have power to shut heaven, so that no rain falls in the days of their prophecy; and they have power over waters to turn them to blood, and to strike the earth with all plagues, as often as they desire. (Rev. 11:5–6)

The miracles these men will perform closely mirror those of Moses and Elijah (Exod. 7:14–10:29; 1 Kings 18:16–39; 2 Kings 1:9–10). Beyond that, God says that Elijah himself will return (Mal. 4:5–6; Mark 9:13), and the Transfiguration may give us an indication of the identity of the second witness (Matt. 17:3). So these men quite possibly may be Moses and Elijah.

And why will God send them? The Bible says, "When they finish their testimony" (Rev. 11:7). What kind of testimony? The testimony of prophecy is the Spirit of Jesus—so these men will be incredible evangelists. Sure, they'll have miraculous powers. And sure, they're going to prophesy. But they'll also preach the Word of God.

In his grace and mercy, God will do just what he did in Old Testament days. He will supernaturally empower an Elijah and a Moses to speak his message. Everyone will see them on the news, proclaiming the truth. CNN's cameras will swarm Jerusalem and the message of these two witnesses will air all over the world.

At the end of three-and-a-half years, the Bible says these two witnesses will be killed. The world will watch their deaths on television and will observe their corpses lying in the street. Three-and-a-half days later, the Lord will mercifully bring his two servants back to life and call them up to heaven—an astonishing miracle that the world also will witness (Rev. 11:7–12).

Why will God go to all of this trouble? One reason: to convince humankind of his reality. How can one deny the supernatural when it multiplies on every hand?

4. God Will Prepare a Special Place for His Special People.

As bad as the first half of the Tribulation will be, the second half will be far worse. At the midpoint of the Tribulation, the Antichrist will desecrate the rebuilt Jerusalem temple in order to proclaim himself God (Dan. 9:27; Matt. 24:15–25; 2 Thess. 2:3–4). Any promises he made to Israel regarding her protection will vanish like smoke, and he will try to destroy the Jewish nation (pictured in Revelation as a woman), beginning the worst persecution in history (Rev. 12:13, 15).

But then God steps in.

Revelation 12 says of Israel:

> Then the woman fled into the wilderness, where she has a place prepared by God, that they should feed her there one thousand two hundred and sixty days . . . But the woman was given two wings of a great eagle, that she might fly into the wilderness to her place, where she is nourished for a time and times and half a time, from the presence of the serpent. (vv. 6, 14)

God will lead his people—maybe a million or more Jews—into the wilderness. Most prophecy scholars think they'll head to Petra, the rock city in Edom. There the Lord will nourish Israel for three-and-a-half years, safe from satanic attack.

"Wow," you say, "what a strange thing to do." Maybe—but do you remember the Exodus? What a weird thing *that* was for God to do! Here God will replicate the Exodus, this time on the "wings of a great eagle." Something supernatural is going to happen, by which God will protect a million or more Jews, setting them down in a place where they will be kept safe from the Antichrist and Satan. The evil ones will run free across the face of the earth to destroy just about everything else they please, but they won't be able to touch that select group of Jews. Why not? Because God promised he would rescue them, provide for them, and nourish them throughout the second half of the Tribulation.

Isn't it mind-blowing? The supernatural God of heaven has announced ahead of time how he will protect and save his people. The Antichrist will persecute them, but God will save them. During that compressed time of three-and-a-half years, they will have the opportunity to choose: Whom are you going to serve? Are you going to obey Antichrist? Or are you going to call on the name of the Lord? Fortunately, even in this time of utter chaos, many will call on the name of the Lord.

And once again, the Lord will plainly demonstrate his abundant grace and mercy.

5. *God Will Send an Angel to Proclaim the Eternal Gospel.*

As the Tribulation nears its fiery conclusion, another incident will occur, something that sets my imagination aflame. For the first time in history, God will commission an angel to preach the gospel: "Then I saw another angel flying in the midst of heaven, having the everlasting gospel to preach to those who dwell on the earth—to every nation, tribe, tongue, and people" (Rev. 14:6).

This has to be the most incredible evangelistic outreach in Bible history. Nowhere else in Scripture does an angelic being preach the gospel. In the past, God has used an angel to tell one human where he could go to hear another human preach the gospel (Acts 10), but never has an angel done the preaching.

This angel is said to have "the everlasting gospel." He's going to be like Michael or Gabriel, a supernatural being who publicly speaks God's message of salvation. The only gospel that exists (Eph. 4:4–6; Jude 1:3) declares that Jesus, God's only Son, died for our sins, was buried, and rose again the third day. So that is the message the angel will preach.

And to whom will he preach? To "every nation, tribe, language, and people." I am sure that in the Tribulation, as now, there will yet remain some remote tribes of whom we have never heard. God, the Sovereign of the universe, will look over all these billions of people, and he will see a tribe here and a city there that hasn't yet had the opportunity to respond to his message. So what will he do? He's already sent the Holy Spirit; he's already sent the 144,000; he's already sent the two witnesses. But just to make sure that everyone gets the message, he will send a special angel to preach the everlasting gospel.

Aware that his Son will return to earth in just a few months and that the Millennium will immediately follow, God will do everything he can to make sure that everyone has the best opportunity to make a wise spiritual decision. So by the end of the Tribulation, everyone who needs to hear the gospel, will hear the gospel. Isn't that amazing?

6. God Warns His People to Flee Babylon.

At the very end, just before the battle of Armageddon and the return of Jesus, God will do one more thing to demonstrate his staggering mercy and grace. The time will have finally come for the destruction of commercial and governmental Babylon and its arrogant, idolatrous lifestyle. But before God's hand of judgment falls, the Lord will declare to those with ears to hear, "Come out of her, my people, lest you share in her sins, and lest you receive of her plagues" (Rev. 18:4).

Babylon will be destroyed just moments before the Lord Jesus comes to set up his thousand-year kingdom. At that time a supernatural voice will speak in the capital city of the world, warning God's people to flee the wrath to come. Even at the eleventh hour, even as angelic swords of doom stand poised to strike, the God of heaven will take time to urge anyone who will hear, "Come to me."

These are not the actions of a bloodthirsty God eager to terrify. This is not the behavior of a deity who revels in destruction. These are not the deeds of a supernatural being who relishes judgment.

But it is exactly what we might expect from a loving God who delights in mercy.

Avoid One, Enjoy the Other

As I said, the Bible gives more space to the Tribulation than it does to any other period in history. In fact, we're told far more about the Tribulation than about the Millennium, although the Tribulation lasts only seven years while the Millennium endures for a thousand. The Millennium outlasts the Tribulation by a ratio of 142.8 to 1, yet it gets less biblical ink. Why?

We guessed earlier that it's because God would rather have us *read* about the Tribulation than experience it. He wants us to glimpse many of its gory details so that we might be motivated to escape it. Therefore he describes for us the seal judgments in the first twenty-one months, followed by the awful trumpet judgments. Then it gets worse. The Antichrist is revealed, the false prophet joins him, and believers are martyred on a worldwide scale. Last come the bowl judgments. For good reason, Jesus called this period the "great tribulation."

But remember, all during this dark time, God will be working to get people to make a decision for him. Why? The Millennium is coming! After Jesus comes in power and great glory, he's going to set up his kingdom and he will allow only those who have chosen to call upon the name of the Lord to enter.

God doesn't give us a lot of details about the Millennium; he would rather have us experience it than get sidetracked by a literary description. Therefore he tells us only a little, just enough to whet our appetites for the real thing.

We must understand the Tribulation in the light of the Millennium. God wants us to avoid the first and enjoy the second. The Millennium will be so much greater than anything we've ever experienced! It will be a magnificent time, the significance of which we can hardly imagine.

God Wills That All Be Saved

All my life I have wished that, just one time, God would bare his omnipotent arm and say in an unmistakable way, "I'm here!"

I hear so many skeptics revile God and shake their fists in his face as if he didn't exist, then go on their merry way. And so I say, "Lord, wouldn't you—*just one time*—give them a little bolt of something that might wake them up?"

But I know he's unlikely to do that . . . until after the Rapture. And then he'll provide a boatload of bolts!

The time quickly approaches when the Great Deception will occur, the worst fraud in history. When Satan gets cast out of heaven and realizes his time is short, this deceiver of mankind will unleash everything in his diabolical arsenal—counterfeit miracles and all kinds of lying signs and wonders—in order to deceive men and women into worshiping him (see Matt. 24:4–5, 11, 23–26; 2 Thess. 2:9–10; Rev. 12:12). That's his ultimate purpose in the Tribulation: to usurp the Lord's place and receive the worship that belongs to God alone.

And yet, even during the Tribulation, God in his marvelous grace will intervene. Even during Satan's "hour—when darkness reigns" (Luke 22:53 NIV), God will literally move heaven and earth in order to entice men and women into his kingdom of light.

May I ask a personal question? Can you say, along with the apostle Paul, "If God is for us, who can be against us" (Rom. 8:31)? When you pray, when you seek the Lord, do you remember that he is *for* you? Believe me, there is no one in this world who is so for you as God.

In fact, to prove just how *for* us he is, our God has given us adequate warning about the seven hellish years of coming Tribulation. People who reject God think it's terrible that he would ever show his wrath. They refuse to surrender to him, they arch their backs, and they continue to defy him. So they go the way of all willful people who depart from God—and one day, billions of such individuals will find themselves in the Tribulation.

It comes down to this: What will you do with Jesus Christ? Is Jesus Lord and Christ? Or just a good man? Should you decide that he is Lord, then take the next step, that he will be *your* Lord. Receive him and surrender your life to him and become his willing servant. That's the decision that God wants everyone to make, even during the Tribulation.

Remember the prophet Joel? What he said thousands of years ago remains true today:

> "Now, therefore," says the LORD, "Turn to Me with all your heart, with fasting, with weeping, and with mourning." So rend your heart, and not your garments; return to the LORD your God, for He is gracious and merciful, slow to anger, and of great kindness; and He relents from doing harm. (Joel 2:12–13)

In the same spirit, Jesus once said, "it is not the will of your Father who is in heaven that one of these little ones should perish" (Matt. 18:14).

So what is the will of God? The will of God is that everyone should come to faith in Jesus Christ. Peter said it explicitly: "The Lord is . . . longsuffering toward us, not willing that any should perish but that all should come to repentance" (2 Pet. 3:9). God does not change, and his will is always that everyone come to repentance.

Even in the Tribulation.

11

❧

Jesus' Most Hope-Filled Prophecy: The Second Coming

Everywhere I go, I find exploding interest in the second coming of Christ. Why?

For one thing, the return of Jesus is the next major event on the prophetic calendar of God. Nothing else needs to happen before Christ will come in the clouds for his church. But a second reason also helps to explain the public's mounting fascination with the Second Coming: many among us feel scared to death of the future.

Several years back, the cover of *Psychology Today* featured a picture of a nuclear bomb blowing up the world. The accompanying article reported that many children today live with the fear of never growing up.

And it's not only children who feel apprehensive and anxious. Intelligent, mature adults agonize that modern technological advances in nuclear, biological, and chemical weapons—as well as the sophisticated delivery systems that allow enormous payloads to hit targets thousands of miles away—make it next to certain that we will one day exterminate ourselves. They worry that terrorist cells or rogue nations already have such fearsome weapons, and they understandably fret that some madman will soon use them.

Two millennia ago Jesus foresaw all of this modern mayhem and yet declared, "See that you are not troubled" (Matt. 24:6). In fact, he bluntly stated, "when you hear of wars and commotions, do not be terrified" (Luke 21:9).

Now, how can that be? How could Jesus tell his followers, in effect, "Don't worry about it"? Does he know something that we might not, something that might calm our fears and comfort our hearts?

As a matter of fact, he does.

God's Master Plan

When Jesus told his disciples to shelve their fears, he didn't mean that they should stick their heads in the sand and pretend that heaven already had arrived. Nor did he want them to disregard the world's problems or to disengage from the task of helping to alleviate human suffering. Quite the contrary. He told them point-blank, "As long as it is day, we must do the work of him who sent me" (John 9:4 NIV). And in a famous parable he urged his followers to get to work "until I come back" (Luke 19:13 NIV).

So what did he mean? Why did Jesus tell his disciples not to fear the future?

The biblical context makes his reason plain: his followers were to reject worry regarding ominous future events because God has in place a master plan for the world, an unshakeable strategy that calls for Jesus to return to earth and reign over it from the throne of David. God promises to so superintend history that, regardless of disaster or ruin or catastrophe, the world will continue to exist until his Son returns to rule it "with a rod of iron" (Ps. 2:9; see also Rev. 2:27, 12:5, 19:15).

Through his reliable Word, Jesus assures us that God really does have everything under control. We needn't fret, because God loves us more than we can imagine and dotes over us, even to the extent of knowing the exact number of hairs that populate every believer's head (Luke 12:5–7).

So does that mean that bad things won't ever happen to us? No, indeed. We may be called upon to suffer trouble, hardship, persecution, famine, nakedness, danger, or sword (Rom. 8:35). Yet none of those things can separate us from the love of God, and none of them can even approach us without God's consent (John 19:11). Because God has said to us, "I will never leave you nor forsake you," we can say with confidence, "The LORD is my helper; I will not fear. What can man do to me?" (Heb. 13:5–6).

Remember, God gave us Bible prophecy to build our confidence, not to make us fearful about the future. "Do not fear, little flock," Jesus said, "for it is your Father's good pleasure to give you the kingdom" (Luke 12:32). Why does Jesus tell us not to worry about the future? Because he will surely return to this planet, and no madman is going to destroy our world before the Lord comes back to take us to his Father's house.

Even so, Jesus knows that anxious thoughts about the future can play havoc with our hearts. For that very reason, he told us exactly what to expect on the day (or night!) he returns to claim his own.

In the Father's House

As the hour of his arrest and crucifixion grew near, Jesus focused his efforts on preparing his disciples for the awful events that lay ahead. When he explained that he would soon be leaving them, his men reacted with alarm. They did not want him to go—but if he did have to depart, they said they wanted to go with him. Clearly, they did not understand what was about to happen.

But Jesus did understand. He also fully appreciated the turmoil of mind that plagued them; that is why he took care to reassure his disciples with hopeful words that continue to comfort us today. "Let not your heart be troubled," he said, "you believe in God, believe also in Me. In My Father's house are many mansions; if it were not so, I would have told you. I go to prepare a place for you. And if I go and prepare a place for you, I will come again and receive you to Myself; that where I am, there you may be also" (John 14:1–3).

This passage in John 14 is the first teaching about the Rapture in the Bible. The Lord Jesus uttered these words at a strategic time, just hours before his arrest in the Garden of Gethsemane. In these words our Lord gave us a treasure that you and I can take to the bank of eternity. This is Jesus' guarantee that one day he's coming back for us. This world has not seen the last of Jesus Christ!

The Bible's Second Most Common Doctrine

While John 14 remains a personal favorite of mine, the Bible overflows with promises of Jesus' second coming. The return of Christ is the second most common doctrine in the Bible; in fact, the majority of the Bible's yet-to-be-fulfilled prophecies concern the second coming of Jesus Christ.

Did you know the Bible contains *almost three times as many* promises of Jesus' second coming as of his first coming? Scripture boasts 129 prophecies regarding Jesus' first coming, but 329 predictions regarding his second coming. Since his first coming occurred just as prophesied, we can anticipate that the second coming is three times as certain as his first.

Jesus is coming again! He said it: "I will come again" (John 14:3). The angel said it: "This same Jesus, who was taken up from you into heaven, will so come in like manner as you saw Him go into heaven" (Acts 1:11). Paul said it: "For the Lord Himself will descend from heaven" (1 Thess. 4:16). Enoch said it: "Behold, the Lord comes" (Jude 1:14). The writer to the Hebrews said it: "He who is coming will come and will not tarry" (Heb. 10:37). Peter said it: "And when the Chief Shepherd appears, you will receive the crown of glory that does not fade away" (1 Pet. 5:4). John said it: "Behold, He is coming with clouds" (Rev. 1:7).

Jesus is coming again in power and great glory, just as the Hebrew prophets and the apostles and Jesus himself foretold.

Yet Scripture indicates that the second coming of Christ will occur in two phases: the Rapture of the church; and at least seven years later, the Glorious Appearing, when Jesus will come physically to the earth.

Let's take a quick look at these two phases of Jesus' return and see how perfectly they fit together.[1]

The Church Snatched Away

The most comprehensive passage about the Rapture appears in the fourth chapter of 1 Thessalonians, where the apostle Paul wrote:

> But I do not want you to be ignorant, brethren, concerning those who have fallen asleep, lest you sorrow as others who have no hope. For if we believe that Jesus died and rose again, even so God will bring with Him those who sleep in Jesus. For this we say to you by the word of the Lord, that we who are alive and remain until the coming of the Lord will by no means precede those who are asleep. For the Lord Himself will descend from heaven with a shout, with the voice of an archangel, and with the trumpet of God. And the dead in Christ will rise first. Then we who are alive and remain shall be caught up together with them in the clouds to meet the Lord in the air. And thus we shall always be with the Lord. (vv. 13–17)

Paul told us here that Jesus will one day return in the air to "snatch away" his followers. The spirits of dead believers, all of whom will return with him, will at that time receive new, glorified bodies. A fraction of a moment later, living believers will rise to meet Christ in the air, where they, too, will receive supernatural bodies. "Therefore comfort one another with these words," Paul wrote (v. 18).

I maintain that the only concept of Christ's coming that truly encourages us is the "preTribulation Rapture"—that is, the teaching that Jesus will gather his church before the start of seven prophesied years of divine wrath. When Jesus comes, he will save all believers from the Tribulation—a time specifically revealed as "the great day" of the "wrath of the Lamb" of God (Rev. 6:16–17)—while the rest of the world will have to go through it. Paul pointedly said that Jesus "delivers us from the wrath to come" (1 Thess. 1:10).

And how does he rescue us? Through the Rapture.

The fourth chapter of Revelation provides us with a picture of the Rapture. The apostle John wrote: "After these things I looked, and behold, a door standing open in heaven. And the first voice which I heard was like a trumpet speaking with me, saying, 'Come up here, and I will show you things which must take place after this.' Immediately I was in the Spirit; and behold, a throne set in heaven, and One sat on the throne" (vv. 1–2).

John, a member of the body of Christ, got this message around A.D. 95 while exiled to the Greek Isle of Patmos. All the other disciples were long dead; he represented the last of them. By this time, the message of the Second Coming had spread throughout the church. Paul had taught it several decades prior, then gone on to his reward. Just before John died, he—as the last eyewitness of the Lord Jesus—had this remarkable vision in which God took him up to heaven as a member of the body of Christ. Through his experience, we see a picture of the Rapture.

While I would never base the Rapture teaching on this single passage, I do think it paints a good image of the Rapture, a doctrine more fully disclosed in other texts. The Rapture is the next major event on God's prophetic calendar.

When will the Rapture happen? I don't know, and neither does anyone else. Paul likened the Lord's return to a "thief in the night" (1 Thess. 5:2)—unexpected, unforeseen, sudden. The apostle borrowed this picture from the Lord himself, who told his disciples to be ready for his return at any time, "for the Son of Man is coming at an hour you do not expect"—just like a thief (Luke 12:40).

That's the first phase of the Lord's return, when he comes in the air to snatch the church away from earth. He will then take his redeemed and glorified followers to his Father's house, where they are to celebrate what is called "the marriage supper of the Lamb" (Rev. 19:6–9) and where each believer will receive whatever rewards he or she may have earned (2 Cor. 5:10; 1 Cor. 3:10–15; Rom. 14:9–12).

Meanwhile on earth, civilization will descend into chaos. Seven horrific years of Tribulation are going to engulf the world as the Antichrist and his satanic forces devastate the planet. Billions will die through war, persecution, disease, famine, and awesome divine judgments. Nevertheless, through it all God will mercifully lavish eternal life on all those who turn to him in repentance and faith. When at last the world teeters on the brink of extinction, God once more will intervene and end those terrible days "for the elect's sake" (Matt. 24:22). And how will God end those days?

By sending his Son to earth, at which time Jesus will set up a kingdom lasting for a thousand years. That's the second phase of his return, which we call the Glorious Appearing.

The Glorious Appearing

A recent poll showed that an astonishing 62 percent of the American public believes that Jesus Christ is physically coming back to this earth. I consider that amazing, since the same poll revealed that only 41 percent of respondents have committed their lives to Christ.[2] That means that a quarter of all Americans who believe Jesus is coming again are not ready for his arrival. That's one out of four!

Jesus offered a parable and a word of advice for every man and woman among that unprepared 25 percent. All of us would do well to pay careful attention to his words:

Watch therefore, for you do not know what hour your Lord is coming. But know this, that if the master of the house had known what hour the thief would come, he would have watched and not allowed his house to be broken into. Therefore you also be ready, for the Son of Man is coming at an hour you do not expect. (Matt. 24:42–44)

As I said, I can't reveal when the Rapture is going to take place. Jesus declared, "But of that day and hour no one knows, not even the angels of heaven, but My Father only" (Matt. 24:36). He reiterated his point just before the Ascension when he told his disciples, "It is not for you to know times or seasons which the Father has put in His own authority" (Acts 1:7).

But I can tell you exactly when the Glorious Appearing is going to occur; none of us needs to remain unprepared for it. Jesus ended his description of the gruesome Tribulation period with these words:

> *Immediately after the tribulation of those days* the sun will be darkened, and the moon will not give its light; the stars will fall from heaven, and the powers of the heavens will be shaken. Then the sign of the Son of Man will appear in heaven, and then all the tribes of the earth will mourn, and they will see the Son of Man coming on the clouds of heaven with power and great glory. (Matt. 24:29–30, italics added)

Everyone who heard Jesus make this statement that day knew he was borrowing some language from the prophet Daniel. Hundreds of years before, Daniel described a vision in which:

> I was watching in the night visions, and behold, One like the Son of Man, coming with the clouds of heaven! He came to the Ancient of Days, and they brought Him near before Him. Then to Him was given dominion and glory and a kingdom, that all peoples, nations, and languages should serve Him. His dominion is an everlasting dominion, which shall not pass away, and His kingdom the one which shall not be destroyed. (Dan. 7:13–14)

In words designed to make sure everyone understood his point, Jesus publicly declared that he would come again to set up the everlasting kingdom predicted by Daniel. And when would this happen? He also made that very clear: *"Immediately after the tribulation of those days."* Jesus promised he would come again at the conclusion of the Tribulation. For that reason, we know exactly when the Glorious Appearing will take place; the Bible has given us the countdown clock. Note the fluorescent hands on its dial:

- We know that the Tribulation will begin with the signing of some kind of treaty between the "many" (Israel) and the Antichrist, which he will break halfway through the term of the agreement (Dan. 9:27).
- We know the Tribulation will last seven years (Dan. 9:27; Rev. 11:2–3; 12:6, 14; 13:5).
- We know that the Glorious Appearing phase of his return will come "immediately after the distress of those days" (Matt. 24:29).
- Therefore we know that Jesus Christ will return physically to earth at the conclusion of the seven-year Tribulation.

Jesus is coming again! During the second and final phase of his return to earth, the world will at last come face-to-face with the one it rejected. This time he will come, not as a Lamb led to slaughter, but as a Lion "with power and great glory" (Matt. 24:30). Chills must have raced up and down the apostle John's spine when he saw a startling vision of Jesus at the end of the Tribulation:

Now I saw heaven opened, and behold, a white horse. And He who sat on him was called Faithful and True, and in righteousness He judges and makes war. His eyes were like a flame of fire, and on His head were many crowns. He had a name written that no one knew except Himself. He was clothed with a robe dipped in blood, and His name is called The Word of God. And the armies in heaven, clothed in fine linen, white and clean, followed Him on white horses. Now out of His mouth goes a sharp sword, that with it He should strike the nations. And He Himself will rule them with a rod of iron. He Himself treads the winepress of the fierceness and wrath of Almighty God. And He has on His robe and on His thigh a name written:

KING OF KINGS AND LORD OF LORDS.
(Rev. 19:11–16)

Such will be the awesome scene when Jesus returns physically to this earth. No one will be able to tear his or her eyes away from the glorious sight.

"Behold," says John:

He is coming with clouds, and every eye will see Him, even they who pierced Him. And all the tribes of the earth will mourn because of Him. Even so, Amen. (Rev. 1:7)

Not the Same Event

Not everyone who studies Bible prophecy believes that Jesus' return will occur in two stages. Many diligent scholars teach that the Rapture will not occur until immediately before Jesus sets foot on earth at the end of the Tribulation—but such a proposed scenario doesn't appear to square with the biblical facts. When one looks closely at the passages detailing the Rapture and the Glorious Appearing, it becomes obvious that several irreconcilable differences exist between them.

I see at least fifteen major differences between the Rapture and the Glorious Appearing. When you compare these differences side by side, you see instantly that Scripture must be talking about two separate phases of one major event. There is simply no other way to reconcile the marked differences. But judge for yourself whether descriptions of the Rapture and the Glorious Appearing describe the same phase of the same event:

Rapture	**Glorious Appearing**
1. Christ comes *for* his own	1. Christ comes in the *air with* his own to earth
2. Believers taken up	2. No one taken up
3. Christians taken to the Father's house	3. Resurrected saints do not see the Father's house
4. No judgment on earth	4. Christ judges the inhabitants of earth
5. The church is taken to heaven	5. Christ sets up his kingdom on earth
6. Imminent; could happen now	6. Can't occur for at least seven years
7. No signs for the Rapture	7. Many signs for Christ's coming
8. For believers only	8. Affects all mankind
9. A time of joy	9. A time of mourning
10. Occurs before the day of wrath	10. Occurs immediately after the Tribulation
11. No mention of Satan	11. Satan is bound in the bottomless pit for one thousand years
12. The Judgment Seat of Christ	12. No time or place for the Judgment Seat
13. Wedding of the Lamb	13. His Bride descends with him
14. Only his own see him	14. Every eye shall see him
15. Tribulation begins	15. One-thousand-year kingdom of Christ begins

I don't see how these two sets of wildly different descriptions could possibly refer to the same thing. Do you? I think it much more likely—in fact, necessary—to see them as two distinct phases of Christ's long-prophesied coming.

Besides, if Jesus comes for his church at the end of the Tribulation, as some Christians believe, how could the judgment of the sheep (believers) and the goats (unbelievers) occur, as described in Matthew 25:31–46? All the believers would have been taken up to him; only the unbelievers would be left. And since the latter will all be cast into "everlasting punishment" (v. 46), no one would be left in their natural bodies to go into the Millennium and populate that thousand-year kingdom. And if that were true, then what group rebels at the end of the Millennium (Rev. 20:7–9)? Consequently, a post-Tribulation Rapture is impossible.

Once before in history some individuals made the mistake of rejecting Christ because he didn't seem to fit the Bible's prophecies of a powerful King who would rule the world with an iron scepter. Those folks didn't understand from Scripture that Jesus would come twice; the first time as a sacrifice for their sin, the second time as an omnipotent King.

Let's not make a similar mistake this time around. Jesus *is* coming again, but he will do so in two distinct phases: first the Rapture, in which he comes in the air for his church; and second the Glorious Appearing, in which he comes to earth to set up his one-thousand-year kingdom.

We should all join with the apostle John in saying, "Amen. Even so, come, Lord Jesus" (Rev. 22:20).

Everything Points to Jesus' Return

The second coming of Christ occupies such an important place in Christianity that it colors almost every element of the faith. Whether we consider doctrine or practice, celebrations or behavior, most everything in our faith anticipates the return of Jesus Christ.

God tells us a great deal about the Second Coming in order to motivate us, encourage us, and give us hope. Reflect on how the Bible weaves the return of Jesus into the fabric of our faith.

The Lord's Supper

Every time believers take Holy Communion, they do so not only in memory of the crucifixion of Christ, but in anticipation of his second coming. The apostle Paul told us, "For as often as you eat this bread and drink this cup, you proclaim the Lord's death till He comes" (1 Cor. 11:26). Jesus himself took the cup at the very first Lord's Supper and said, "For this is My blood of the new covenant, which is shed for many for the remission of sins. But I say to you, I will not drink of this fruit of the vine from now on until that day when I drink it new with you in My Father's kingdom" (Matt. 26:28–29).

Worship

Whenever Christians gather for worship, by this very act they look forward to the return of Jesus. "Therefore, since we are receiving a kingdom which cannot be shaken," said the writer to the Hebrews, "let us have grace, by which we may serve God acceptably with reverence and godly fear" (12:28).

Prayer

Our prayers gain focus and power when we consciously remember that Jesus is coming again: "the end of all things is at hand; therefore be serious and watchful in your prayers" (1 Pet. 4:7).

Ministry

God encourages ministers of the gospel to keep in mind the Second Coming so that their service will remain both effective and relevant: "I charge you therefore before God and the Lord Jesus Christ, who will judge the living and the dead at His appearing and His kingdom: preach the word! Be ready in season and out of season. Convince, rebuke, exhort, with all longsuffering and teaching" (2 Tim. 4:1–2).

Funerals

When we stand before a casket containing the remains of a Christian brother or sister, the Lord wants us to remember that Jesus is coming back: "But I do not want you to be ignorant, brethren, concerning those who have fallen asleep, lest you sorrow as others who have no hope. For if we believe that Jesus died and rose again, even so God will bring with Him those who sleep in Jesus" (1 Thess. 4:13–14).

Patience

It's easy to grow impatient or irritable with others when we forget that the Lord could return at any time. Therefore God instructs us: "Therefore be patient, brethren, until the coming of the Lord. See how the farmer waits for the precious fruit of the earth, waiting patiently for it until it receives the early and latter rain. You also be patient. Establish your hearts, for the coming of the Lord is at hand" (James 5:7–8).

Friendship

Even the quality of our friendships improves when we take seriously the truth that Jesus could return to earth at any time: "For what is our hope, or joy, or crown of rejoicing? Is it not even you in the presence of our Lord Jesus Christ at His coming? For you are our glory and joy" (1 Thess. 2:19–20).

Spiritual Vigilance

Since the Lord could return for his church at any hour of the day or night, we are to keep vigilant: "Watch therefore, for you do not know when the master of the house is coming—in the evening, at midnight, at the crowing of the rooster, or in the morning—lest, coming suddenly, he find you sleeping. And what I say to you, I say to all: watch!" (Mark 13:35–37).

Sex and Marriage

The return of Jesus affects even such "earthy" relationships and activities as marriage and sex: "Marriage is honorable among all, and the bed undefiled; but fornicators and adulterers God will judge" (Heb. 13:4).

Finances

If Christ's imminent return is to influence the way we conduct our marriages and sex lives, then it should not surprise us that it is also to shape the way we relate to money. Peter said that God does not want us to be "greedy for money, but eager to serve; not lording it over those entrusted to you, but being examples to the flock. And when the Chief Shepherd appears, you will receive the crown of glory that will never fade away" (1 Pet. 5:2–4 NIV).

God never intended that the return of Christ should become merely a quirky doctrine on the outskirts of Christian theology. From the very beginning, our Lord expected that the truth of his Son's return would shape and color every aspect of our lives as Christians. The Second Coming is *that* important.

No Need to Fear

Jesus is coming again! That's the hope we have in this life—so long as we know him personally. Everywhere that the Gospels talk about the coming of Christ, knowing him is always the condition for blessing. That's the secret! If you call on the name of the Lord, you will be saved—not only from eternal condemnation, but also from the horrors of the Tribulation. Once we call on him, we can "serve the living and true God, and . . . wait for His Son from heaven, whom He raised from the dead, even Jesus who delivers us from the wrath to come" (1 Thess. 1:9–10). Are you going to the Father's house? Have you made your reservations in advance? Have you called on the name of the Lord Jesus Christ? If so, you needn't fear, "even though the earth be removed, and though the mountains be carried into the midst of the sea; though its waters roar and be troubled, though the mountains shake with its swelling" (Ps. 46:2–3). Why not? Because "God is our refuge and strength, a very present help in trouble" (Ps. 46:1).

No matter what happens in the world, Jesus says we can keep fear at bay. Bible prophecy can give us the confidence we need to live courageously, regardless of world events. So the apostle Peter said, "we have the prophetic word confirmed, which you do well to heed as a light that shines in a dark place, until the day dawns and the morning star rises in your hearts" (2 Pet. 1:19). That star rises as a person studies Bible prophecy and begins to see it, feel it, and know that Jesus is coming back and has a plan for him or her.

Lest anyone think such an idea absurd, remember that the morning star rose in the heart of Simeon and Anna as they studied the prophecies of the Word of God (Luke 2:25–38). For his efforts, Simeon was privileged to hold the Christ child, pray over him, and dedicate him to God. What an honor! The morning star dawned in the heart of Simeon for Jesus' first coming. In the same way, if we study the prophets, the morning star could dawn in our own hearts regarding the second coming of Christ.

Although no one knows the day or the hour of Jesus' return, I recommend that you ask, every morning when you first awake, "Could this be the day?" One of these days, it *will* be the day. That's why we should live every moment in preparation for his coming.

PART THREE

WHY DOES IT MATTER?

12

God's Wonderful Plan
for Your Present

When I graduated from high school at age seventeen, I tried to sign up for the Air Force. World War II was raging and I wanted to become a fighter pilot. I finally got in, but not until my eighteenth birthday.

In the interim I decided to attend Moody Bible Institute in Chicago to begin training for the ministry. Evangelism instructors taught us to begin conversations with prospective converts by asking, "Do you know that you're a sinner, bound for hell?"

What a pleasant way to start! But as good, fundamental Christians, we believed that individuals *were* going to hell if they didn't receive Jesus. Why not tell them where they stood with God, right up front?

Then my dear friend Dr. Bill Bright came along. He published a little booklet called *The Four Spiritual Laws*, and the whole landscape of evangelism changed forever.

I could hardly believe his first law: "God has a wonderful plan for your life." Now, *that's* the way to start! His startling words hit with unexpected power, but also with the force of biblical truth. Didn't Scripture say in John 3:16, "For God so *loved* the world that He gave His only begotten Son"? Bill simply took that scriptural idea and framed it in terms appropriate to our age. *God has a wonderful plan for your life.* Even today, the words reassure and relax.

As I write, my friend Bill Bright is cleaning up his affairs and preparing to be with his Lord, whom he has faithfully served for sixty years. Our merciful God gave him many months' warning of his impending death, but today he's losing strength and is on oxygen. He suffers from pulmonary fibrosis, an incurable lung condition that doctors say causes excruciating pain.

Not long ago Bill met with his staff and handed the reins of Campus Crusade for Christ—the organization that he began fifty years ago—to Steve Douglass, a trusted and capable long-term associate. In a few months, barring a miracle, Bill will be with the Lord, of whom he's testified to so many.

I've often thought that Bill has probably won more men and women to Christ, both personally and by training others, than anyone since the apostle Paul. I can't wait until heaven to stand in line and watch Bill Bright receive his rewards. For sixty years he has been Johnny One Note, always winning the world for Christ—his passion for more than half a century.

Today, Campus Crusade has more than 21,000 full-time staff members worldwide and an army of volunteers, all effectively sharing their faith. It was also Bill's brainchild to create the *Jesus* film that, so far, has been shown to more than 500 million viewers in scores of languages around the world.

And it all started with "God has a wonderful plan for your life." When Bill came up with those words five decades ago, I'm sure he had no idea how wonderfully God planned to use him in spreading the message of Jesus. Still, he believed in the truth of the statement and dedicated his life to spreading the Good News. Millions of men and women are safely in God's kingdom today because they, too, believed that God had a wonderful plan for their lives. And they should believe it, for the Bible says it so many times and in so many ways.

The Practical Nature of Bible Prophecy

After studying Bible prophecy for my entire adult life, I can testify, along with Bill Bright, that God really does have a wonderful plan for your life. You're not an accident, but a much-loved creation of God who has come from someplace and is going someplace. In the next chapter, we'll glimpse the wonders of the place that awaits us.

Bible prophecy, however, doesn't merely announce that God has a wonderful plan for our future; it also proclaims that he has a wonderful plan for our *present*. God wants you and me to spend our years on earth in confidence and hope, enjoying his goodness and delighting in his grace. And prophecy shows the way.

Sadly, many of us never grasp the intensely practical nature of Bible prophecy. We too easily forget that God never reveals information about future events merely to tickle our fancy, but to encourage us to live in such a way today that we may fully enjoy the extreme pleasures of tomorrow. More than that, God uses Bible prophecy to enable us to enjoy life to the maximum *right now*. Time after time in the Scriptures, God uses prophecy about the future to show us how to live joyfully in the present.

If we were to scan the prophetic texts of the New Testament, we would see passage after passage that shows how God intends knowledge of the yet-to-come to improve our lives in the here-and-now. Consider just ten areas of earthly life in which Bible prophecy is to exert a powerful and practical influence on us.

1. Taking Heart When Things Go Awry

In an affluent, technologically advanced society, sometimes we forget that we live in a fallen world where disaster strikes unexpectedly and disease can quickly rob us of our health. If we also forget the marvelous future that our merciful God has promised to us, misfortune or hardship can cause us to lose heart. We can even find ourselves in an emotional free fall.

To keep that from happening, God reminds us that better days are coming. Notice how he connects a prophecy about the future with an encouragement to keep going in the present. Paul wrote:

> He who raised up the Lord Jesus will also raise us up with Jesus, and will present us with you. For all things are for your sakes, that grace, having spread through the many, may cause thanksgiving to abound to the glory of God.
>
> Therefore we do not lose heart. Even though our outward man is perishing, yet the inward man is being renewed day by day. For our light affliction, which is but for a moment, is working for us a far more exceeding and eternal weight of glory, while we do not look at the things which are seen, but at the things which are not seen. For the things which are seen are temporary, but the things which are not seen are eternal. (2 Cor. 4:14–18)

At this very moment God is working to renew our inner man, and he will finish the job in the future when he refashions our outer man. "Therefore," Paul said, "since we have this ministry, as we have received mercy, we do not lose heart" (2 Cor. 4:1).

In other words, God uses prophecy about the future to encourage us in the present.

2. Forgiving Others

Bible prophecy concerns itself not only with momentous events and trends at the end of history, but with practical instruction intended to make life better for everyone right now. Jesus once told a parable to illustrate his strong desire that his followers forgive those who had wronged them, and he motivated them to obey by adding a severe prophecy.

Jesus spoke of a king who discovered that one of his servants owed him a gargantuan amount, impossible to repay. When the king threatened to throw the man and his family into prison, the servant begged for mercy. The king relented and the ungrateful servant immediately left the palace to find a man who owed him some trifling sum. When this second man begged for time to repay the debt, the servant scorned his request and had him tossed behind bars. When the king heard what had happened, he summoned the unforgiving servant into his presence and said, "You wicked servant! I forgave you all that debt because you begged me. Should you not also have had compassion on your fellow servant, just as I had pity on you?" (Matt. 18:32–33).

Jesus then ended his story with some sobering words: "And his master was angry, and delivered him to the torturers until he should pay all that was due to him. So My heavenly Father also will do to you if each of you, from his heart, does not forgive his brother his trespasses" (Matt. 18:34–35).

This remarkable combination of parable and prophecy provides us with crucial guidelines for living. Jesus requires his followers to forgive those who injure them, and he used prophecy to show that an unforgiving spirit reveals an unrepentant heart.

3. Refusing to Judge Others

I admit that I felt a little surprised when I discovered how many Bible prophecies focus our attention on the dangers of passing judgment on others, especially when it concerns motivations of the heart. We simply don't know what is going on inside someone else, so we have no business judging personal motivations. God alone is able to discern "the thoughts and intents of the heart" (Heb. 4:12), so he alone is capable of passing judgment.

This is why the apostle Paul counseled us to "judge nothing before the time, until the Lord comes, who will both bring to light the hidden things of darkness and reveal the counsel of the hearts. Then each one's praise will come from God" (1 Cor. 4:5).

In another prophetic passage, the apostle connected our future judgment before Christ with a strong instruction that we refrain from arrogantly dismissing our fellow believers. Paul said:

Christ died and rose and lived again, that He might be Lord of both the dead and the living. But why do you judge your brother? Or why do you show contempt for your brother? For we shall all stand before the judgment seat of Christ. For it is written: "As I live, says the LORD, every knee shall bow to Me, and every tongue shall confess to God."

So then each of us shall give account of himself to God. Therefore let us not judge one another anymore, but rather resolve this, not to put a stumbling clock or a cause to fall in our brother's way. (Rom. 14:9–13)

Judgment of internal motivations and character—not necessarily of public behavior (see number 4 below)—belongs to God alone. Ironically, those who do pass illegitimate judgment on others are often guilty of the very offenses they condemn, and so will bring judgment on themselves (Matt. 7:1–2; Rom. 2:1–11). Therefore, in a very practical word of instruction given a sharp point by prophecy, God tells us to keep our personal judgments to ourselves.

4. Handling Legal Disputes

While many name "Judge not, lest ye be judged," as their favorite Bible verse, Jesus clearly did not mean that we should consider all behavior equally acceptable. He himself told the crowds, "Do not judge according to appearance, but judge with righteous judgment," and "Yes, and why, even of yourselves, do you not judge what is right?" (John 7:24; Luke 12:57). The apostle Paul, following the lead of the Spirit, instructed the Corinthian church to expel a professing believer who was sleeping with his stepmother, telling them, "What business is it of mine to judge those outside the church? Are you not to judge those inside? God will judge those outside. 'Expel the wicked man from among you'" (1 Cor. 5:12–13 NIV).

That said, the apostle brought up another problem that had been unsettling the church. Some believers had accused fellow church members of defrauding or taking financial advantage of them, and they sought legal relief in the municipal courts—giving the church a big, public black eye. This Paul refused to leave unchallenged. He wrote:

> Dare any of you, having a matter against another, go to law before the unrighteous, and not before the saints? Do you not know that the saints will judge the world? And if the world will be judged by you, are you unworthy to judge the smallest matters? Do you not know that we shall judge angels? How much more, things that pertain to this life?
>
> If then you have judgments concerning things pertaining to this life, do you appoint those who are least esteemed by the church to judge? I say this to your shame. Is it so, that there is not a wise man among you, not even one, who will be able to judge between his brethren? But brother goes to law against brother, and that before unbelievers! Now therefore, it is already an utter failure for you that you go to law against one another. Why do you not rather accept wrong? Why do you not rather let yourselves be cheated? No, you yourselves do wrong and cheat, and you do these things to your brethren! (1 Cor. 6:1–8)

How did the apostle try to motivate the Corinthians to settle their differences outside of the civic court system? Answer: by appealing to prophecy, reminding them that one day they would judge both the world and angels. In view of their future, he advised them to get a little practice by arbitrating *in the church* whatever financial disputes might arise between believers. And once again, we see how God uses prophecy to give us practical guidance on how to obtain a better life on earth.

5. Encouraging Each Other

All of us need a little encouragement in this world. Life throws a thousand things at us at once, and we can feel overwhelmed when we try to deal with everything by ourselves. Yet that is just the genius of the church—God does not want us to struggle through on our own. He desires that we get connected to other believers in relationships so close that we can legitimately call our fellow Christians "brothers" and "sisters."

And how does God sometimes choose to motivate us to encourage one another? Through prophecy! "For God did not appoint us to wrath," Paul wrote, "but to obtain salvation through our Lord Jesus Christ, who died for us, that whether we wake or sleep, we should live together with Him. Therefore comfort each other and edify one another, just as you also are doing" (1 Thess. 5:9–11). The writer to the Hebrews added, "Let us not give up meeting together as some are in the habit of doing, but let us encourage one another—and all the more as you see the Day approaching" (10:25 NIV).

Our merciful God uses prophecy to prompt us to encourage one another—and the nearer the day of Jesus' return, the more we are to encourage. These days really ought to be the most encouraging the church has ever known!

6. Finding the Confidence to Live Well

Life plays out so much better when we move through it with confidence. God does not want us to become timid souls, shrinking in fear from whatever terrifies those who do not know him. Instead, he desires that his children live boldly, secure in the conviction that he has prepared an overwhelmingly positive future for them.

Prophecy helps us to do this. "And now, little children, abide in Him," wrote the apostle John, "that when He appears, we may have confidence and not be ashamed before Him at His coming" (1 John 2:28). To feel real confidence, however, involves much more than merely avoiding pangs of shame. Once again, the job of building our confidence falls to prophecy.

The apostle Paul told us that even if our bodies are destroyed, we look forward to new bodies "not made with hands." He admitted that on this earth we "groan, being burdened," but he reminded us that God has "given us the Spirit as a guarantee." And what is the result? "So we are always confident,

knowing that while we are at home in the body we are absent from the Lord. For we walk by faith, not by sight. We are confident, yes, well pleased rather to be absent from the body and to be present with the Lord" (2 Cor. 5:1–8).

Do you want to feel confident? Do you want to live boldly? Do you want to reject timidity and embrace a life of spiritual adventure? If so, then fill your mind with the prophetic Word of God.

7. Gaining Courage and a Desire to Work Hard

As we draw ever nearer to the end of the age and the return of Jesus Christ, we need courage as never before. We need courage to boldly proclaim the name of Jesus, and we need courage to continue our efforts at living for him. Through prophecy, God intends to give us the courage we need to work hard for his kingdom.

Therefore he tells us through the apostle Paul that "we shall all be changed—in a moment, in the twinkling of an eye, at the last trumpet." And on that day, "then shall be brought to pass the saying that is written: 'Death is swallowed up in victory,'" for God "gives us the victory through our Lord Jesus Christ." And how should this knowledge affect us? Paul made it clear: "Therefore, my beloved brethren, be steadfast, immovable, always abounding in the work of the Lord, knowing that your labor is not in vain in the Lord" (1 Cor. 15:51–52, 54, 57–58).

We do not have to allow hardships to discourage us, nor do we have to "grow weary while doing good, for in due season we shall reap if we do not lose heart" (Gal. 6:9). There is a race to be run, the apostle reminded us, and prophecy instructs us to "run in such a way as to get the prize. Everyone who competes in the games goes into strict training. They do it to get a crown that will not last; but we do it to get a crown that will last forever" (1 Cor. 9:24–25 NIV).

Now is no time to give up, God says. Therefore he lovingly and firmly reminds us to keep going.

8. Pursuing Holiness

God probably devotes more prophetic passages to holy living than he does to any other set of "practical prophecies" in the Bible. Ephesians 5:3–7 provides a good example of these prophecies:

> But fornication and all uncleanness or covetousness, let it not even be named among you, as is fitting for saints; neither filthiness, nor foolish talking, nor coarse jesting, which are not fitting, but rather giving of thanks. For this you know, that no fornicator, unclean person, nor covetous man, who is an idolater, has any inheritance in the kingdom of Christ and God. Let no one deceive you with empty words, for because of these things the wrath of God comes upon the sons of disobedience.

The apostle Peter also connected prophecy to holy living:

> But the day of the Lord will come as a thief in the night, in which the heavens will pass away with a great noise, and the elements will melt with fervent heat; both the earth and the works that are in it will be burned up.
>
> Therefore, since all these things will be dissolved, what manner of persons ought you to be in holy conduct and godliness, looking for and hastening the coming of the day of God? (2 Pet. 3:10–12)

Many similar prophecies might also be cited (see 1 Cor. 6:12–14; Col. 3:4–10; 1 Thess. 4:3–8), all with the same message: Live today in a way that pleases God, for tomorrow we will all "appear before the judgment seat of Christ, that each one may receive the things done in the body, according to what he has done, whether good or bad" (2 Cor. 5:10). Holy living *now* pays off handsomely *then*!

9. Standing Firm in the Faith

None of us knows when we might be called upon to suffer persecution for the name of Christ. In many parts of the world,

Christians are at this moment dying for their faith. America has long enjoyed freedom of religion, but no one can guarantee that such a happy situation will long endure.

So how are we to stand firm for the Lord, even in the face of terrible persecution? Prophecy lends us a strong hand. After describing a hostile group he called "enemies of the cross of Christ," the apostle Paul encouraged his readers to remember:

> Our citizenship is in heaven, from which we also eagerly wait for the Savior, the Lord Jesus Christ, who will transform our lowly body that it may be conformed to His glorious body, according to the working by which He is able even to subdue all things to Himself . . .
>
> Therefore, my beloved and longed-for brethren, my joy and crown, so stand fast in the Lord, beloved. (Phil. 3:20, 4:1)

Jesus himself warned that his followers would be dragged into court for their faith, but told them not to worry because they could expect some supernatural help: "Now when they bring you to the synagogues and magistrates and authorities, do not worry about how or what you should answer, or what you should say. For the Holy Spirit will teach you in that very hour what you ought to say" (Luke 12:11–12).

Hard times will come, God warns us, but in his mercy he also foretells how things will turn out. Because he will never abandon us, we can stand strong for him, even in the most terrible of circumstances.

10. Getting Ready

All of these "practical prophecies" basically come down to one thing: Be ready! Because Jesus is coming again; because believers will receive new, supernatural bodies; because everyone will give an account to God of his or her life; because the Lord will remake the heavens and the earth in righteousness and holiness—therefore we ought to conduct ourselves in a way that most pleases God.

Jesus encouraged his disciples to remain vigilant by saying:

> Let your waist be girded and your lamps burning; and you your-
> selves be like men who wait for their master, when he will return
> from the wedding, that when he comes and knocks they may
> open to him immediately. Blessed are those servants whom the
> master, when he comes, will find watching. Assuredly, I say to
> you that he will gird himself and have them sit down to eat, and
> will come and serve them. And if he should come in the second
> watch, or come in the third watch, and find them so, blessed are
> those servants. (Luke 12:35–38)

What a promise! For good reason one scholar calls this "the
Bible's most astonishing image of Christ's second coming."[1]
Why so astonishing? Because the King of kings and Lord of
lords, the Lion of the tribe of Judah, Jesus Christ, prophesied
that upon his return in power and glory he will "gird himself,
and have them [read: "us"!] sit down to eat, and will come and
serve them"! Normally, servants attend to the needs of their
master, not the other way around. Yet Jesus said here that
those who conduct themselves in a godly way while he's gone
will have something extraordinary to enjoy upon his return.
Who can fully imagine what Jesus meant when he said, "It will
be good for those servants whose master finds them ready"
(v. 38, NIV)? Who can guess the lengths to which he will go to
bless his faithful servants? No one. He simply said, "It will be
good."

What an excellent reason to "be ready"!

Whatever the Future Holds

What does the immediate future hold? I don't have a clue. I've
studied Bible prophecy so I know a lot about the major events
yet to occur, but I don't know either the short-range future or
even my personal future. I have a hunch the Rapture will happen soon, but what's going to occur between now and the Rapture, I have no idea.

I might lose my health. I might be injured or killed in an accident. My investments might go up in smoke in a market crash, a bank collapse, or a financial panic. I might face all kinds of difficult circumstances.

But whatever happens, I know I'll be all right. Prophecy assures me that our God is gracious, loving, merciful, and kind. He is quick to hear, eager to forgive—and he has promised never to leave me or forsake me! All that any of us have to do is to look to him in our time of need.

God wants you and me to embrace the future with confidence, because we know that he holds that future. More than that, he wants us live with boldness and assurance in the present, come what may. He has designed Bible prophecy as a kind of divine searchlight, cutting through the darkness and fog to show us the best path to a full life, even on this side of heaven. When I think of an outstanding example of someone who depended fully upon that heavenly searchlight, even as the sun slowly set on her earthly journey, I always think of my mother.

Faithful to the End

At eighty-one years of age, my dear mother sensed that she didn't have long to live. Her health began to fail and she suffered intense discomfort.

Still, the pain never weakened her strong will; she expected us to do what she ordered. I saw her in the hospital on a Thursday, just after the doctor told me that her heart had nearly worn out. I was scheduled to speak at a seminar somewhere, so I stood at my mother's bedside and said, "Mom, I think I'll call and cancel my seminar. I don't like to do that, but I think I should be with you."

"You will *not*," she commanded. "You go up there and do what you have to do."

Like a dutiful son, I obeyed. But before I left I said, "Well, at least we ought to pray. Do you have anything you'd like to have me remember in prayer?"

"Yes," she replied, "two things. One, ask the Lord to take me right away; I'm in terrible pain. And two, I want to lead one more person to Jesus before I go."

I took one look at all the tubes and gadgets going in and out of her and thought, *Who knows? Miracles happen.* So I prayed, left town, and did my seminar.

That Saturday while I was gone, she told the doctor she wanted to return home. She knew she was about to die and insisted she wanted to do so in familiar surroundings. Since the doctors could do nothing more for her, they sent her home. Moments after she sat in her own easy chair, waiting to join her Lord, a woman telephoned and rather hesitantly said, "Margaret, I know you're in pain and you're not doing well, but would you mind manning the Crisis Pregnancy Line for about three hours? We don't have anyone to cover the calls."

"Oh, sure," Mom replied, "I'm just sitting here in my easy chair."

The woman rerouted the pregnancy line to reach Mom's number, and sure enough, her phone soon rang. A seventeen-year-old girl, unmarried and pregnant, was on the other end of the line, sobbing and unsure what to do. In a few minutes my mom led this troubled young girl to Jesus.

Three days later, we held Mom's funeral. God honored both of her requests!

That's the kind of merciful, gracious God we serve. He delights in blessing his faithful servants with the desires of their hearts. For that very reason he also gives us prophecy, not only to prepare us for momentous events such as the return of Christ and the beginning of the millennial kingdom, but also to assure us that he has a wonderful plan for our lives, *right now.* All he asks is that we trust him.

13

God's Wonderful Plan
for Your Future

When you stop to think about the future, what feelings rise to the top? Excitement? Fear? Anticipation? Dread? Most of us have opinions about the days to come, and few of us feel hesitant to express them.

If you're Canadian educator Marshall McLuhan, you doubt we can know much at all about what lies ahead: "We drive into the future using only our rearview mirror," he said.[1]

If you're author J. G. Ballard, the coming years offer little appeal: "I would sum up my fear about the future in one word: boring. And that's my one fear: everything has happened; nothing exciting or new or interesting is ever going to happen again . . . the future is just going to be a vast, conforming suburb of the soul."[2]

If you're celebrated scientist Albert Einstein, you see no point in pondering what great events may overtake us: "I never think of the future. It comes soon enough."[3]

If you're actor Sir Arthur Wing Pinero, you expect no real surprises: "I believe the future is only the past again, entered through another gate."[4]

And if you're social critic George Orwell, you see a doomed planet with only a bleak and brutal destiny: "If you want a picture of the future, imagine a boot stomping on a human face—forever."[5]

How glad I am that we needn't take our cues from mere mortals! When we allow God to shape our thoughts and feelings about the future, anticipation replaces fear and excitement pushes out dread. For the Bible makes one thing certain: God has a wonderful plan for our future, a blockbuster destiny so thrilling it will take eternity to fully enjoy. Through prophecy, God reveals the high points of the glorious future he has prepared for us. So Scripture can declare:

> "Eye has not seen, nor ear heard, nor have entered into the heart of man the things which God has prepared for those who love Him." But God has revealed them to us through His Spirit. (1 Cor. 2:9–10)

Relax and Look Forward

God, in his great mercy and grace, wants us to relax and look forward to the future he has in store for his cherished people. "There is surely a future hope for you, and your hope will not be cut off," he tells us in Proverbs 23:18 (NIV).

What kind of hope? The prophet Isaiah felt great excitement over the future that God had planned, because he knew the Lord took eons of time to design and bring about exactly the right chain of events (Isa. 25:1).

David's heart also thrilled over the future, for he knew that when God decides to bring huge blessings upon his people, he doesn't skimp in the details. "*Many*, O LORD my God, are Your wonderful works which You have done; and Your thoughts toward us cannot be recounted to You in order; if I would declare and speak of them, they are more than can be numbered" (Ps. 40:5, italics added).

But how can we be sure that great wonders and marvels yet await us? Because God himself has promised exactly that. The

Lord designs all of his plans to prosper us, not harm us, to give us a bright hope and a solid future (Jer. 29:11).

Nor should we think that anyone can frustrate or derail the plans for blessing that God long ago set into motion for us, his people. In fact, just the opposite is true: "The LORD brings the counsel of the nations to nothing; He makes the plans of the peoples of no effect." On the other hand, "The counsel of the LORD stands forever, the plans of His heart to all generations" (Ps. 33:10–11).

What an amazing future awaits us, for all those who put their faith in the death and resurrection of Christ as a full payment for their sins! While God revealed bits and pieces of his amazing plan to such giants of the faith as Moses and David and Isaiah, yet he reserved its final outpouring for us, "upon whom the ends of the ages have come" (1 Cor. 10:11). While God commended all his loyal servants for their faith, none of them received the full complement of what he promised. Why not? Because the Lord had planned something better for us so that only together with us would the saints of old be made perfect (Heb. 11:39–40).

I can't help but believe that the time may well be near for God to bring to completion his eternal plan. Many prophecy scholars believe that the stage is already set, that no more signs need to occur before Christ could come to rapture his church. That event will trigger the thrilling things God has in store for all humankind. And if we can't get excited about the amazing events to come, then either we haven't really understood, or someone ought to pull a sheet over our head and call for the coroner.

Beauty for Ashes

What does lie ahead in the plan of God? Next on the divine agenda is the Rapture; then the seven-year Tribulation; and then a fabulous time of peace and prosperity we call the Millennium.

The Millennium takes its name from Revelation 20:1–10, where we learn that Satan will be bound "for a thousand years." Resurrected believers will reign with Christ "a thousand years" and they will be "priests of God and of Christ, and shall reign with him a thousand years."

Six times, Revelation 20 refers to a kingdom that lasts for a thousand years. The word *millennium* comes from the Latin term *millesimus*, which means "a thousandth." Therefore the Millennium refers to the thousand-year rule of Christ on earth. Some Christian brothers who allegorize or spiritualize Scripture interpret this thousand years symbolically, but there is no logical or grammatical reason for doing so. When Scripture says six times that this period will last "a thousand years," we are more than justified in taking it to mean a literal one thousand years.

And what will this rule look like? The Old Testament provides far more information on the nature of the Millennium than does the New Testament. Isaiah 61:2–7 tells us that God will use this time:

> ". . . to comfort all who mourn, to console those who mourn in Zion, to give them beauty for ashes, the oil of joy for mourning, the garment of praise for the spirit of heaviness; that they may be called trees of righteousness, the planting of the LORD, that He may be glorified."
>
> And they shall rebuild the old ruins, they shall raise up the former desolations, and they shall repair the ruined cities, the desolations of many generations. Strangers shall stand and feed your flocks, and the sons of the foreigner shall be your plowmen and your vinedressers.
>
> But you shall be named the priests of the LORD, they shall call you the servants of our God. You shall eat the riches of the Gentiles, and in their glory you shall boast. Instead of your shame you shall have double honor, and instead of confusion they shall rejoice in their portion. Therefore in their land they shall possess double; everlasting joy shall be theirs.

The Millennium will be the most blessed time the world has known since the idyllic days of the Garden of Eden. It will be a time of unprecedented prosperity, a time of astonishing fruitfulness, and a time devoid of war, crime, and perversity.

This is the kingdom to which Jesus referred in Matthew 25 when he prophesied that, as the returning King, he would tell his faithful followers to take their inheritance. He called it, "the kingdom prepared for you from the foundation of the world" (v. 34). This is the kingdom over which Jesus must reign "till He has put all enemies under His feet" (1 Cor. 15:25). This is the kingdom of Christ that Daniel described as "an everlasting kingdom" in which "all dominions shall serve and obey" Jesus (Dan. 7:27).

Utopia is coming! Can you imagine anything like ten centuries of righteousness, when Satan will be bound and unable to deceive anyone? There'll be no pornographers, no gangsters, no drug dealers, no terrorists, no arsonists or scam artists or counterfeiters. Nothing that's bad about today's society will exist during that time.

To top it off, everyone will know the truth about God, "for the earth shall be full of the knowledge of the LORD as the waters cover the sea" (Isa. 11:9). Everyone will be able to see what God is really like, for Jesus will reign from Jerusalem as King of kings and Lord of lords. In short, the Millennium will exceed our fondest expectations—and best of all, believers in Christ will get to live in it! Why? Because we're smart? Because we've done anything special? Not at all. Rather, we'll be there because "God so loved the world that He gave His only begotten Son, that whoever believes in Him should not perish but have everlasting life" (John 3:16). The Bible makes it clear that we don't have to do anything to be a part of the Millennium—other than trust Christ with our lives.

Oh, what a time this will be! The Bible sees it as the golden age, the time of great blessing, an era of unbroken peace. We'll enjoy a thousand years without war. A thousand years of plenty. A thousand years of harmony. No wonder the population will swell beyond anything that's ever been known!

It's hard for us to imagine what a thousand years of peace

and righteousness might look like, but perhaps we can get a few clues by looking at revivals of the past. At certain times in history, God has moved powerfully among his people and in their communities to bring about seasons of "Millennium-like" conditions.

Consider the Welsh Revival of 1904–05, almost a century ago. God used a praying young Welshman named Evan Roberts to spark a spiritual movement in which an estimated 100,000 men and women came to Christ in just six months.[6] Not only did church attendance mushroom and prayer groups multiply, but the whole tenor of life in many towns and villages radically changed.

"The mighty and unseen breath of the Spirit was doing in a month more than centuries of legislation could accomplish," reported the London *Times* on January 1, 1905. David Lloyd-George, who later became British Prime Minister, told the *Times* nine days later that the Welsh revival gave him hope that "at the next election Wales would declare with no uncertain sound against the corruption in high places which handed over the destiny of people to the horrible brewing interest." In one town, he told the newspaper, the local tavern sold only nine cents worth of liquor the previous Saturday night.

As the revival spread, political meetings and soccer matches were postponed in favor of prayer, and infighting between trade-union workmen and non-unionists greatly abated. Employers remarked how their workers vastly improved their efforts on the job.

"Everything sprang into new life," said one contemporary historian. "Former blasphemers were the most eloquent, both in prayer and praise . . . Drunkards forgot the way to saloons . . . With ever increasing momentum, the movement advanced, creating unprecedented excitement among the churches and the secular institutions outside."

Some judges showed up at their benches, only to find they had no cases to try. Alcoholism fell by half. The famous preacher, G. Campbell Morgan, told how one manager in the mines reported to him that, "The haulers are some of the very lowest. They have driven their horses by obscenity and kicks. Now they can hardly persuade their horses to start working, because they have no obscenity and kicks."

When Christ truly begins to rule in the hearts of large numbers of men of women who live together in peace, we begin to *see* what it means for God's will to "be done on earth as it is in heaven" (Matt. 6:10). In revival, we see hints and echoes of what will happen fully and in a sustained way in the Millennium.

And yet, remarkably, the Bible says the Millennium will end in war.

Scripture tells us that after the thousand years of peace have ended, God will release Satan from his prison and the devil will "deceive the nations which are in the four corners of the earth" (Rev. 20:8). Despite the peaceful conditions of the Millennium, a huge multitude like "the sand of the sea" will reject Christ's leadership and march out in battle to surround "the camp of the saints and the beloved city" (v. 9).

It won't be much of a war, though; John testified simply that "fire came down from God out of heaven and devoured them" (Rev. 20:9). Only then will Satan be thrown into the lake of burning sulfur, where he will spend eternity.

Now, try to imagine what John described here. At the end of a thousand years of paradise, all it will take is the release of Satan to reveal the wicked souls of millions of unredeemed humankind. The Millennium will conclusively answer the age-old question of nature or nurture: do we go bad because of a faulty environment, or are we bad because of a corrupt heredity? The open rebellion of an unconverted multitude will prove, once and for all, the sinfulness of the human race and the necessity of Christ's death. The Millennium will prove that even a perfect environment cannot cure the spiritual disease that eats at the soul of every man, woman, and child. Only the death of Christ can deal with such depravity.

And so the Millennium will come to a sudden end, glorifying

not only the goodness of God's provision, but also the infinite worth of Christ and the utter indispensability of his death on the cross. Once those questions have been settled, nothing remains to be proved . . . other than an unending display of the wisdom, holiness, and love of God.

And that's something we call "heaven."

Better than the Millennium

What could be better than the Millennium? Only one thing: heaven! We aren't told a great deal about the eternal future God has planned for us, but what we are told staggers the imagination.

Imagine never growing old, but enjoying a body that remains eternally strong, perpetually healthy, and forever beautiful.

Imagine living in a vast community of godly men and women, all of whom possess bright minds, unique viewpoints, and delightful passions—and that you know each of them by name, without ever needing an introduction.

Imagine having a long conversation with a favorite hero of the faith—whether Abraham or Ruth or Paul or Mary or Martin Luther or Amy Carmichael—and never having to worry that you'll run out of time for a million other such talks.

Imagine exploring the new heaven and new earth that God creates for the enjoyment of his people, and being able to whisk in and out of wildly exotic places at the speed of thought.

Imagine gazing upon the face of Jesus Christ and upon that of his Father as they blaze forth in unquenchable light—brilliant, dazzling beams of glory that make obsolete the dull rays of the sun and moon—and yet you feel no pain, no discomfort, only indescribable joy.

Imagine drinking in a pure creation of infinite beauty, visually staggering in its endless variety. For your pleasure God eternally rolls out inimitable shapes, impossible colors, delightful textures, and enormous proportions.

Imagine . . . but what's the use? The glories of heaven lie radically beyond human expression. When the apostle Paul was "caught up" to heaven—whether physically or in a vision, he never knew for sure—he reported hearing "inexpressible words, which it is not lawful for a man to utter" (2 Cor. 12:4). One translator rendered the apostle's sputtering words like this: "[I] heard things so astounding that they are beyond a man's power to describe or put in words (and anyway I am not allowed to tell them to others)" (TLB).

The Bible does not tell us much about heaven, largely because at this point we couldn't begin to comprehend its wonders. Of what we *do* know about heaven, Revelation 21 gives us more information than any other passage. Consider, first, some of the items that heaven will *lack*:

A temple (21:22)
A sea (21:1)
Tears, death, sorrow, crying, and pain (21:4)
Fear (21:12)
Sun and moon (21:23)
Night (21:25)
Sin and evil (21:27)

Revelation 22 adds that heaven will have no room for disease and physical or emotional injuries (v. 2) or any remnant of the curse (v. 3).

As good as God reveals himself to be in what he bars from heaven, he shows himself to be even more generous by what he brings to the eternal celebration. Note just a few of the benefits God plans to build into heaven:

Nonstop camaraderie with God (21:3, 7, 22)
Everlasting newness (21:5)
Limitless water of life (21:6)
Inexpressible beauty (21:11, 21)
Perfect safety (21:12)

Complete unity among believers (21:12, 14)
Infinite holiness (21:27)
Staggering size (21:16)
Incalculable riches (21:18–21)
Perpetual light (21:23)
Unrestricted access (21:25)

Other Bible passages tell us that heaven will offer its residents unceasing fruit from the tree of life (Rev. 22:2); creative opportunities to serve God (Rev. 22:3); eternal privileges of rule (Rev. 22:5); reenergizing rest (Heb. 4:1–11); vast knowledge (1 Cor. 13:12); extreme joy (1 Thess. 2:19); vibrant worship (Rev. 7:9–12); and breathtaking glory (2 Cor. 4:17).

All this awaits everyone who says "Yes!" to Jesus Christ. And while we don't yet walk those famous streets of transparent gold, the moment we say "yes" to Jesus, God makes us full citizens of heaven and hands to us our divine passports. But don't take my word for it. Listen to the apostle Paul: "For our citizenship is in heaven, from which we also eagerly wait for the Savior, the Lord Jesus Christ, who will transform our lowly body that it may be conformed to His glorious body, according to the working by which He is able even to subdue all things to Himself" (Phil. 3:20–21).

Competing Views of the Afterlife

In this day of intense interest about what lies ahead for the world, Christians have by far the most attractive message available. I believe that no religion, no philosophy, no faith in the world comes close to what Jesus, the Spirit of prophecy, offers those who follow him. His vision of the future far surpasses anything else on the market.

Compare Jesus' offer of eternal life in heaven with the expectations and hopes proposed by the major strands of the world's great religions:

Buddhism

Since Buddhism teaches that evil comes from pursuing desire, its goal is to extinguish all desire, to lose all sense of self. The word *Nirvana* literally means "blowing out," as in extinguishing a candle flame. It says little of the afterlife, other than it is a transcendental, permanent state. It is often likened to a lotus flower unfolding in the sun.[7]

Confucianism

Confucianism is really not so much a religion as a philosophy. It encourages adherents to follow principles of good conduct, to seek practical wisdom, and to engage in proper social relationships. It offers only vague ideas of an afterlife.[8]

Daoism

The goal of Daoism (*dao* = "way") is to empty one's self of all doctrines and knowledge, to transcend life and death. When one reaches unity with the Dao, one is supposed to get mystical power.[9]

Existentialism/Secular Humanism

Existentialists and secular humanists believe that nothing exists beyond the material world and that death marks the end of the person. The molecules of one's body survive, but all consciousness is lost. An Internet enthusiast named Horatio recently explained his secular view of the afterlife: "when you die you die. And I dont have any dilema comprehending that life is meaningless its just something to cope with" [sic]. Bob agreed with him: "After you die you turn into a piece of dirt and then into mud and from there, nevermind . . . After you die your dead. there."[10]

Hinduism

Most Hindus desire to escape from an endless cycle of birth, death, and rebirth by achieving a state in which all personality dissolves into the "unimaginable abyss" of Brahman. In this state, one merges with pure consciousness and "wakes up" from the nightmare of individuality.[11]

Islam

The Quran, the scripture of Islam, describes (often in vivid detail) the afterlife. It pictures paradise as a garden full of sensual delights. In a chapter ("surah") titled "The Event," the Quran says:

> Those are they who will be brought nigh in gardens of delight; a multitude of those of old and a few of those of later time, on lined couches, reclining therein face to face. There wait on them immortal youths with bowls and ewers and a cup from a pure spring wherefrom they get no aching of the head nor any madness, and fruit that they prefer and flesh of fowls that they desire. And there are fair ones with wide, lovely eyes, like unto hidden pearls, reward for what they used to do.[12]

Some Islamic theologians consider such descriptions allegorical, but others insist on their literal character.

Judaism

Ancient Hebrews believed in *Sheol*, a dark and ill-defined abode of the dead. By the time of Daniel, the idea of bodily resurrection and divine judgment had appeared, complete with separate realms for the wicked and the righteous. But beyond that, little more was taught about the afterlife. Modern orthodox Jews accept the traditional view, but secular and Reform Jews do not necessarily agree on any particular understanding of the afterlife (if there is one).

Do you see why I believe nothing else comes close to the Bible's teaching on the afterlife? In the New Testament, God outlines the world's greatest plan for the future—in my opinion, the only future worth looking forward to.

I treasure the hope we have in Jesus Christ, the Son of God who died on a cross to win for us a magnificent future. No wonder the Bible calls it a "blessed hope" (Titus 2:13)—properly interpreted, a "blessed expectation." We enjoy a fabulous expectation that lasts for eternity—and it is guaranteed to us by the Hebrew prophets, by the apostles, by Jesus Christ, and by God himself. What a future!

Comfort at Death

The Christian teaching on heaven and the afterlife shows its power most clearly, not in abstract discussions of how it compares to other faiths, but in how it brings real comfort and strength to Christians when loved ones die.

Only Jesus gives real hope for the future. When a fellow believer dies, we grieve, but not as others grieve. Why not? Because we know we will see our loved one again when we meet the Lord in the air. The Bible tells us that, at the resurrection, every believer in Christ will receive a glorified body, much like the one the Lord had after his own resurrection (1 Cor. 15:35–57; 2 Cor. 5:1–5; 1 John 3:2).

My father died when I was only nine years old. I remember him as a gregarious man who worked in a factory and had only an eighth-grade education. Eight years before he died, he invited Jesus into his life; four years later, I accepted Christ.

I felt devastated when my father died. His death traumatized me more than any other experience in my life, before or since. I couldn't stop crying—the hero of my life was gone! I didn't even want to go to his funeral. Seeing his lifeless body lying immobile in that casket was almost more than I could bear. Things got no better at the graveside service. I saw Dad's friends put the casket on those straps, and knew that in a few moments they were going to lower it into a hole, shovel dirt on it, and that would be the end of Dad.

I wept uncontrollably. It seemed as though my life had ended.

Everything changed, however, when the minister of our church said, "This is not the last of Frank LaHaye. The day is coming when the Lord Jesus is going to shout from heaven and the dead in Christ—including Frank LaHaye—will be caught up together in the air. They'll be transformed and caught up, resurrected together with us in the clouds." Those marvelous words gave me hope that has lasted a lifetime. I have had confidence for more than sixty-five years that I will see my dad again. All Christians can share that same confidence about their saved loved ones.

What a wonderful meeting time it will be when Jesus comes back in the clouds! Even better, the Bible says, "So shall we ever be with the Lord" (1 Thess. 4:17 KJV).

We have a magnificent hope, a hope that brings comfort even when death comes knocking. While no one wants to volunteer for death until the embers of life grow dim, David, armed with a strong faith in God, could say to his Lord, "though I walk through the valley of the shadow of death, I will fear no evil; for You are with me" (Ps. 23:4). I've noticed that those who lack such a comforting faith tend to crumble when death hits.

A deacon in a church I served, Charles Malone, suffered thirty-eight heart attacks. A congenital heart defect stalked his family, and all four boys died in their fifties. Charles lived to be fifty-eight, while this three brothers died five or six years before reaching that mark.

Charles walked with God, and every time he'd suffer a heart attack, he'd say something like, "Well, if I live, praise the Lord. If I die, praise the Lord. In any case, I'm ready to meet the Lord." An attitude like that relaxes one's heart and encourages a longer life.

Finally, however, even Charles's heart gave out. I will never forget his memorial service. His lifetime partner and wife, Olivia, felt heartbroken and missed her husband terribly. She grieved, but not like her sister, Esther, who had come for the funeral. Esther didn't know Christ. At the funeral I saw what a difference faith makes.

As we headed back to the cars to leave the cemetery, Esther

began to weep and sob hysterically. Olivia put her arm around her sister and said, "Esther, don't take on so. I'll see him again."

That's the difference! Esther had no hope, while Olivia enjoyed abundant hope in Christ Jesus. Olivia demonstrated for me that day how the God of prophecy has removed the sting even of death.

Perhaps you have lost a loved one, maybe a partner of many years, or a darling child. The God of prophecy says, "It's all right to sorrow, but you needn't grieve as do the hopeless." When we put the bodies of those we love in the ground, we know it's only a temporary good-bye. Soon Jesus will resurrect all the dead in Christ and bring us all back together. And so will we be with the Lord forever. No other religion in the world offers this kind of confidence.

Jesus Holds the Keys

Many cultures, faiths, and books portray death as a doorway to another realm. The Bible also uses this image, but it adds something crucial: Jesus holds the keys to the door! "I am He who lives, and was dead, and behold, I am alive forevermore. Amen. And I have the keys of Hades and of Death," Jesus said in Revelation 1:18.

Many of us fear the future because we know Hades is exactly the wrong place to be. But Jesus holds the keys to Hades! In fact, he owns the keys to the whole future. If you know Jesus, you can rest secure.

Years ago I visited a federal penitentiary in St. Cloud, Minnesota, to see an inmate. I will never forget the sound of heavy doors slamming shut and locking behind me. I had to walk through about twelve gates before finally reaching the interior. Still, I never felt overly nervous, because the guard who accompanied me carried all the keys. I knew he could open all those hard-sounding gates and that soon I would again breathe freedom.

That's how eternity is. I don't know all the answers to the future, but I do know that Jesus holds all the keys. Therefore I know that one day I will breathe the free air of heaven.

Another deacon friend of mine, Frank Gleena, died one Thursday after a nine-month illness. The following Saturday a cousin came to visit Frank's widow, because the couple had no children. At the breakfast table, the cousin later reported, Frank's wife slumped over, dead. Frank had been her life and everybody in the church knew how much they loved each other.

So do you know what we did? We held a joint memorial service in the church, the only one I ever conducted. We held a praise service, not a funeral service. How could we do anything but celebrate when two faithful Christians were absent from their bodies and present with the Lord (2 Cor. 5:6)?

The story of Frank and his wife continues to remind me that God has a marvelous plan for our future. Because of what God's Son did on Calvary's cross, we can live eternally with him—safe in the arms of our merciful, loving Lord.

What do *you* think about the future? I hope that you can agree with two great saints of God who have gone ahead of us to heaven. Dutch fireball Corrie ten Boom, whose story is told in the film *The Hiding Place*, said, "Never be afraid to trust an unknown future to a known God." And William Carey, who spent his life telling others about Jesus Christ, reminded us, "The future is as bright as the promises of God."

You can't get any brighter than that.

14

Lives Changed

What you believe about God determines everything in your life. What you think of him influences the way you handle yourself, how you use your time and your talent, what you do with your money, the nature of your interpersonal relationships, and every decision you make. In fact, what you think about God determines both the direction and the quality of your life.

If you think God is an angry taskmaster, hard to please and surly most of the time, then it will be difficult for you to trust anyone. If you believe God is cold and distant, or that he doesn't exist at all, then you'll act as though you're in this world all by yourself.

On the other hand, if you believe in a merciful and kind God who cares whether you live or die; if you trust in a gracious heavenly Father who cares whether you're in good health or bad; if you depend upon a loving Lord who pays attention to every detail of your life—then, as the apostle Peter wrote, you can cast "all your care on Him, for He cares for you" (1 Pet. 5:7).

And how do we cast our care on such a God? How does one approach such a merciful, loving Lord? We puny humans tend to think of God as the Supreme Master of heaven and earth, the Creator of all things, the august and terrible God—and he is all of that. But we never have to pray, "O omnipotent God, ruler of heaven and earth, hear now the supplication of this, thy worm." Instead, our Lord instructs us to pray, "Our Father, who art in heaven." We pray as dearly loved sons and daughters of a merciful heavenly Father.

Isn't that magnificent? We can approach God in all of his glory and in all of his power, all the while knowing that he is our loving Father. Therefore we are to "come boldly to the throne of grace, that we may obtain mercy and find grace to help in time of need" (Heb. 4:16). What a privilege that you and I can pray to God as our Father!

And beyond that, if we understand God as he really is and trust him with our lives, we can rest confidently no matter what happens around us. When some adversity busts through the door of our life, we can look to God and say, "Lord, what are you going to do about this?" Years ago I used to say, "What are *we* going to do?" but I soon found out that he was the one who eventually worked things out.

What we believe about God makes an enormous difference in the way we approach life. With him, the Bible says, all things are possible (Mark 10:27)—and therefore we can stride into life with confidence. Without him, however, the possibilities rapidly diminish, along with any assurance that things really will turn out okay in the end.

The apostle Paul must have had this in mind when he wrote, "If God is for us, who can be against us?" (Rom. 8:31) How much better to live, knowing that God is for us than to think he is against everything we do or that he couldn't care less about us.

So—what do *you* believe about God? How do you picture him? It really does make a great deal of difference.

Changing for the Better

One of the most hopeful verses in the Bible comes on the heels of one of the most encouraging prophetic passages in Scripture. Second Corinthians 5 proclaims that all believers can look forward to inhabiting a supernatural body (a body specially modeled after Christ's own resurrection body, according to Philippians 3:21). The apostle Paul encouraged us to confidently accept God's promise of a new-and-improved body, because already he "has given us the Spirit as a deposit, guaranteeing what is to come" (v. 5 NIV).

The apostle declared that wonderful changes lie in store for every believer in Christ—but that doesn't mean we have to wait until heaven for many of those changes to occur! Because God wants us to get a little taste of heaven right here on earth, he sends his Holy Spirit to live within every individual who trusts in Jesus Christ. And when the Lord takes up residence within our hearts, he makes possible radical changes in behavior and character that even our closest friends might find hard to imagine. When God comes to live within us, true personal change becomes possible.

Paul said it like this: "Therefore, if anyone is in Christ, he is a new creation; old things have passed away; behold, all things have become new" (2 Cor. 5:17) And don't think for a minute that Paul spoke metaphorically in this verse; he meant precisely what he said. In an earlier letter to the Corinthians, he reminded his friends that, before they came to Christ, many of them had been "sexually immoral," "idolaters," "adulterers," "male prostitutes," "homosexual offenders," "thieves," "greedy," "drunkards," "slanderers," and "swindlers." Yet all of this lay in the past, before their conversions. So Paul wrote, "And that is what some of you *were*. But you were washed, you were sanctified, you were justified in the name of the Lord Jesus Christ and by the Spirit of our God" (1 Cor. 6:11 NIV, italics added).

Radical changes reshaped these men and women of ancient Corinth once they submitted their lives to Christ. They exchanged ruined lives of sexual immorality and thievery and alcoholism and hate for hopeful lives of faithfulness and generosity and sobriety and love. In a word, they became "new creations."

Would you like to become a "new creation"? Would you like the old to go and the new to come? Believe me, that is just as possible for you as it was for the ancient Corinthians, and as it has been for countless others through history. In fact, I'd like to introduce you to a few individuals who became "new creations" the moment they placed their faith in Jesus Christ, the Son of the merciful God of heaven.

Blue Lewis Comes to Faith

America spends about 40 billion dollars annually on criminal reform. Do you know the success rates for these secular attempts at change? Approximately 90 to 95 percent of all violent criminals who are released commit another crime and are once again incarcerated.[1]

Everyone regrets such grim statistics—yet there is a way to markedly improve them. Many studies have shown that prisoners who place their faith in Christ while behind bars stand an enormously greater chance of staying out of jail once they win their release. In fact, 90 to 95 percent of prisoners who become born-again Christians *never* go back to jail.[2]

The prison recidivism rate merely illustrates the enormous power of the cross. What one believes about God exerts a tremendous influence on how that person lives. Released prisoners who never bow their knee to a loving Lord stand an overwhelming chance of returning to jail; released prisoners who welcome God's love through his Son, Jesus Christ, stand an overwhelming chance of remaining free for the rest of their lives. What is this but a breathtaking testimony to the power of change made possible by the indwelling Spirit of God?

Blue Lewis knows all about this life-changing power. Convicted at age sixteen of killing a man in a street fight, he received a life sentence for murder. He started boxing in prison and eventually won the crown of the entire federal boxing system. Yet despite his fame as a boxing champion, everyone—

fellow prisoners and guards alike—kept their distance from this angry, powerful, and violent young man.

One tiny woman, however, showed no fear of Blue Lewis. For twenty-three years, my widowed mother, a five-foot-tall dynamo, served as the Child Evangelism Director for Lansing, Michigan. She strove to present the gospel wherever she could, and one Easter weekend she arranged to speak to inmates at the Ionia, Michigan, federal prison. She brought in the flannelgraph board she used with children, along with cutout figures of Pilate, Jesus, and other characters, and she used them to describe the crucifixion, burial, and resurrection of Jesus Christ. Several prisoners committed their lives to Christ after her first presentation, and she quickly became a popular and regular visitor to the prison.

When one of the new believers told Blue about "the little lady," he came to see her for himself. Soon he also committed his life to Christ. But was it a real conversion? Fellow prisoners, guards, and his family all watched closely to see. But no one could mistake the signs: a new spirit of love and cooperation, a changed vocabulary, a controlled temper. Many prisoners came to Christ by witnessing the major changes in Blue.

Still, I admit that I worried about my mother in the presence of so many violent inmates. But she told me to relax. "The Lord and Blue take good care of me," she said. "The other prisoners are so afraid of Blue they wouldn't dare hurt me."

One night my mother found out exactly how committed Blue was to her safety. In the middle of a flannelgraph presentation, an electrical storm doused all the lights in the chapel. Blue had been standing at the back of the room, "keeping order" as usual, but in the darkness Mom felt terrified to be standing in a room full of violent men. She reflexively took two steps backward . . . and ran into a large body that hadn't been there just moments before. Before she could scream, she heard Blue's deep voice whisper, "Don't be afraid, Margaret, I'm here." Blue the Intimidator had become Blue the Protector.

Sometime later, prison officials transferred Blue to another location about fifty miles away. One day some of the most violent prisoners in the facility took thirteen guards hostage and held them for several days. In an effort to peacefully resolve the volatile situation, the warden asked Blue to serve as a mediator.

"Why me?" Blue asked. "Can't you find someone experienced in such things?"

"Blue," the warden replied, "you're the one man in this prison whom both the prisoners and the staff respect. You have the reputation that you keep your word."

Blue agreed to do what he could and eventually negotiated a deal that won the safe release of all hostages as well as several improvements in living conditions for the prisoners. Shortly afterward the warden recommended that Blue be paroled, and several months later, just days before his thirty-second birthday, this once-violent offender walked out of prison a free man. In time Blue married a fine Christian woman (my mother and a friend attended the wedding) and the new couple had several children.

Today, you can number Blue Lewis among the 90 to 95 percent of paroled felons who never return to prison after committing their lives to Christ. He demonstrates how radical personal change is possible for those who come to believe in a merciful, gracious, loving God.

A Changed Man in Minneapolis

Before I moved to San Diego to pastor, my wife and I spent six wonderful years in Minneapolis at a growing church. I was young and experimenting with how best to preach the Bible, and one morning I decided to speak on the Great White Throne Judgment (see Rev. 20:11–15).

I have never forgotten the reactions of two people in the audience. One haughty lady—well dressed with a big, fancy hat—shook hands with me but with fire in her eyes said, "Young man, that's the *worst* sermon I've ever heard. You're four hundred years behind the times."

Now, when you're twenty-five years old and struggling to find your identity, a statement like that rocks you. As I stood there, reeling from her piercing words, several others walked by. I don't remember any of them—except a young man named Bob. He grabbed my hand, squeezed it, and wouldn't let go. He looked me in the eye and said, "Tim, may I come to your office tomorrow night at seven o'clock? I want to get saved."

Only three months earlier I had met Bob for the first time, at the urging of his wife and daughter. Bob was a nice guy with no time for God. He didn't mind that his wife and daughter attended church; he just didn't think he needed "religion." Many times his wife had said to me, "Please pray for my husband. On Sunday he golfs or fishes or whatever he wants to do. And he thinks all preachers are stuffed shirts."

One day while driving by his house, I saw him washing his car. I stopped the car, got out, and introduced myself—not sure whether he would spray me with the hose or shake my hand. I asked him what he did for a living.

"I'm a buyer at Dayton's," he said.

"You are? So's my wife," I replied.

"She is? What department does she work in?"

"The bills I get," I remarked with a smile, "she works in *all* the departments."

Bob laughed, and the next Sunday I saw him in church. So it was that, about three months later, he was shaking my hand and saying, "I want to come to your study and get saved." When he arrived for our meeting, I hit him with all kinds of Bible verses about salvation; I confess I dumped the whole wheelbarrow on him.

"I know all that," he said impatiently. "Tim, I just want to get saved."

So at his urging we both got down on our knees, and Bob prayed the most beautiful prayer for salvation that I ever heard. To this day I can remember his words.

In 1998 this church celebrated its one-hundredth anniversary. As part of the celebration, the church's leadership asked me to fly back to Minneapolis to be a guest speaker. In my remarks I told this story—and suddenly I wondered, *What if he hasn't been living for the Lord? This is his community; they all know him.*

I didn't know Bob himself was sitting in the audience.

After the service I shook hands with a lot of old friends and new acquaintances. In the middle of several glad reunions, Bob walked up, put his arms around me, gave me a big hug, and said, "Tim, I want to thank you for leading me to Jesus."

At that moment it dawned on me at that, in all these years, while many wonderful people have written me letters and e-mails or spoken to me in person to thank me for this or that, not one person has ever complained, "Why did you lead me to Jesus? Why didn't you let me go on in my sin and my ignorance and my emptiness?" Not one!

As I write, Bob's conversion took place almost fifty years ago. He's as happy in the Lord as he has ever been.

I can't imagine what happened to the lady with the big hat.

Dying Without God

If today you came to the end of your life and found yourself staring death in the face, would you be satisfied with the output of your years? Would you welcome your imminent audience with God, or would his judgment make you tremble?

All of us intuitively know that judgment follows death. Not only does the Bible insist on a coming divine judgment—"Man is destined to die once, and after that to face judgment" (Heb. 9:27 NIV)—but it's also written on the tablet of every human heart.

The fear and hatred of divine judgment have no doubt prompted some men and women to become atheists. It's not that they can't see the handiwork of a supreme being all around them; rather, they desperately need some way to assure themselves that they will never have to stand before God to give an account of their life's work. And the best way to solve that problem is to convince themselves, *There is no God.*

Such a solution, however, usually misfires as death approaches.

I've read the last words of many famous atheists, and I have to say that their sad statements only confirm my theory. It's remarkable how many longtime atheists leave this world kicking and screaming and fearful of entering the presence of the God they claim doesn't exist.

As the historian and atheist Edward Gibbon lay dying, for example, he looked up at the friends and family gathered by his bedside and declared, "This day may be my last. I will agree that the immortality of the soul is at times a very comfortable doctrine. All this is now lost, finally, irrevocably lost. All is dark and doubtful."[3]

Thomas Hobbes, the renowned English political philosopher and skeptic who died in 1674, said as he took his final breaths, "If I had the whole world, I would give it to live one day. I shall be glad to find a hole to creep out of the world at. About to take a leap in the dark!"[4]

Perigood-Talleyrand built for himself a formidable reputation in service as foreign minister to both Napoleon and King Louis XVIII. As he lay dying, his king asked him how he felt. "I am suffering, Sire, the pangs of the damned," Talleyrand replied.[5]

The French skeptic Voltaire wrote and spoke often against Christianity. About Christ he once said, "Curse the wretch!" He also boasted, "In twenty years Christianity will be no more. My single hand shall destroy the edifice it took twelve apostles to rear." Yet a few months after his death, the house in which he printed his tracts and books became a warehouse for the Geneva Bible Society, from which copies of Scripture made their way across the globe. A doctor named Trochim, attending Voltaire at his death, said the desperate man cried out, "I am abandoned by God and man! I will give you half what I am worth if you will give me six months' life. Then I shall go to hell; and you will go with me. O Christ! O Jesus Christ!"[6]

But perhaps no atheist ever suffered a more dreadful exit from this world than Kay, who with his final breath shouted incessantly, "Hell! Hell! Hell!" His terrible shouts so unnerved his family that they fled from his room until they were sure he was dead.[7]

Compare such difficult deaths to that of Catherine Booth, who with her husband, William, founded the Salvation Army. "The waters are rising, but so am I," she declared just moments before she died. "I am not going under but over. Do not be concerned about dying; go on living well, the dying will be right."[8]

How could Catherine die so "right"? Because she fully believed in a merciful, gracious, loving God who in moments would gladly welcome her into his bright presence. Catherine could die well because she had lived well, faithfully following in the footsteps of her Lord, Jesus Christ.

Before Catherine Booth left this earth to stand face-to-face with her God, she helped thousands of others to prepare for that day when they, too, would step into his holy presence. She had seen the power of God change even the most corrupt and depraved of human hearts, and she rejoiced that no one, not even atheists, lay beyond God's ability to save anyone who would come to Jesus Christ in faith.

Catherine died in 1890, and today, more than a hundred years later, I can give personal testimony that God remains in the business of rescuing anyone, even atheists, from a deathbed of regret and fear. I know this is true because of a precious letter I received just a few months ago.

A Longtime Atheist Comes to Christ

Jerry B. Jenkins and I get thousands of letters and e-mails from readers of our end-times fiction series. One woman wrote to thank us for writing the books. She said that her father had for many years been a true atheist. He allowed his family to worship God, but he wanted no part of it and forbade his wife and children from talking in his presence about spiritual things. He did permit them to say grace at meals.

Years later, the man came to stay in his daughter's home. She told him, "Dad, we pray at our home. We pray at mealtime; we pray at night. And if you live in our home, you'll have to sit here for prayers."

"You had to obey my rules when you lived in my home," he replied. "Now I have to obey your rules in your home."

And so he'd sit there politely and let the family pray to a God in whom he didn't believe.

Three years later, the old atheist became very ill and lost his sight. He loved to hear his daughter read to him, so they made a bargain that she would do so if she could select the reading. So she started in on *Left Behind*. To her surprise, he liked the story, despite its religious nature. She continued the series, reading through *Tribulation Force* and *Nicolai*. By the time she got to *Soul Harvest*, she could see something happening in her dad's crusty old heart.

One morning she entered her father's room and he said, with a big smile on his face, "Honey, you don't have to worry about me anymore."

"Why not?" she asked.

"Last night, I prayed the prayer of Rayford Steele," he replied. Rayford Steele is one of our fictional characters who prayed to accept Christ after the Rapture.

For two months afterward, this woman read to her father from the Bible. To her joy, he showed all the signs of truly coming to know Christ. Then he passed away.

Her story told, this woman had a question for me: "Pastor La-Haye," she wrote, "is it possible that God would accept a man who had rejected him for all those years, eighty-four years of life, and then just before he dies, reverse his opinion and say 'yes' to Jesus?"

What a beautiful question. And there's a beautiful answer:

Yes! It was a delight to show her a number of verses of Scripture that declare how God is able to save to the uttermost everyone who calls on him. And I gave her an illustration.

Do you recall the thief on the cross, one of two criminals crucified with Jesus? At first, he cursed and reviled Jesus, along with everyone else (Matt. 27:44). But as he watched how Jesus died, something caused him to turn to the Lord and say, "Lord, remember me when You come into Your kingdom" (Luke 23:42).

Now, if anyone seems unworthy of salvation, it has to be this thief on the cross. What did he do to deserve mercy? He had spent his whole miserable life robbing innocent victims. And yet Jesus, the spirit of prophecy—the one who came to proclaim the year of the Lord's favor—replied, "Assuredly, I say to you, today you will be with Me in Paradise" (Luke 23:43).

Isn't that a marvelous guarantee? Whatever our dirty backgrounds, our merciful and loving Lord can cleanse us through faith in Jesus Christ, God's dear Son.

Many people through the years have told me that God has poured out his mercy upon them. In their grief, he has become utterly real to them. In their hour of trial, he has become their ever-present supply. Why? Because he is a gracious, merciful, long-suffering, eager-to-forgive heavenly Father.

Someday in heaven, you might want to ask an eighty-four-year-old former atheist about that. And if you'd like, you can call in a former thief for corroboration.

15

Then They Will Know

When you really love someone—when that love is deep, genuine, and persistent—you want the object of your affection to know how you feel. You don't want that person to remain in the dark, to wonder whether you really care. You want your loved one to know beyond a shadow of a doubt that she or he has captured your heart.

Do you realize that you have captured God's heart and that he wants you to know it?

Because the Lord wants us to know how much he loves us, he has given us prophecy. He speaks to us of the future, not only to prove the identity of his Son and to prepare us for eternity, but to help us know, without question, that he loves us and that he wants the best for us, both now and for eternity. He has a tremendous desire that we know who he is and that he cares for us. And he wants us to freely choose to worship him so that we can enjoy him forever.

Years ago I ran into a man who did not know of God's love for him. In fact, he identified himself as "an unscientific atheist." He visited our church one Sunday and told me, "I've never studied Christianity. I was raised in an atheistic home and I went to liberal schools."

But while earning his master's degree at Stanford University, this man learned that he should never make a final conclusion about anything until he had carefully examined all sides of the evidence. Eager to shed the "unscientific" part of his identity, he told me: "During these nine months in San Diego, while I'm working for General Dynamics as an engineer and before I enroll at Brandeis University to work on my Ph.D., I'm going to attend your church and give you an opportunity to expose me to Christianity."

I relished the challenge and with great delight asked him to meet with me once a week. During our times together, we considered many evidences for the truth of the Christian faith, especially data concerning the resurrection of Jesus. Before he finished one year of doctoral work, this young man gave his life to Christ, concluding that Jesus Christ really was the Son of God. He had discovered five times as many reasons to believe in the bodily resurrection of Christ as to reject it—and of course, the resurrection of Jesus is the very foundation of the Christian faith.

Why hadn't this bright young man become a Christian earlier? Only one reason: He had never been exposed to the evidence. He wasn't familiar with the many proofs of our faith that God gives us in his Word and in history. And because of that, he didn't know how deeply God loved him.

That's one piece of ignorance that God wants to wipe out. He not only loves us, he wants us to *know* that he loves us. And he's on a mission to see that everyone gets the fantastically good word concerning his caring, compassionate heart.

God Wants Us to Know

One of the most common statements to be found in the Bible is some form of "Then they will know." God does not want the world to remain ignorant of either his will or his love. Therefore he pulls out all the stops to let us know what he's really like.

Through the prophet Isaiah, God reminded the nation Israel that only he could accurately foretell the future and reveal the truth about the past. Why did he make such a declaration? He himself explained: "That you may know and believe Me, And understand that I am He" (Isa. 43:10). He did the same with Jeremiah (Jer. 16:21) and Daniel (Dan. 8:16, 19).

God wants us to understand, to comprehend, to know. Perhaps no prophet of God grasped this overpowering divine desire so well as Ezekiel. At least twenty-one times in his book the prophet used some form of the phrase, "Then you will know."[1] Ezekiel made it clear that God gave Bible prophecy so that we would know and understand both the plan and the love of the Lord.

Consider just one of Ezekiel's prophecies, concerning a future time when Russia and her allies will invade Israel, "coming like a storm, covering the land like a cloud" (38:9). At that time God will stand up and supernaturally wipe out the invaders. Why? "So that the nations may know Me," God said. "Thus I will magnify Myself and sanctify Myself, and I will be known in the eyes of many nations. Then they shall know that I am the LORD" (38:16, 23).

Several times in chapters 38 and 39 (38:16, 23; 39:6, 7, 22, 23, 28) God says that he will perform a great miracle on Israel's behalf in order to declare that he's alive and well. Through that miracle (which will occur just before the Tribulation), millions will see the Lord for who he really is and will recognize their need for salvation.

Clearly, God wants us to know how much he truly loves us.

God Goes to Great Lengths

So urgently does God want us to understand his mercy and grace that he goes to great lengths to show us the depths of his love.

In Ezekiel's time, the people of God had wandered far away from pure devotion to the Lord and instead had attached themselves to foreign gods—dead idols of wood and stone. The Israelites had earned terrible divine judgment for their open rebellion, but still God did everything he could to turn their hearts back to him before it became too late.

In one of the great "object lessons" of the Bible, God told Ezekiel to dress himself like a captive and act out before his people what was about to happen, should they refuse to repent. "Therefore, son of man," God said, "pack your belongings for exile and in the daytime, as they watch, set out and go from where you are to another place. *Perhaps they will understand,* though they are a rebellious house" (Ezek. 12:3 NIV, italics added).

No doubt Ezekiel felt foolish as he played the unusual role God had assigned to him. But if there were even a slim chance that the people would understand their danger by watching the prophet act out his peculiar role, the exercise would be worth it in the eyes of a merciful God.

Jeremiah also described the lengths to which God is prepared to go in order to enable confused human minds to understand his true nature and will. The "weeping prophet" described unspeakable calamities to come, judgments that would grow increasingly severe if the people refused to turn from their folly. "The anger of the LORD will not turn back until He has executed and performed the thoughts of His heart," Jeremiah said. He then added the telling thought, "In the latter days you will understand it perfectly" (Jer. 23:20). God will use dramatic measures to help us understand, even if that means something as terrible as the Great Tribulation.

Yet God delights in blessing, not devastation. If to get us to understand he goes to the extreme in his righteous judgments, he goes to even greater extremes in his overflowing blessings. So he promised through Isaiah:

> I will open rivers in desolate heights, and fountains in the midst of the valleys; I will make the wilderness a pool of water, and the dry land springs of water. I will plant in the wilderness the cedar

and the acacia tree, they myrtle and the oil tree; I will set in the desert the cypress tree and the pine and box tree together, that they may see and know, and consider and understand together, that the hand of the LORD has done this, and the Holy One of Israel has created it. (Isa. 41:18–20)

Isaiah declared in this passage that:

- God wants us to "see."
- God wants us to "know."
- God wants us to "consider."
- God wants us to "understand."

So earnestly does the Lord want us to see, know, consider, and understand, that he will go to great lengths to make it happen. When such tremendous events take place, those who see them unfold will naturally gape in wonder. Witnesses will marvel at the extreme commitment of God to spreading the truth concerning himself—but God will not marvel. After all, he planned these astonishing events long ago. He has long desired to lavish on his people the abundant riches of his love and mercy.

God Still Works Passionately for Our Salvation

It would be a grave mistake to think that, while God may have performed great marvels in the past to help people to understand his love and his will, and in the future will execute similar feats, in the present he almost hides. The truth lies elsewhere. In fact, God is even now working passionately to show men and women his love.

Luis Palau tells of meeting a middle-aged Arab woman from a wealthy and powerful family. "As soon as she entered the room," Luis reported, "I felt as though the Queen of England had appeared—only more so. She spoke with authority, exuded class, and carried herself with regal bearing. She spoke French, English and Arabic, and had memorized most of the Quran. Her father held the #2 post in her country."[2]

None of the perquisites of this woman's lofty situation, however, gave her peace. She felt empty inside and began quietly searching for spiritual reality. God is always on the lookout for such sincere seekers, and one evening Jesus appeared to this woman in a dream. He told her that soon she would meet someone who could point her in the right spiritual direction. She believed what he told her even though no churches existed in her country, she knew little about Jesus, and had never seen a Bible.

One day she had a chance encounter with a visiting foreigner. He secretly gave her a Bible and a copy of the *Jesus* video—and within five years of first seeing the vision, this woman, her children, her father, and many of her friends had all accepted Jesus Christ as their Savior and Lord.

But get this: Luis says the woman's visionary encounter is far from unique. "Jesus often breaks through in the Muslim community today through dreams and visions," he says. "I'm told he always appears in white, accompanied by music. No kidding! I've heard the story repeatedly from Muslims who have come to Christ through these unusual visitations. They tell me, 'The Lord said to me, "I am Jesus, of whom you read in the Quran. You don't know much about me yet, but I'm real. And I'm alive. I'm your Savior. Trust Me! Obey Me. And I will be speaking more to you soon."'"[3]

How's that for going to great lengths to help men and women understand God's marvelous mercy and love? But don't imagine that the Middle East has a monopoly on such stories.

Andre Boshmakov pastors a growing church in Voronesh, Russia, about three hundred miles southwest of Moscow. Some time ago he decided that more of his countrymen could hear about the grace and mercy of God if he could get the message out on local TV airwaves—no easy task, since the state owns the television stations. He investigated the cost of such a project and discovered that he and his church had nowhere close to the funds needed. So he began to pray.

"Lord," he said, "if this idea is from you, then please increase the yield of our crops to pay for the expense." Boshmakov and his family farmed a small plot of land to help make ends meet, a fairly common practice for Russian pastors. Months later, at harvest time, Boshmakov discovered that God had answered his prayer—with a yield about *four times* the usual, amounting to about three thousand dollars of additional money. The abundant harvest prompted the pastor to wonder if he shouldn't use part of the money to help his own struggling family. When he told his wife about his new idea, she replied that the extra money—all of it—was to go to the project he had prayed about. End of discussion.

Boshmakov then visited the television station manager to describe his proposed program and to inquire about the costs of airing it. The manager listened politely, then informed the stunned pastor that airtime would run about five hundred dollars a month—far in excess of Boshmakov's budget. The pastor left the station, discouraged, but still praying. A few weeks later he returned to the station and again pleaded his case. Much to his surprise, the formerly disinterested station manager offered him six months of airtime *at no cost*. Although the man didn't believe in Boshmakov's message, he decided the show might have promise and okayed it without Moscow's consent.

Now Boshmakov had to buy the equipment needed to produce his half-hour show. He quickly discovered the necessary gear would cost more than five times what he had available. So he and his church began praying once more . . . and soon acquired everything they needed, and then some.

Almost as soon as the show began broadcasting, it became a hit. Other stations in the area began inquiring about getting tapes of the program to air for their own audiences. Today the show can be seen not only in Voronesh, but also in St. Petersburg and Kosovo. And now Boshmakov is praying about raising additional funds to buy tape duplication equipment, to provide the program to more stations that say they want it.

God still does his utmost to get out his message—all over the world, in the most unlikely countries. My collaborator for this book, Steve Halliday, last year visited Nellore in southern India to help out with two conferences for Christian leaders—one for pastors and one for evangelists. While in Nellore he heard several remarkable stories, directly from those involved, about how God is at work in India to reach interested men and women with the gospel of Christ.

Several years ago, the Rev. C. Kamalakar pastored the Nellore Baptist Church. One Sunday morning, he noticed a nervous visitor hanging around the fringe of the crowd after the worship service. One could easily spot the visitor, for he wore clothes typical of a villager (80 percent of India's population of one billion lives outside of the cities). After everyone else had left, Kamalakar asked the man if he could assist him in some way.

"I hope so," replied the man, who then explained that almost everyone in his village had been having the same two dreams, and not even the local witch doctor could suggest what the dreams meant. The shaman suggested that they send a representative into the city to ask someone there about the dreams. So this man showed up at Kamalakar's church, seeking answers from another kind of "holy man."

He described both dreams to the pastor. In the first, men unknown to the village were joyfully dunking the villagers, one by one, in the waters of a nearby river. In the second, the villagers received little pieces of bread to eat and a red liquid to drink. The second dream upset the man and his neighbors, because in their tribal religion, red liquid usually represented something dangerous or evil.

Kamalakar could hardly believe his ears. The villager had unknowingly described, in perfect detail, two Christian rites practiced around the world: baptism and the Lord's Supper. As soon as Kamalakar told the man what the dreams meant, the villager committed his life to Christ. And then he delivered a second message to the pastor: "You must come to my village and tell my people what you have told me."

A few days later, Kamalakar did so, and on the spot almost the whole village made a commitment to Christ. The pastor's experience in this village prompted him to wonder how he might get God's message out to other nearby villages, and over the next few years he began an organization—ALMA, the Abundant Life Ministerial Associates—to train a select number of village Christians to evangelize their own people. Today, about seventy-five evangelists and their wives each work in about three villages apiece. Dirt-poor (they're fortunate if they own a donated bicycle), they faithfully trudge from village to village, bringing the Good News of Jesus Christ to their countrymen.

You can almost hear the voice of the prophets when incidents like these take place: *Then they will know* . . . God wants people all over the world to know of his love and mercy and grace, and he will act dramatically to get that knowledge to them.

And how about here, in the West? To what lengths does God go to get our fellow countrymen to understand and know his true nature? While God may use dreams and visions and remarkable answers to prayer and miracles anywhere he wants, more often than not he tends to reach Westerners through more "ordinary" means. I believe the recent upsurge of interest in Bible prophecy is one of God's chosen ways to help men and women to know and understand his merciful, gracious nature. The very fact that you hold this book in your hands demonstrates his earnest desire to help *you* understand.

Reports from this country and from across the world confirm that God will use any legitimate means necessary to reach us with his love. Yet I have to express one word of caution: we must never attempt to dictate to God how and when he should communicate his message. He tends to like surprises, as the contemporaries of Jesus discovered. And we should never expect him to do anything that contradicts his Word as revealed in the Bible.

God Acts in Unexpected Ways

We could all spare ourselves a lot of grief over how God reveals his goodness if we would spend a little time in the seventh chapter of John's Gospel. There we learn that while God loves to help men and women understand his loving nature, he sometimes offers his help in unexpected ways.

By this point in John's narrative, Jesus was avoiding Judea because of official opposition to his message. As an important national feast approached, however, Jesus and his disciples wanted to celebrate in Jerusalem. Jesus' brothers—who did not yet believe in him—knew that he wanted to spread his message, and so they cynically urged him to leave Galilee. "Depart from here and go into Judea, that Your disciples also may see the works that You are doing," they said. "For no one does anything in secret while he himself seeks to be known openly. If you do these things, show Yourself to the world" (vv. 3–4).

And how did Jesus reply to his unbelieving brothers? "My time has not yet come . . . You go up to this feast. I am not yet going up to this feast, for My time has not yet fully come" (vv. 6, 8). Christ's answer revealed the first of four important lessons to be gleaned from John 7.

1. God Accomplishes His Mission on His Own Timetable.

Yes, Jesus wants others to understand the merciful, gracious nature of God. Despite his brothers' cynicism, Jesus intended to spread God's Word at the feast. Yet he would do so on his own timetable; no one could force him to work according to his or her schedule.

John's record tells us that after Jesus spoke with his brothers, "He remained in Galilee. But when His brothers had gone up, then He also went up to the feast, not openly, but as it were in secret" (vv. 9–10). Jesus had every intention of attending the feast in Jerusalem and of broadcasting his message there, yet *he* would be the one to choose how and when he would spread his message. And so he taught us a second lesson about God's methods:

2. God Accomplishes His Mission in His Own Way.

Once Jesus arrived in Jerusalem, he went to the temple and began teaching the crowds. His listeners marveled at his words, for they knew he had never received a formal education. Yet his enemies also heard him, and they planned to arrest him and so stop him from spreading his message. John said, "They sought to take Him; but no one laid a hand on Him, because His hour had not yet come" (v. 30). This verse provides a third important lesson concerning God's methods of communicating his message of hope:

3. Nothing Stops God's Plan to Reach Out with the Good News.

Why couldn't Jesus' opponents arrest him at the feast, thereby preventing him from telling the crowds about God's amazing love? Because, John said simply, "His hour had not yet come." God's methods not only differ from what we expect; they also cannot be frustrated.

As Jesus continued to speak at the feast, "many of the people believed in Him" (v. 31). Alarmed by the Lord's growing popularity, frightened religious leaders sent officers to arrest Jesus—but the officers soon returned, empty-handed. "Why have you not brought him?" their superiors demanded. "No man ever spoke like this Man!" the officers replied (vv. 45–46). Their words revealed that some in the crowds believed Jesus and his message, while others discounted both him and his words. John summarized, "So there was a division among the people because of Him" (v. 43)—providing us with the final lesson about God's methods of helping people understand his loving nature:

4. God's Message Often Receives Mixed Reactions.

God goes out of his way to ensure that interested men and women hear and grasp his message—but it is up to the hearers to decide how they will respond.

May I ask, how have *you* responded?

Because the Lord may use whatever means he deems necessary to get out his word, we should never feel surprised at the methods he actually chooses. Phillips Brooks, the nineteenth-century author of the Christmas carol, "O Little Town of Bethlehem," reminded us of this when he said:

Oh, how we make God a method, a law, a habit, a machine, instead of a great, dear, live, loving Nature, all afire with affection and radiant with light! How we have taken that great word *faith* and made it to mean the holding of set dogmas, when it really means the wide openness of a whole life to God! How we have limited and stereotyped the range and possibility of a miracle until only what God *has* done we think God *can* do, and so do not stand ready for the new light and mercy and salvation which the Infinite Love and Power of God has to give!

Open your heart today. God cannot merely do for you over and over again what He has done in the past; He must do *more*.[4]

"Now I Know"

Throughout Bible history and on into today, God strives to help us understand what he's doing in the world. His ultimate goal is not to get some nameless, faceless mob to know him, but to enable individual men and women, boys and girls, to say with utter conviction, "Now *I* know him!"

We can be sure of this because it's happened many times already.

After God brought the Israelites out of Egyptian captivity, their leader, Moses, described to his Midianite father-in-law the great miracles God had performed along the way. In response, Jethro declared, "*Now I know* that the LORD is greater than all the gods" (Ex. 18:11, italics added).

After God cured Naaman, the Syrian general, of a terrible skin disease, the grateful soldier returned to the prophet Elisha and proclaimed, "Indeed, *now I know* that there is no God in all the earth, except in Israel" (2 Kings 5:15, italics added).

After God sent an angel to free Peter from prison and an almost certain execution, the apostle cried out, "*Now I know for certain* that the Lord has sent His angel, and has delivered me from the hand of Herod" (Acts 12:11, italics added).

Every time God says, "Then they will know," what he really

wants in return is a multitude of joyful voices proclaiming, "Now I know for certain!"

So that brings the question: Do *you* know that there is no god in all the earth, except for the God of Abraham, Isaac, and Jacob?

Do *you* know that the Lord is greater than all gods?

Do *you* know for certain that the Lord wants to deliver you from the hand of the evil one?

It really comes down to this. God wants us to know and understand him, not so that we can correctly answer a few questions to a religious edition of *Trivial Pursuit*® but so that we can enjoy eternity with him. He wants us to know the tremendous hope found only in him. And hope really is the issue, as God declares through the prophet Isaiah:

> Kings shall be your foster fathers, and their queens your nursing mothers; they shall bow down to you with their faces to the earth, and lick up the dust of your feet. Then you will know that I am the LORD, for they shall not be ashamed who wait for Me. (Isa. 49:23)

16

Seven Reasons Why Prophecy Matters

Does Bible prophecy really matter? Is it relevant to the nitty-gritty, practical issues of day-to-day living?

Had you been a Christian living in ancient Jerusalem around A.D. 70, such a question never would have crossed your mind. Why not? Because Bible prophecy probably saved your life.

In A.D. 70, the Romans' four-year campaign against Jewish revolutionaries came to a bloody end with the obliteration of Jerusalem. Angry legionnaires broke through the city's northern defenses, torched the temple and the city, and slaughtered its residents wherever they could find them. Some accounts place the death toll at upwards of one million. The armies of Rome leveled the ancient city, leaving only three towers standing (one of them, named Phasael, still remains).

Yet most Christians escaped the carnage, having fled to the mountains—many to Pella in Perea—after heeding a stern warning of impending doom.[1] And what authority issued the warning?

Bible prophecy.

The ancient historian Eusebius recorded in his *Ecclesiastical History* that as the Christian residents of Jerusalem saw Roman legions beginning to encircle the city, they remembered a

prophecy uttered by Jesus some forty years before:[2] "But when you see Jerusalem surrounded by armies, then know that its desolation is near. Then let those who are in Judea flee to the mountains, let those who are in the midst of her depart, and let not those who are in the country enter her. For these are the days of vengeance" (Luke 21:20–22).

Believers in Christ took their Master's prophetic warning literally. They left the city in droves, fleeing to the mountains before Roman soldiers closed off all avenues of escape. And so God spared their lives.

A dramatic illustration, you say? Certainly, but just as true as it is dramatic. Bible prophecy *matters*, even making the difference between life and death.

Does It Make a Practical Difference?

"But wait a moment," someone may say. "A single illustration, no matter how dramatic, does not prove that Bible prophecy makes a bit of difference to contemporary life. How does it help me to pay my bills, rear my kids, succeed at my job? I don't see how Bible prophecy can help me to live better from day to day. If I live in Jerusalem and see the city surrounded by armies, okay, I'll get out of there—but if I make my home outside of Israel, how can prophecy matter all that much to me?"

I hope that in this book I've already provided several strong reasons to show why prophecy should matter to all of us. Bible prophecy helps us to face the future with courage, gives our lives meaning in the here and now, and comforts us at the passing of believing loved ones. God designed Bible prophecy to enrich and strengthen every aspect of our lives.

For the moment, however, let's put all of that aside and ask, *What practical difference does Bible prophecy make to everyday living? Why should I bother with it?*

Based on the thousands of letters I have received from readers of my previous books on prophecy, and based on my own experience over the past five decades of active ministry, I can

testify that a concentrated focus on Bible prophecy yields countless practical benefits. Since this book considers the nature of God as revealed through Bible prophecy, let's narrow our focus and ponder how prophecy's compelling picture of God helps us to live well. What we believe about God affects every aspect of our lives—so let's look at seven prophetic "snapshots" of God that shape every facet of our lives as modern human beings.

I think you'll see that Bible prophecy makes a *huge* difference.

1. A Loving God

We say that "love makes the world go 'round," and that "what the world needs now is love, sweet love,"[3] but unless we consider the white-hot furnace of love aflame in the heart of God, we miss the genuine article.

The prophets of God could not help but marvel at the Rock of love that was their eternal Sovereign. "Though the mountains be shaken and the hills be removed," God said through Isaiah, "yet my unfailing love for you will not be shaken" (Isa. 54:10 NIV). Likewise, after God led the nation of Israel out of slavery in Egypt, Moses and his sister, Miriam, sang a prophetic song in which they declared to God, "You in Your mercy have led forth the people whom You have redeemed" (Ex. 15:13). And Zephaniah the prophet saw God as a great Lover who yearned to bless his people:

> The LORD your God in your midst, the Mighty One, will save; He will rejoice over you with gladness, He will quiet you with His love, He will rejoice over you with singing. (Zeph. 3:17)

When we know we're loved, we gain a confidence unavailable through any other means. Love strengthens us when we feel weak, lifts us up when we feel down, gives us courage when we feel like running, and inspires us when we feel tapped out. More than once in my ministry the love of my wife has kept me going when I felt like giving up.

We cannot fully comprehend the astonishing power of love. And when we know that it is God, the Almighty himself, who loves us and who will never stop loving us—just as the prophets declare—then what enemy could possibly drive us to live in tents of gloom?

When the apostle Paul asked that question, he answered his own query in an exclamation full of passionate, prophetic conviction:

> For I am persuaded that neither death nor life, nor angels nor principalities nor powers, nor things present nor things to come, nor height nor depth, nor any other created thing, shall be able to separate us from the love of God which is in Christ Jesus our Lord. (Rom. 8:38–39)

If you rest secure in the love of God as pictured by the prophets, *nothing* can ultimately move you. Death can't. Life can't. Angels can't. Demons can't. The present cannot defeat you, nor can the future ruin you. No power in heaven above or in hell beneath or in any other dimension can separate you from the love of God in Christ.

You cannot find anything that "matters" more than this! And neither will you find a guarantee better than this anywhere outside of the prophetic Word of God.

2. A Faithful God

When you give your word to someone, does that person feel confident that you will keep it? When you make a promise, do your hearers feel certain that you will do exactly what you say?

In other words, do others consider you *faithful*?

"We have all known the hurt of unfaithfulness," wrote author Myrna Alexander.

> We have wondered whom we can depend on. The Scriptures give us great hope by coupling the truth that God is faithful with the fact that He cannot change. "For I the LORD do not change" (Malachi 3:6). God will always be faithful to you because it is im-

possible for Him to change. For God to be unfaithful even once would cause Him to change. God's very name is "Faithful" (Revelation 19:11), for He is perfect in faithfulness. Imagine, there *is* Someone who will never let you down, who will never break His promise to you![4]

The prophets reveled in the knowledge that God acts with perfect faithfulness in all he does. "Therefore know that the LORD your God," Moses told the Israelites, "He is God, the faithful God who keeps covenant and mercy for a thousand generations with those who love Him and keep His commandments" (Deut.7:9).

So what does that mean for us? How does God's faithfulness make a difference in our daily lives? In what ways should this beloved truth of Bible prophecy matter to us? Listen to Myrna Alexander once more:

> What does this mean to you? God *will* be, *must* be, faithful to His Word and to every promise He has made to you in it: "Faithful is he that calleth you, who also will do it" (1 Thessalonians 5:24 KJV). That means:
>
> *Faithful* is He who calls you as an encourager to your spouse with his or her unique needs; He will also give you grace to meet those needs.
>
> *Faithful* is He who calls you as mother or father to your children with their individual physical limitations, temperaments, and mental capacities; He will also enable you to work properly with them.
>
> *Faithful* is He who calls you to a seemingly impossible task; He will also give you whatever ability you need to accomplish that task (Hebrews 4:16).
>
> Since God is perfect, he cannot fail you even once! What security, what peace, what confidence is now possible for you! God is faithful. He will never fail to keep His promises to you.[5]

God promises to be faithful to believers by giving them the strength to overcome whatever temptations threaten to tear them down (1 Cor. 10:13). He promises to remain faithful by keeping them strong to the end so that they may greet the returning Lord Jesus with great joy (1 Cor. 1:8–9). No wonder the apostle Paul could pray so confidently for the young believers he nurtured through his letters! He prayed that they might become more and more like Jesus, that they might be found "blameless" when their Lord returned. How could he be so confident? Because he believed with all his heart, "He who calls you is faithful, who also will do it" (1 Thess. 5:23–24).

3. A Patient God

Although I live, like you, in a technological age full of gee-whiz wonders, I confess that, so far at least, I haven't availed myself of one of its most ubiquitous offerings: e-mail. Although my wife gleefully scurries around the Internet, swapping messages and files with cohorts around the globe, I remain contentedly mired in the world of postage stamps, faxes, and Federal Express. Why? For one thing, I suppose I just don't have the patience to learn the inscrutable ways of bits and bytes (an attitude my daughter describes as "cute").

While my Linda may think me adorable for my aversion to e-mail, a lack of patience can often get one into trouble. For lack of patience, thousands of mismatched couples have foolishly waltzed down the aisle; scores of inventors have quit just before making a fabulous breakthrough; and untold nations have marched their finest young soldiers off to war.

Can you imagine what life would be like for us if *God* lacked patience? If God were easily frustrated and quickly lost patience when we failed to measure up to his perfect standards—where would any of us be? I know at least two things for sure: I wouldn't be writing this paragraph, and you wouldn't be reading it.

But God *is* patient with us, as the New Testament prophet, Peter, declared: "The Lord is not slow in keeping his promise, as some understand slowness. He is patient with you, not wanting anyone to perish, but everyone to come to repentance . . . Bear in mind that our Lord's patience means salvation" (2 Pet. 3:9, 15 NIV).

If you think of God as a nail-biting, cosmic policeman, impatient and ill-tempered with our frequent screwups, then you have missed the prophets' consistent message through the ages: *patience* lights up God's character. In the passage we just read, Peter simply spelled out for his generation what previous prophets had proclaimed to their own. When the Israelites rebelled against the Lord in the wilderness, Moses asked God to forgive their sin and reminded him of a lesson taught not long before: "The LORD is *slow to anger*, abounding in love and forgiving sin and rebellion" (Num. 14:18 NIV, italics added). Moses' phrase "slow to anger" is simply another way of saying *unbelievably patient.*

God is exactly that: unbelievably patient. We don't deserve it, we don't earn it, we often don't even appreciate it—but there it is, anyway: God exercises unfathomable patience toward us (see Neh. 9:19; Ps. 86:15; Nahum 1:3).

Think about what this means for you. God does not fly off the handle the moment you mess up. He does not lose his temper when you take a wrong turn. He does not give up on you when you fail, and he does not hurl thunderbolts the second you step off the right path. He is patient with you, and that makes all the difference.

The father of a friend of mine is in God's kingdom today because of God's great patience. For more than thirty years this man resisted his family's efforts to get him to consider the Good News of Jesus Christ. He never railed against their faith nor even scoffed at it; he simply didn't think it was for him. One evening, after waiting for his father to finish reading the newspaper, his son asked, "Dad, what do you think about God?" The man immediately picked up his already-read paper, slid behind its fortress-like walls and replied, "Why, does it matter?" So ended that discussion.

Yet God is patient; for good reason some have called him, "the Hound of heaven." The Lord never gave up on this man, and through a series of well-timed events, the man eventually surrendered his life to God, just before he retired. Today he's a happy, growing Christian.

We ought to thank God for his patience, yet never take it for granted. None of us knows how long we have on this planet. "Now" is always the best time to accept God's offer of eternal life.

4. A God of Security

As I write, security is on everyone's mind. Earlier this year the governor of California mobilized National Guard troops to watch over our state's major bridges, reportedly threatened by terrorists. The U.S. House of Representatives and the Senate are working out a compromise bill on new rules for airport and commercial airline security. And just a couple of days ago in the mail we received, "A Message from the Postmaster General." The message begins, "The U.S. Postal Service places the highest priority on the safety of our customers and employees and on the security of the mail." On its reverse side, the card lists a series of answers to two questions: "What should make me suspect a piece of mail?" and "What should I do with a suspicious piece of mail?"

As I said, security's on everyone's mind.

Psychologists tell us that every human being has the need to feel both significant (loved) and secure (safe). When these needs go unmet, significant dysfunction results.

But in these uncertain days, how can anyone feel truly secure? Constant media speculation about terrorists wielding biological, chemical, and perhaps even portable nuclear weapons does nothing to help us feel safe. So where can we turn to regain a sense of security?

God might suggest that we turn to his prophetic Word.

When the prophet Isaiah felt tempted to succumb to the fears running rampant among his people, God told him:

Do not say, "A conspiracy," concerning all that this people call a conspiracy, nor be afraid of their threats, nor be troubled. The LORD of hosts, Him you shall hallow; let Him be your fear, and let Him be your dread. He will be as a sanctuary. (Isa. 8:12–14)

Although God originally addressed these words to Isaiah, we have every right to claim God as a sanctuary for ourselves, as the apostle Peter affirms. Peter quoted these very words to his Cristian friends: "'And do not be afraid of their threats, nor be troubled.' But sanctify the Lord God in your hearts" (1 Pet. 3:14–15). The key to security, according to Peter, is to focus on the Lord. And why should this give us comfort and a deep sense of safety? Because Jesus is Lord of the universe and nothing ever spins out of his control.

Remember when Jesus stood before Pilate, the Roman governor who grew angry that the Lord declined to answer his questions? "Are you not speaking to me?" asked an incredulous Pilate. "Do You not know that I have power to crucify You, and power to release You?" (John 19:10).

Jesus looked steadily at Pilate, then broke his silence: "You could have no power at all against Me unless it had been given you from above" (v. 11). Pilate thought that he remained in total command of the situation; Jesus informed him that, at best, he enjoyed a derivative authority. It almost makes you wonder who the *real* prisoner was in that Jerusalem palace!

Jesus wants us to feel secure in his complete control over all of creation, even in dark days when world events seem to be spinning out of control. God said to Isaiah:

Strengthen the weak hand, and make firm the feeble knees. Say to those who are fearful-hearted, "Be strong, do not fear! Behold, your God will come with vengeance, with the recompense of God; He will come and save you." (Isa. 35:3–4)

So does this mean no tragedy will ever touch God's people? You know better than that. It does mean, however, that when everyone around us trembles in fear, we can stay calm. How?

Through total dependence upon God to take care of us—even in uncertain days.

Jesus predicted that someday believers would be dragged before kings and governors, betrayed by friends and family members alike. "They will put some of you to death," Jesus prophesied. "And you will be hated by all for My name's sake. But not a hair of your head shall be lost. By your patience possess your souls" (Luke 21:16–19).

Now, what on earth could *that* mean? That some will die, but their hair will remain full-bodied and lustrous? No, indeed. Jesus meant that:

> Although they are to suffer physical pain and death, they can never be plucked from the protecting hand of God—nothing will happen to them outside His will, and He will make all things work together for their highest welfare and their eternal salvation, and at His second advent they will arise with glorified, celestial bodies in which there will be no defect or injury.[6]

That is true security. That is total safety. And it is the only sure way to battle fear in an era of terror.

5. A Just God

In some ways we shrink from the idea of God's justice. But the longer we ponder it, the more we see both its necessity and its huge upside.

The fact that God is just means that nobody ultimately "gets away with" any kind of evil. Wicked men may escape the justice of mortals, but they can never escape the justice of God. Peter spoke of this when he reminded his friends:

> You have spent enough time in the past doing what pagans choose to do—living in debauchery, lust, drunkenness, orgies, carousing and detestable idolatry. They think it strange that you do not plunge with them into the same flood of dissipation, and they heap abuse on you. But they will have to give account to him who is ready to judge the living and the dead. (1 Pet. 4:3–5 NIV)

A friend of mine tells me that his mother drilled into his young head the idea of God's infinite justice. Whenever he did something wrong, or even when his mother *suspected* that he had done something wrong, she would quote one of her favorite Old Testament verses: "Be sure your sin will find you out" (Num. 32:23). Jesus added substance to the warning through a prophecy of his own: "I say to you that for every idle word men may speak, they will give account of it in the day of judgment. For by your words you will be justified, and by your words you will be condemned" (Matt. 12:36–37).

If we have made peace with God through faith in his Son, Jesus Christ, we have nothing to fear in the judgment to come. Paul meant to encourage us when he said God "'will render to each one according to his deeds': eternal life to those who by patient continuance in doing good seek for glory, honor, and immortality; but to those who are self-seeking and do not obey the truth, but obey unrighteousness—indignation and wrath" (Rom. 2:6–8).

Thoughts of God's perfect justice not only keep us from wandering onto hurtful and foolish paths, they also keep us from envying those who flout God's laws and yet seem to prosper. This was the great lesson learned by a man named Asaph.

Asaph admitted that as he watched "the boastful" and "the wicked" successfully pull off their sinful schemes, he envied their prosperity. He complained that they had no struggles, that their bodies seemed healthy and strong. In fact, "They are not in trouble as other men, nor are they plagued like other men" (Ps. 73:4–5). To add insult to injury, he couldn't help but notice that they also managed to amass enormous personal fortunes (v. 12).

As Asaph pondered the gross injustices of life, he began to feel sorry for himself. (Don't we all?) "Surely I have cleansed my heart in vain, and washed my hands in innocence. For all day long I have been plagued, and chastened every morning" (v. 13–14).

When finally he could stand it no more—and just before he

prepared to publicly indict God for the whole mess—a sharp prophetic insight kept him on a godly course. He entered the temple and there God let him see the destiny of those he had been envying.

"Oh, how they are brought to desolation, as in a moment! They are utterly consumed with terrors. As a dream when one awakes, so Lord, when You awake, You shall despise their image" (vv. 18–19). As soon as God revealed the future awaiting all the unrepentant, Asaph realized he had chosen the better path. "You will guide me with Your counsel, and afterward receive me to glory," he exulted. "My flesh and my heart fail; but God is the strength of my heart and my portion forever" (vv. 24, 26).

It should encourage all of us that God upholds his infinite holiness by exercising his perfect justice. At the end of history, all the balance sheets will be reconciled and all the debts, paid. And so everyone who loves Jesus Christ will gladly say, "Even so, Lord God Almighty, true and righteous are Your judgments" (Rev. 16:7).

6. A Merciful God

Who among us doesn't, at some point, need mercy? Who among us hasn't longed for compassion or lenience from someone who has us in his or her power?[7]

Nineteen-year-old Jacob Todoriko needed mountains of mercy last fall. When the Oregon State University student fell asleep at the wheel late on a September evening, his pickup slammed into three law enforcement officers who had stopped to assist a stranded motorist along busy I-5. Two of the officers died at the scene; a third remains in a coma.

Todoriko could have faced eighteen months in prison under state sentencing guidelines. Instead, under a plea bargain approved by the victims' families, he pled guilty to criminally negligent homicide and was sentenced to two days in jail, three years of probation, and 660 hours of community service. He also had his driver's license revoked for eight years.

"I'm sorry for what I did," an emotionally distraught Todoriko told the court. "I'm sorry for all the pain I've caused. If I could, I would have given my own life to save them." The victims' families believed Todoriko's repentance to be genuine and said they forgave him.[8]

Mercy: at some point, we all need it. How glad I am that God, the omnipotent Sovereign of the universe, specializes in mercy! The prophet Micah, a contemporary of Isaiah, rejoiced in this truth:

Who is a God like You, pardoning iniquity and passing over the transgression of the remnant of His heritage? He does not retain His anger forever, because He delights in mercy. (Mic. 7:18)

God doesn't merely approve of mercy; he doesn't merely practice mercy; he *delights* in mercy!

When you know that the God you serve delights in mercy, you needn't fear to bring him any problem or hardship or sin. When you believe the prophets and their joyful descriptions of a merciful God, you gladly bring to him all of your troubles and ask him for help.

What if you sinned terribly, hurt someone on purpose, and admit you stand guilty and without excuse? If you know that God is merciful, you approach him as did the psalmist: "LORD, be merciful to me; Heal my soul, for I have sinned against You" (Ps. 41:4).

What if your enemies have plotted your ruin? If you know that God is merciful, you approach him as did David: "Have mercy on me O LORD! Consider my trouble from those who hate me, You who lift me up from the gates of death" (Ps. 9:13).

What if you suffer from some physical problem that makes life almost unbearable? If you know that God is merciful, you cry out to him as did blind Bartimaeus: "Jesus, Son of David, have mercy on me!" (Mark 10:47).

When you know that God delights in mercy, you also know that no heartache or tragedy lies beyond the reach of his merciful hands. When you humble yourself and cast yourself upon God's mercy, there's no telling what wonders he may perform.

Nehemiah could not help but meditate on the mercy of God when the Lord brought his chastened people back to their own land. The governor told his Lord:

> For many years You had patience with them, and testified against them by Your Spirit in Your prophets. Yet they would not listen; therefore You gave them into the hand of the peoples of the lands.
>
> Nevertheless in Your great mercy You did not utterly consume them nor forsake them; For You are God, gracious and merciful. (Neh. 9:30–31)

Why does prophecy matter? It matters because we all need divine mercy, and it is through the prophets that we learn of that amazing mercy. No matter what we have done, no matter how guilty we may feel, God invites us to drink deeply of his mercy:

> Let the wicked forsake his way, and the unrighteous man his thoughts; let him return to the LORD, and He will have mercy on him; and to our God, for He will abundantly pardon. (Isa. 55:7)

7. A God of Hope

Oscar Wilde, the witty Irish author who published *The Ballad of Reading Gaol* two years before his death in 1900, finished his days largely without hope. Perhaps the most famous lines in *Ballad*—a reflection on his years of imprisonment from 1895–1897—testify to his despondency: "We did not dare to breathe a prayer / Or give our anguish scope! / Something was dead in each of us, / And what was dead was Hope."[9]

Wilde ridiculed the Christian faith throughout his life, so it is no surprise that hope fled from him as his days drew to an end. One who lives in the desert should never feel shocked at the drought. Nor should anyone expect to find life-saving medicine in a bottle of poison.

God doesn't want any of us to end our lives without hope. When you approach life with hope, not even black, boiling clouds above can douse the light radiating from your soul. A life lived in hope means all is never lost and the battle is never futile. The road ahead may grow steep and our bodies may grow weary, but hope keeps us moving ahead.

Hope is not some Pollyanna mind-set available only to those who wear rose-colored glasses. Rather, it is the confident expectation that God will always keep his promises, and that in the end, Jesus wins. In hope, we await the day when our bodies will be redeemed, for "we were saved in this hope" (Rom. 8:24).

Hope is a big thing to God—so big that Paul claimed, "whatever things were written before were written for our learning, that we through the patience and comfort of the Scriptures might have hope" (Rom. 15:4).

Did you catch that? *Everything* that was written in the Scriptures, God designed to give us hope. It is always too early to give up!

Do you wake up in the morning disappointed to have to open your eyes? Or do you greet each new day with great anticipation, fueled by an inexhaustible, divine hope? I have discovered that hope is a most practical commodity. It matters. And God wants you to have it in spades.

The Relevance of Bible Prophecy

Does prophecy matter? Is it relevant to the practical issues of day-to-day life in the modern world?

Yes! A thousand times, yes! God inspired courageous prophets to speak his words of love, faithfulness, patience, security, justice, mercy, and hope. Today his words continue to strengthen, encourage, and equip us in ways that make life better now and assure us of a fabulous future tomorrow.

Can anything be more relevant or practical than that?

17

Can You Love a God Like That?

I got out an old photograph the other day while working through some material for a speaking engagement. My daughter saw the picture and asked, "Dad, who is that woman?"

I looked again at the fading photo, my heart fluttering a bit, and said, "Honey, that's your mother."

I held Bev's high school graduation picture for several moments and stared at the picture. I'm no fool; I picked a beauty. In those days she had soft, wrinkle-free skin, beautiful teeth, luxurious hair, and gorgeous eyes. My daughter didn't recognize her own mother from the picture because today Bev looks very different than she did back then—yet before God, after fifty-four years of marriage, I can say she's more beautiful today than when I met her. I look through the eyes of love and see the incredibly lovely person inside.

Have you ever observed an elderly couple holding hands, and instantly known they'd be in eternity in just a few months or years? Yet you smile because you see they clearly love each other more than life itself; through the years they have grown intensely special to one another.

God's love for us is like that. We are intensely special to him. We are God's wonderfully made and much-loved creatures.

We're not mere robots; we're not accidents; we're not the products of time and chance, a "fortuitous concourse of atoms," as Richard Bentley once put it.[1] No, we are specially made creatures beloved by God.

Therefore we don't have to wake up in the morning and say, "Oh no, another day! I wonder what bad thing is going to befall me?" No, we can greet the day with thanksgiving, knowing that the God who loves us is going to be with us again.

Sure, we'll face some problems, more on some days than on others. But however life treats us, we can move forward confidently, convinced that God loves to do good to us. Our Lord is gracious, merciful, slow to anger, and rich in mercy.

Can you love a God like that? Can you trust a God like that? Can you commit your way, your whole life, to a God like that?

God Is Willing to Forgive

It's time to put away our childish and backward ideas of God, and get it into our heads that the Lord is a merciful, gracious, loving and long-suffering God. He is not trying to hurt anyone. He is trying to usher as many of us as possible into his everlasting kingdom.

Can you love a God like that?

Do you recall the scene just before the crucifixion of Jesus, when a mob brought the Savior to Pilate for judgment? The crowd, stirred by violent hatred, called for the execution of Jesus. Pilate, the Roman governor, examined Jesus and then announced, "I find no fault in Him at all" (John 18:38). And how did the mob reply? "Away with Him, away with Him! Crucify Him!"

"Shall I crucify your king?" Pilate asked.

"We have no king but Caesar!" the chief priests screamed (John 19:15).

Pilate's wife had told her husband that she had "suffered many things today in a dream" because of Jesus, and so warned him to have nothing to do "with that just Man" (Matt.

27:19). Pilate therefore ordered a bowl of water to be brought to him, washed his hands in front of everyone, and declared, "I am innocent of the blood of this just Person. You see to it" (v. 24).

And then came the awesome reply, "His blood be upon us and on our children" (v. 25). Chilling words!

Yet do you remember what Jesus prayed as he hung on the cross? "Father," he pled, "forgive them, for they do not know what they do" (Luke 23:34). Even as the mob committed a heinous sin—killing not just a good man, but the very Son of God—Jesus prayed, "Forgive them."

Let's put this in perspective. If you or I had been God, and if that had been our son hanging on the cross, and if we had omnipotence at our disposal, we would have obliterated every one of those who dared to injure Jesus. None would have walked off of Calvary's hill alive.

But God withheld his anger. Why? He so loved the world, that he gave his only begotten Son. God permitted Jesus to pour out his blood on our behalf, the only thing that could cleanse us from our sin (Heb. 9:22).

So did God hear and answer Jesus' prayer? You decide. Fifty days later, Peter got up and preached on the day of Pentecost, looked at those who had demanded the crucifixion of Jesus, and said, "You, with the help of wicked men, put him to death by nailing him to the cross" (Acts 2:23 NIV). When they heard his words their hearts felt pricked with conviction and they asked what they ought to do (v. 37).

"Repent, and let every one of you be baptized in the name of Jesus Christ for the remission of sins," replied Peter, "and you shall receive the gift of the Holy Spirit" (Acts 2:38). That very day, three thousand guilty men placed their faith in Christ.

And who were these newest church members? Just fifty days earlier, many of them had cried out, "Crucify him!" Yet when they repented, God forgave them.

How can you understand a faith like that, unless the Author of the faith is a merciful, long-suffering, gracious God?

He Loves Us Regardless

When we sin, many times we feel afraid of God. We think of ourselves as unworthy of his love and forgiveness—and we are. But that makes no difference to God. He tells us to acknowledge him in all our ways, to seek him while he may be found and to call upon him while he is near. And he warns us not to take his invitation lightly. What God said through the apostle Paul to an ancient audience, he says to us today:

> Therefore let it be known you, brethren, that through this Man is preached to you the forgiveness of sins; and by Him everyone who believes is justified from all things from which you could not be justified by the law of Moses.
>
> Beware, therefore, lest what has been spoken in the prophets come upon you: "Behold, you despisers, marvel and perish! For I work a work in your days, a work which you will by no means believe, though one were to declare it to you." (Acts 13:38–41)

God offers to forgive us of our sins and to give us a new, vibrant life of faith with him, if only we will turn from our sin, call upon the name of Jesus Christ, and commit our lives to the gracious, merciful God of heaven.

Now—can you love and serve a God like that?

God Wants Us to Live Forever with Him

We all aspire to a long life, and the older we get, the more we want to add years to the calendar. But all of us know one thing about life: it ends, sooner or later. And what *then?*

We're all born with the knowledge that we are not meant only for this world. We intuitively believe we will live again. Almost every religion in the world has some idea, no matter how vague, of life after death. Where did they all get such an idea? Collusion? A desperate desire to deny human mortality? No. Ecclesiastes 3:11 tells us that God has "set eternity in the hearts of men" (NIV).

God loves us, and wants us to spend eternity with him in heaven. That's why Jesus came to earth, to make it possible for his Father's desire to be fulfilled. "Whoever lives and believes in Me shall never die," he said in John 11:26. Oh, one's body will die, but the real person who indwells that body will live forever.

In heaven at this very moment, Joseph of Arimathea could be having a spirited conversation with Joseph, the former prince of Egypt. Martin Luther could be discussing theology with Augustine of Hippo. And Mary Magdalene might be sipping celestial tea around a table of friends, perhaps with the former judge Deborah, the former nun Teresa of Avila, and the former nurse Florence Nightingale. They're all enjoying eternal life in the presence of God.

Jesus did all he could to broadcast the wonderful message of life in him. In one of my favorite passages, he told a crowd, "Most assuredly, I say to you, he who hears My word and believes in Him who sent Me has everlasting life, and shall not come into judgment, but has passed from death into life" (John 5:24).

What are the keys? The Bible gives us two: *hearing* the word of Jesus and *believing* it. The word "believe" in the passage we just read could be translated "commit." Whoever believes enough in Jesus to commit his or her life to him has everlasting life. What person with any sense would refuse the offer of eternal life?

When we know we have received life everlasting, we no longer have to fear death. As a pastor for many years, I've stood at the bedside of many individuals who were either dying or on the verge of death. While Christians aren't anxious to die, they're not afraid, either. In fact, many believers get a premonition when it comes time to go home.

Just recently I heard about a seriously ill believer who told his friends that he really wanted to live. But one day he changed his tune. He calmly announced, "The Lord told me I'm going to die." Six days later, he slipped away, without any fear and with absolute peace.

How could a sinful human being ever die so serenely? How could a flawed mortal slip into eternity without the slightest bit of apprehension? Believers in Jesus can do so, because "the testimony of Jesus is the Spirit of prophecy," and he wants to give us the assurance of eternal life.

Now, can you love a God like that?

The Time of Choice

Decisions chart the course of your life. The quality of your life—no matter how much talent you have, no matter how good-looking you are, no matter how much education you possess—will be determined by the right decisions you make. You will make a jillion decisions during your lifetime, some minor, some monumental. But you will never face a decision more critical than the one you make about Jesus Christ.

Our merciful God has given you the ability to choose your eternal destiny. You can choose this day whom you will serve. It's a choice God gives people in every age. He gave the choice to the children of Israel (Deut. 30:19), to Paul and his contemporaries (2 Cor. 6:1–2), and he gives it to you and me.

If you're asking yourself, *What am I going to do with the rest of my life?* let me suggest that the best thing you can do is to say, "Lord, I want to submit all my plans to you. You can have my life." The best bargain you can ever make is to give your life to God. He'll take it and use it beyond your fondest expectations.

Throughout history, from Adam and Eve to the present hour, God leaves it up to individuals to choose whether they will follow him. That was the choice in the Garden. That was the choice in ancient Israel. And that is the choice that faces you and me.

When we're young, we think, *I have a lot of time.* But as we get older and the miles pile up on our speedometer, we start hurrying. We know we have less time than we used to. May I suggest that the most important thing you can do is to guarantee your future? Turn it over to Jesus, receive him as the one and only

Lamb of God who takes away the sin of the world, and then live the rest of your life in obedience to him.

If you haven't yet made this choice, could I urge you to make it today? Look into your heart and ask yourself, *Am I ready? Have I prepared my soul for what's to come by calling on the name of the Lord?* In the quiet of your heart, believe that Jesus died on the cross for your sin and rose again, then call on his name. Pray a simple prayer like this: "Oh God, I am a sinner. I believe that Jesus died for my sin. I now receive him as my Lord and Savior. I give my heart to you. Amen."

Once you make this choice, you can have the confidence that when Jesus shouts from heaven to collect all who belong to him, you'll be among them. That choice, you alone can make.

Can you love a God who gave his only begotten Son, just so you could make that choice? Can you love a God like that?

The Easiest Thing in the World

Salvation is the easiest thing in the world to obtain for those who willingly turn from themselves and say, "Oh, God, I need you!" Yet that's just the sticking point for some of us.

A man on a plane said to me recently, "You know, what you're saying is just too easy. I have to *do* something for it."

"It's easy for us," I replied, "but not for Jesus. Jesus paid his whole life for our salvation. He paid it all. All you have to do is receive it like a gift."

This man, like many others, has a hard time receiving gifts. Perhaps he feels better about himself by believing he can add something of critical value to his salvation. Yet the Bible tells us that no amount of work can earn the least bit of our salvation; only the blood of Christ has any value in bringing us to God— and it has infinite value! Therefore the only thing we can do is to receive his gift with thanksgiving.

What right do we have to salvation? None, in and of ourselves. Only because of who God is and what he's done for us can we look forward to eternal life. God is the merciful one, the gracious and loving and kind Lord who is quick to forgive. Whatever your sins may be, if you will just call upon this wonderful God, he will wipe them out and remove them as far as the east is from the west.

This period we call "time" could easily be termed the time of choice. The decision you make now about Jesus will last forever. And just as there is a wonderful plan for those who receive him, there is a terrible plan for those who reject him. You alone make the choice, and that choice will determine where you spend eternity.

The Long War for Human Souls

In one way, this world is only a grand battle between God and Satan for the souls of men and women.

Don't be fooled: Satan is after your soul. The devil is an accomplished liar and a cunning deceiver. He'll never come to you saying, "Bow down and serve me." Instead, he'll whisper, "Who has the right to tell you how to live? You don't need anyone telling you what to do. You're as smart as anyone else. So do your own thing." But when you do your own thing, you defy God—exactly what Satan wants.

God, on the other hand, is honest. He comes to you and says, "Present your body as a living sacrifice to me. Come and follow me. I'll bless your obedience. Come and serve me."

From the very beginning, when God challenged Adam and Eve to obey him and Satan enticed them to rebel and "do their own thing," the war has raged between God and Satan for human souls. God's arsenal includes the Bible, godly prophets, and the Holy Spirit. Satan uses the weapons of idolatry and false prophets and necromancers and soothsayers. All of this takes place so that each of us can have a choice. Will we obey God or disobey him?

"But what about those who don't live in a place where the gospel is preached?" someone asks. Jesus said that if anyone really wants to know God's will, they can find him (John 7:17).

In heaven we'll discover millions of men and women who throughout history managed to find God, no matter their situation. One of the fun things about heaven will be to hear their stories and see just how merciful and loving our God has been.

Now, can you love a God like that? Can you trust a God like that? Can you serve a God like that for your entire life?

Better Than Anything You've Known

God has a wonderful plan for your future, but the only way to enjoy its benefits is to voluntarily fall on your knees before the cross of Jesus Christ and be born again. Then the God of prophecy will cleanse your soul and conscience. He'll guide you, not only in the future, but right now.

Do you want something better than anything you've ever known? Or do you want something more terrible than your worst nightmare? The stakes are that high. And the choice is yours.

Through the many prophecies of the Bible, the merciful God of heaven has shown us what he's really like. Prophecy describes the wonderful plan he has for those who receive him and love him. It also reveals that God wants us to share his amazing future with us, as his friends and as members of his own dearly loved family.

This God, who goes to such incredible lengths to save to the uttermost anyone who calls upon him, must be worth trusting.

Can you trust a God like that? Can you love a God like that?

I pray that you will, and that you will join me in accepting our merciful God's astonishing offer of eternal life. And I hope that you will walk with God:

> . . . until our Lord Jesus Christ's appearing, which He will manifest in His own time, He who is the blessed and only Potentate, the King of kings and Lord of lords, who alone has immortality, dwelling in unapproachable light whom no man has seen or can see, to whom be honor and everlasting power. Amen. (1 Tim. 6:12, 14–16)

PART FOUR

APPENDICES

Appendix A

Questions and Answers

The study of Bible prophecy often generates important questions. In the material that follows, I have tried to provide brief answers to some of the most commonly asked questions.

Isn't there a difference between the God of the Old Testament and the God of the New Testament?

Some people talk as though the Bible presents two vastly different pictures of God, a severe God of wrath in the Old Testament and a tender God of love in the New Testament. Yet the Bible itself never even hints at such a distinction; both testaments reveal the very same God.

Both testaments use the same phrase—"the God of Abraham, Isaac and Jacob"—to describe God (Exod. 3:16; cf. Matt. 22:32). So even by the way it refers to the Lord, Scripture makes it clear that God is exactly the same now as he was in the Garden of Eden. Wrote the psalmist:

> Of old You laid the foundation of the earth, and the heavens are the work of Your hands. They will perish, You will endure; yes, they will all grow old like a garment; like a cloak You will change them, and they will be change. But You are the same, and Your years will have no end. (Ps. 102:25–27)

This is why the New Testament can declare, "Jesus Christ is the same yesterday, today, and forever" (Heb. 13:8).

The Old Testament reveals God as holy and infinitely righteous, but also as merciful and gracious and loving (see chapter 2 of this book). The New Testament highlights exactly the same divine qualities. Even "the apostle of grace," Paul, urged us to "consider the goodness *and* severity of God" (Rom. 11:22, italics added).

Everyone universally acclaims Jesus as a preacher of love and forgiveness, yet repeatedly he said that he got his message from his heavenly Father (John 8:28, 12:50). Jesus claimed that if observers watched him, they could know what God was like (John 14:7).

Finally, many Bible passages tell us that God continues to work out today the plan that he designed ages ago (Rev. 13:8; Rom. 1:20; Eph. 3:11), demonstrating that he does not change from age to age. We can take great comfort in the fact that God remains the same forever, for it is this fact that guarantees that he will never change his mind about doing good to us: "I am the LORD, I do not change; therefore you are not consumed" (Mal. 3:6).

How could a God of love allow something like the Tribulation to happen? How could he permit so much suffering?

Love always wants what's best for the beloved, not necessarily what feels good at the time. A father who discovers his precious daughter has cancer pursues the course of treatment that stands the best chance of curing her—and much of that treatment may hurt frightfully. The daughter may even be tempted to think that, because her father does not call off the treatments, he could not possibly love her. Yet it's precisely because the father does love her—precisely because he wants the best for his child—that he continues the medical regimen, even though it causes terrible discomfort. It might be easier to let a seriously ill daughter die, but a loving father will always fight to keep her alive.

We should think of the Tribulation as God's severe medical regimen to bring millions of men and women to spiritual health. He will use extraordinary measures in this "time of trouble" to awaken those who sleep spiritually and to bring them into his eternal kingdom. If he did not love them so much, he could simply let them go on in their rebellion and sin, comfortably riding into a hellish eternity without him. But he loves his creatures too much to skip the medicine, no matter how much pain it may cause.

Life is at stake, and God is committed to using whatever measures may be necessary to lead as many people as possible into eternal life. We must not forget that it is through the Tribulation that "a great multitude which no one could number, of all nations, tribes, peoples, and tongues" end up "standing before the throne and before the Lamb, clothed with white robes, with palm branches in their hands, and crying out with a loud voice, saying, 'Salvation belongs to our God who sits on the throne, and to the Lamb!'" (Rev. 7:9–10) The Tribulation may be a severe mercy, but it is mercy nonetheless.

Why should I care about prophecy when I'm having enough trouble in the here and now?

I can almost hear some parents saying, "Why should I bother about the coming Antichrist when my teenager is acting like the Antichrist right now?" In other words, if prophecy concerns only the future and gives no help for the present, why spend much time worrying about it?

We need to remember that prophecy concerns much more than coming events. God gave a large percentage of Bible prophecy to help us live well right now (see chapter 12). When we live in the expectation that Jesus could return at any moment, we discover a purpose for life and a passion for living far beyond anything we could know in any other way.

Historically, whenever the church has focused on the second coming of Christ, it has enjoyed a fullness of life and a breadth of influence far exceeding what it has experienced at other times. In fact, the first three centuries and the last three centuries—eras during which the church banked its hope on the Second Coming—have proven to be the most evangelistic periods in church history. A focus on the Second Coming produces three great effects:

- a desire for holy living in an unholy age
- a greater spirit of evangelism
- a greater vision to reach the world for Christ.

Prophecy does give us hope and confidence for the future—but more than that, it offers us great strength and courage so that we may live boldly *today.*

Isn't the study of prophecy discredited by the many failed attempts at determining the time of Jesus' return?

The landscape of history is littered with foolish attempts at divining the time of Christ's return. Many cults are notorious date-setters, and periodically we read of this or that group that claims it has figured out some "hidden code" or "secret message" in the Bible that allows its members to determine when Jesus will come again.

In 1994, for example, a group led by radio preacher Harold Camping felt sure the Lord would return that September. When that date began to look doubtful, Camping recalculated and said that Jesus had to come by October 2. He didn't.[1]

The year 1988 saw the publication of a little book by Edgar Whisenant titled *88 Reasons Why the Rapture Will Be in 1988!* Whisenant sold 4.5 million copies of his book, which nevertheless turned out to be dead wrong. Undeterred, Whisenant announced he had forgotten to account for the year 0, leaving him off by one year. He then published another book, *Final Shout,* claiming that Jesus would *really* return in 1989 . . . and again wound up with egg on his face.[2]

When will we learn? Jesus could not have put it any more bluntly: "But of that day and hour no one knows, not even the angels of heaven, but My Father only" (Matt. 24:36). After his

resurrection, just in case his disciples had forgotten his earlier words, Jesus said again about the time of his return, "It is not for you to know times or seasons which the Father has put in His own authority" (Acts 1:7).

Here's the truth: nobody knows when Jesus will return to this earth to rapture his church. If anyone claims to know that time, we know at least one thing about them: they're wrong. *No one* knows that time, and there exist no secret messages in the Bible that, once decoded, will reveal the hidden information.

On the other hand, the Bible does give us some clues to the *general* time frame in which Jesus will return. In the Olivet Discourse (Matt. 24), Jesus gave us several signs and concluded, "So you also, when you see all these things, know that it is near—at the doors!" (v. 33) He said that we would "see" several signs and thereby know that the time for his return had drawn near. Luke said it like this: "Now when these things begin to happen, look up and lift up your heads, because your redemption draws near" (Luke 21:28).

The apostle Paul gave us further signs of "the end of the age" (1 Tim. 4:1–3; 2 Tim. 3:1–5), as did the apostle Peter (2 Pet. 3:3–4). So God clearly does want us to be watching and vigilant, ready at any moment for Christ to return. I believe that an abundance of current signs confirms that we may well be "the final generation" before Christ returns.[3] On the other hand, it's possible the world may continue for another century or two before the Second Coming. (I doubt that, but who knows?)

The fact that foolish men and women continue to set dates for the return of Christ should not deter anyone from looking to God's prophetic Word for instruction and encouragement. Do we let counterfeiters deter us from spending paper currency? Do we allow frauds in the medical profession to discourage us from seeing a doctor? Do we permit charlatans in the home improvement industry to keep us from getting our roofs fixed? No, indeed. And neither should we allow silly date-setting "prophets" to dissuade us from receiving the instruction and encouragement we need from the prophetic Word of God.

If no one knows "the day or the hour" of Christ's return, why should we bother with studying it?

If you care nothing about whether you make a difference in this world; if you have no desire to live boldly; if you feel ambivalent about giving comfort to those who need it, or apathetic about lending confidence to those who lack it—then you have no need to study the Bible's teaching on the return of Christ.

If, on the other hand, you want to live boldly, effectively, graciously, and courageously in this fallen world, then you need to immerse yourself in what Scripture says about the Second Coming. The study of prophecy is intensely practical.

I could name scores of verses that make this point, but let me quote just one. The apostle John insisted that vibrant and effective living in the present depends upon a vital consciousness of Jesus' second coming: "Beloved, now we are children of God; and it has not yet been revealed what we shall be, but we know that when He is revealed, we shall be like Him, for we shall see Him as He is. And everyone who has this hope in Him purifies himself, just as He is pure" (1 John 3:2–3).

Do you want to be like Christ? Do you want to enjoy the same kind of purity that he enjoys? Then focus on the Second Coming of Jesus Christ. There is no better way.

People hold all kinds of opinions on how to interpret prophecy. How can anyone know which opinion is right?

One of the best ways to identify the "right" method of interpreting prophecy is to see how the Bible itself interprets prophecy. When we investigate the question, time after time we discover that Scripture tends to interpret its own prophecies *literally* (see chapter 5). For example:

- Micah 5:2 said Jesus would be born in Bethlehem; so he was (Luke 2:1–7).
- Isaiah 53:9 said Jesus would die among the wicked and be buried among the rich; so he was (Matt. 27:38, 57–60).

- Jesus said the Jerusalem temple would be torn down
  stone by stone (Matt. 24:1–2); so it was, in A.D. 70.

When the Bible uses poetic terminology, of course, we have to take that into account. We must not try to interpret figurative language as though it were concrete. When Bible characters talk about finding refuge under God's wings (Ruth 2:12; Psalm 36:7; 57:1; 61:4; etc.), for example, we are not to think of God as some sort of gargantuan bird. Still, authors use even figurative language to convey something specific; a text cannot mean whatever we would like it to mean. An old rule of thumb for Bible interpretation stands up pretty well: "If the plain sense makes good sense, then any other sense is nonsense."

Is prophecy always clear and easy to understand?

I wish I could say that Bible prophecy is always easy to interpret and grasp, but that simply is not true. Equally competent and godly believers often come to vastly different interpretations of the same prophetic passage. While their differences may often be traced to whether they interpret the passage literally or symbolically, even those who come to the passage with a commitment to literal interpretation sometimes find themselves at odds over how to best understand the passage.

Consider the Book of Revelation, a work full of strange and startling images. It is not always easy to determine which images are to be taken literally and which are to be interpreted symbolically; both kinds of images exist in the book. In chapter one, for example, Jesus is pictured as having a mouth from which flashes a "sharp two-edged sword" (v. 16). I know of no one who takes this image literally; no one wants to see Jesus with a steel sword for a tongue. On the other hand, at the end of the book we read that God will "wipe away every tear from their eyes; there shall be no more death, nor sorrow, nor crying. There shall be no more pain, for the former things have passed away" (21:4)—and I know of no one who wants to take this in any way *other* than literally. The questions arise when we find images that might be taken either way.

It is also true that God's people frequently have not fully understood some prophetic texts until after the events in question had occurred (see Jer. 23:20, 30:24; Dan. 8:27; John 8:27–28, 12:16, 13:7, 20:9; Mark 9:32; Luke 9:45, 18:34, 24:16). So why did God inspire these prophecies? In most cases, he gave them long before their fulfillment so that those who witnessed the prophecies unfold could take great confidence in God's control of history—and see once more his loving nature.

Not even the disciples understood some prophecies of Jesus until after the Resurrection. Consider just a few examples:

About the Father: "They did not understand that He spoke to them of the Father. Then Jesus said to them, 'When you lift up the Son of Man, then you will know that I am He, and that I do nothing of Myself; but as My Father taught Me, I speak these things'" (John 8:27–28).

About washing their feet: "What I am doing you do not understand now, but you will know after this" (John 13:7).

About the Triumphal Entry: "His disciples did not understand these things at first; but when Jesus was glorified, then they remembered that these things were written about Him and that they had done these things to Him" (John 12:16).

About the Resurrection: "But they did not understand this saying, and were afraid to ask Him" (Mark 9:32). "But they understood none of these things; this saying was hidden from them, and they did not know the things which were spoken" (Luke 18:34). "They still did not understand from Scripture that Jesus had to rise from the dead" (John 20:9 NIV).

So, is Bible prophecy always clear and easy to understand? No. At the same time, however, we must recognize that God intends to "lift the curtain" on Bible prophecy as history winds to a close. The prophet Daniel did not understand some of what God revealed through him, but an angel told him, "Shut up the words, and seal the book *until the time of the end* . . . The words are closed up and sealed *till the time of the end*" (12:4, 9, italics added). As we get nearer to the end, many Bible prophecies become much clearer. I believe this is one reason why we are seeing such an explosion of interest in Bible prophecy today.

Is there no room for differences of opinion on the correct interpretation of prophecy?

First, we have to recognize that the major difference between Christian scholars in the area of prophecy is whether they interpret the text literally or allegorically (or "spiritually"). With such radically different ways of interpreting the Bible, there is no way they *could* agree on most prophetic passages—in fact, they find it hard even to debate the issues. I believe a literal approach best honors the Scripture and most effectively gets at its true meaning (see chapter 5).

Still, we have to recognize that good people hold differing opinions on some prophetic issues. There are many good, faithful Christians who hold views on biblical prophecy different from mine, even though we hold to the same hermeneutical principles.

I try not to argue with these dear friends, because neither their theory nor mine makes any difference to the facts. Jesus will come on *his* schedule, and when he shouts from heaven, we're all going at the same time. In heaven, all our ideas about prophecy and eschatology will get straightened out.

How do current world events fit into Bible prophecy?

While I don't encourage anyone to try matching every current news event with some specific Bible prophecy, I do think that the world appears to be on a fast track to the end of the age.

God's prophetic calendar clearly began speeding up when Israel became a nation in 1948. Since that time, all kinds of events began to fall into place, just as the Bible had foretold. Consider just a few of the major "signs of the times":

- Knowledge and travel have increased exponentially (Dan. 12:4).
- Millions of Jews have returned to their ancestral homeland (Ezek. 11:17).
- Earthquakes, ethnic strife, and wars have multiplied at ever increasing rates (Matt. 24:6–8).
- Jerusalem has become a source of worldwide discord (Zech. 12:2).
- Western, industrialized nations have become increasingly secular and militarized (Dan. 11:38).

No one knows for sure when the Lord Jesus will return to this world with a shout, but the "signs of the times" seem to indicate that the stage is being set for the fulfillment of Bible prophecy—which means that the time for his return may not be far off.

If the world is going to be destroyed anyway, isn't it a waste of time to try to alleviate global suffering? Why polish the brass fittings on a sinking ocean liner?

Those of us who believe that Jesus Christ will return at any time to rapture his church are sometimes accused of encouraging believers to forget about this world, since it's going to be destroyed anyway. Nothing could be more inaccurate.

To the contrary, a deep belief in the soon return of Christ motivates us to do more, not less. Jesus told us to "occupy till I come" (Luke 19:13 KJV), and that means keeping busy at God's work until the moment we rocket through the skies to be at Jesus' side. "As long as it is day, we must do the work of him who sent me," Jesus told us. "Night is coming, when no one can work" (John 9:4 NIV).

As faithful representatives and ambassadors of Jesus Christ, we ought to do all we can to make God look good. The apostle Paul told us, "Make it your ambition to lead a quiet life, to mind your own business and to work with your hands, just as we told you, so that your daily life may win the respect of outsiders" (1

Thess. 4:11–12 NIV). He added, "Be wise in the way you act toward outsiders; make the most of every opportunity. Let your conversation be always full of grace, seasoned with salt, so that you may know how to answer everyone" (Col. 4:5–6 NIV).

That may mean building schools, getting deeply involved in politics, working with the homeless, bringing medical help and facilities to people in need, funding effective charities, leading the charge in economic development—however God has gifted us, we are to use those gifts to serve the Lord by serving men and women made in the image of God. Everything we do ought to glorify God, thereby leading as many individuals as possible into a saving knowledge of Jesus Christ.

I have often been criticized for doing everything I can to get a maximum number of Christians out to vote, when, as my critics say, "The Rapture will solve all our social problems in one second." But what if the Rapture doesn't occur for one or two or five more decades—or even more? The failure of millions of Christians to vote could cause a premature and unnecessary loss of freedom. I consider turning out for Election Day a minimum requirement for today's Christians to help preserve freedom in our land, so that we can continue to preach the gospel around the world.

And that's hardly "polishing the brass fittings on a sinking ship"!

Prophecy tends to scare me. Is it supposed to do that?

It depends on what you mean. If you are camping in the woods and suddenly a U.S. Forest Ranger comes tearing up to your campsite and orders you to get out because a wildfire is roaring your way, his words might frighten you, but he intends them to save your life. Some Bible prophecy is like that; God is telling you to get out of the way of an approaching firestorm. His words may frighten you, but he intends his warning to save your life.

On the other hand, God's bedrock intention in giving us Bible prophecy is to help us feel confident in the glorious future he has planned for us. He wants already fulfilled prophecies to give us confidence that yet-to-be-fulfilled prophecies will take place exactly as foretold. Studying fulfilled prophecy builds our confidence in the rest of the supernaturally inspired Bible and encourages us to place our total trust in the faithfulness and mercy of God. Meditating on the Bible's fulfilled prophecies gives us confidence to follow the Bible's lead when it tells us to "trust in the LORD with all your heart, And lean not on your own understanding; In all your ways acknowledge Him, And He shall direct your paths" (Prov. 3:5–6).

For example, when we consider an ancient prophecy of Daniel that's being fulfilled in our lifetime, we find fresh confidence to believe the rest of God's Word. Speaking of "the time of the end," Daniel said that "many shall run to and fro, and knowledge shall increase" (Dan. 12:4). When you realize that humankind has been able to travel faster than horseback only for a little more than one hundred years, Daniel's prophecy demands that we sit up and take notice. Today, thanks to an exploding knowledge base, we can travel in space at speeds of up to 24,000 miles per hour; and even on earth, bullet trains travel at more than two hundred miles per hour.

How did the prophet know, some 2,600 years ago, that an increase in knowledge would make possible greater and faster travel? Divine revelation!

I often think of Daniel and his prediction regarding travel whenever I add more air miles to the five million I already have, "running to and fro" to spread the Good News of Jesus Christ. And I have to tell you this: I feel more confident today in God's Word and in his promise to fulfill that Word—and thus take care of all his children—than I ever have. Far from frightening me, prophecy thrills me. And I think God wants the same experience for you.

Appendix B

Discussion Guide

The following discussion guide has been prepared to help readers better grasp the content of the book and to give them a greater appreciation for the mercy of God as Bible prophecy proclaims it. Each study—suitable either for individuals or groups—relates to a corresponding chapter in the book and features two main sections:

- Questions for discussion, designed to get readers thinking about the topic under review;
- Selected Bible passages, paired with questions designed to investigate what God has to say.

May God bless your efforts as you seek to know, love, and serve him better!

Chapter 1:
God Has Gotten a Bad Rap

1. What images normally come to mind when you think of prophecy? Describe them. From where do you think these images have generally come?

2. What feelings surface when you think of Bible prophecy? Does pondering Bible prophecy generally make you frightened? Confident? Curious? Alarmed? Explain.

3. Do you think God has gotten "a bad rap" through a widespread misunderstanding of Bible prophecy? Why or why not?

4. Tim describes how he once had very different opinions of Jesus Christ and of God the Father; he loved Jesus but didn't much care for God. Have you ever felt this way? If so, describe how you felt (or feel), and what prompted those feelings.

5. Read Luke 15:11–32.
   A. What do you learn about the younger son in this story?
   B. What do you learn about the older son in this story?
   C. What do you learn about the father in this story?
   D. What picture of God was Jesus trying to paint through this story? Does your picture of God mirror this one? Explain.

6. Read Matthew 18:12–14.
   A. Who set out after the "lost sheep" in this story? Why did he go out to look for the sheep?
   B. To whom did Jesus compare the shepherd in his story? What are we to learn about God through the story?

7. Read John 6:37–40.
   A. Who gives individuals to Jesus so that they may obtain the bread and water of life?
   B. Describe the mission that Jesus received. From whom did he receive this mission?
   C. What is the Father's will, according to verse 40? What does this tell you about his nature?

8. Read 1 Timothy 2:1–4.
   A. What pleases God, according to verse 3? What does this reveal about his character?

B. What does God desire, according to verse 4? What does this reveal about his character?

9. Read Genesis 3:14–15.
   A. What curse did God pronounce on the serpent for deceiving Eve into eating the forbidden fruit?
   B. What do you think this prophecy means: "He will crush your head"? (See also Col. 2:15; Heb. 2:14–15; Rev. 20:10.)
   C. What do you think this prophecy means: "You will strike his heel"? (See also Luke 22:3–6; John 13:2, 18, 27–30.)

10. Read Psalm 66:5.
    A. What invitation is given in this verse?
    B. For whose benefit is the invitation extended?
    C. Have you accepted this invitation? Explain.

Chapter 2:
The God of the Prophets

1. What do you know about the prophets of the Bible? What made them different from other figures in Scripture?

2. If you could ask one of the Old Testament prophets a single question about God, what prophet would you pick, what would you ask him, and why?

3. Why would Tim say that the prophets "were the best God had"? What made them so special? Why can we trust their testimony concerning the character of God?

4. Read Deuteronomy 18:20–22.
   A. What tests of a true prophet does this passage give?
   B. What practical ways do we have of detecting a false prophet?

5. Read 2 Peter 1:20–21.
   A. What is the origin of Bible prophecy? Why does this make a difference?

B. What does it mean to be "carried along" by the Holy Spirit?

6. Read Jonah 4:2–11.
   A. How did Jonah explain his flight to Tarshish?
   B. What five traits of God did Jonah list in verse 2? What does each of these traits teach us about God?
   C. What further lesson did God give Jonah about his character? What can we learn about God's nature from this incident?

7. Read Joel 2:12–13.
   A. What request did God make of his people in verse 12?
   B. What do we learn of God's character in verse 13? How does this make it easier to comply with his request?

8. Read 2 Chronicles 30:6–9.
   A. What request did King Hezekiah make of the people of Israel?
   B. What result did Hezekiah expect if the people complied with his request?
   C. On what basis did Hezekiah expect such a result (v. 9)?

9. Read Psalm 86:15 and 103:8–12.
   A. What do you learn about God in Psalm 86:15?
   B. What do you learn about God in Psalm 103:8?
   C. How do these traits affect the way God deals with his people (vv. 9–12)?

10. Read Exodus 33:19–34:8.
    A. What request did Moses make of God in 33:19? What do you think this means?
    B. What do you learn about God's nature in this passage?
    C. How did Moses respond to this revelation of God's character? How does an accurate knowledge of God's nature change the way we live in the modern world?

Chapter 3:
The God Who Reveals Secrets

1. Have you ever read tabloid stories about modern predictions? If so, what do you remember about them? Why do you think so many people seem so interested in such stories?

2. Tim says that God already has fulfilled about five hundred prophecies to this point in history, and that another five hundred remain to be fulfilled. Does such a prophetic track record give you confidence about what the Lord says concerning the future? Why or why not?

3. Tim calls prophecy "history written in advance." What does he mean by this? If his description is accurate, how should it encourage you about your own future?

4. Read Isaiah 46:9–10.
   A. What do you learn about God in verse 9?
   B. How did God validate his credentials in verse 10? How does this show his utter uniqueness?
   C. What did God say about how his plans will turn out? How should this give us confidence?

5. Read Ezekiel 8:3–18.
   A. Where was Ezekiel taken in this vision? Why is that significant?
   B. What atrocity did he see in verses 5–6? What does this show you about the spiritual condition of the people?
   C. What scandalous thing did he see in verses 7–13? What does this show you about the spiritual condition of the people?
   D. What shocking activities did he see in verses 14–15?
   E. What abomination did he see in verses 16–17?
   F. How did God swear to respond (v. 18)? What does this demonstrate about God's character?

6. Read Isaiah 47:12–15.

   A. What sins had Babylon committed, according to this passage?

   B. How would God respond to these sins (v. 14)?

   C. Why did God make his final statement in verse 15? Who *could* save these erring people?

7. Read Numbers 11:4–20, 31–34, and Psalm 106:14–15.

   A. Why were the Israelites complaining in the Numbers passage? How did God respond?

   B. How did God predict the people would react to getting their illegitimate wishes?

   C. How does the psalm passage summarize what happened in Numbers 11? How can it be a warning for us?

8. Read Daniel 2:1–49.

   A. What demand did King Nebuchadnezzar make of his magicians? Why did they consider this an impossible demand?

   B. What request did Daniel make of his God? How did God respond?

   C. Did Daniel take credit for being able to meet the king's demand (v. 27)? Why is this significant?

   D. How did Daniel picture God in verse 28? How is this significant?

   E. What do you learn about the future in verses 44–45? How does this make you feel? Explain.

   F. How did Nebuchadnezzar characterize God in verse 47? How should this encourage us today?

9. Read Amos 3:7.

   A. What general principle did Amos lay out in this verse?

   B. How can knowledge of this principle give us courage, even in difficult times?

Chapter 4:
Why Prophecy?

1. Has someone ever given you a "heads up"? If so, what was it? Did it help? Explain.

2. In what way is prophecy God's "heads up" to us?

3. How does Tim explain the fact that God gives us much more information about the relatively short period of judgment that's coming than he does about the very long future period of divine blessing? Do you agree with him? Why or why not?

4. Read Isaiah 44:6–8.
   A. How did God describe himself in this passage?
   B. What challenge did God issue in this passage?
   C. Why did God tell his people not to fear the future?

5. Tim says that prophecy answers the five major questions of life:
   A. *Who am I?* Read Isaiah 43:7.
      1. For what reason did God create human beings, according to Isaiah?
   B. *Where do I come from?* Read Genesis 1:26, 9:6.
      1. In whose image did God create human beings?
      2. What is significant about this special origin? How should it change the way we view life?
   C. *Why am I here?* Read John 3:16.
      1. What is God's purpose for human beings, according to John?
      2. How do we enter into his purpose in this life?
   D. *Where am I going?* Read Acts 24:14–16 and Matthew 25:31–32, 46.
      1. What future lies ahead for the world?
      2. What two classes of people does Jesus foresee in the future?
      3. To which class do you think you belong? Explain.

E. *How do I get there?* Read 1 Peter 3:18 and Romans 1:16–17.

   1. How do these verses tell us to fulfill God's purpose for us? What do we have to do?

   2. Do you know where you're going when this life is over? Explain.

6. Tim says that Bible prophecy shows God's love for at least three categories of people:

   A. *To godly believers, warning them of rough times ahead.* Read Matthew 10:17–18, 21–22.

      1. What kind of rough times lay ahead for believers?

      2. In what way does God intend such knowledge to encourage or help these believers?

   B. *To struggling believers, encouraging them to return to the path of life.* Read Revelation 2:5, 21–23.

      1. What was the spiritual problem of the believers described in this passage?

      2. What remedy did Jesus give to them for their condition?

      3. Do you see yourself in any of these verses? Explain.

   C. *To honest seekers, to help them find the source of life.* Read Acts 17:27–31.

      1. How did Paul picture God in this passage?

      2. How did Paul use prophecy to encourage his hearers to commit their lives to God?

      3. How does this future event relate to you? Do you look forward to it? Why or why not?

7. Read 2 Timothy 4:8.

   A. To what did Paul look forward in this passage?

   B. How did this expectation encourage and strengthen the apostle?

   C. What promise did Paul give to other believers here?

   D. Do you look forward to the fulfillment of this prophecy in your own life? Explain.

Chapter 5:
Just As He Said He Would

1. What does a "literal" approach to interpreting Scripture mean to you? How would you explain such an approach to someone else?

2. What dangers might you see in a symbolic or metaphorical approach to interpreting the Bible?

3. Why should the way God fulfilled his prophecies in the past suggest to us how we should interpret his prophecies concerning the future? How *has* God typically fulfilled his prophecies in the past?

4. Read Jeremiah 40:2–3.
   A. What prophecy had God given concerning the city of Jerusalem in Jeremiah's day? What happened?
   B. In what way does verse 3 give us a pattern for how God normally fulfills the prophecies that he gives us?

5. Read Joshua 6:26 and 1 Kings 16:34.
   A. What did Joshua prophesy concerning the city of Jericho?
   B. How was this prophecy fulfilled in 1 Kings 16:34?

6. Read 2 Samuel 12:7–10.
   A. What did David do to become the recipient of such a harsh prophecy? What was the prophecy?
   B. How was this prophecy fulfilled throughout Israel's history? Does this give us any clues as to how to interpret most prophecy? Explain.

7. Read 1 Kings 21:19, 23, 1 Kings 22:34, and 2 Kings 9:30–33.
   A. What prophecy did Elijah give concerning King Ahab? How did God fulfill this prophecy?
   B. What prophecy did Elijah give concerning Queen Jezebel? How was this prophecy fulfilled?

8. Read Ezekiel 26:3–14 and 28:20–23.
   A. Name six specific predictions Ezekiel made concerning the city of Tyre, and review how each prediction was fulfilled in history.
   B. How did Ezekiel's predictions concerning Sidon differ from those of Tyre? Why is this significant, given the fact that the cities lay only about twenty-five miles from each other?

9. Read Jeremiah 23:3 and 24:6.
   A. What prediction concerning the regathering of Israel to her homeland did Jeremiah give in these texts?
   B. Why did these predictions seem almost impossible until they started to come to fulfillment in 1948?
   C. How does the fulfillment of these prophecies instruct us about the best way to interpret Bible prophecy?

10. Read Daniel 12:4.
    A. What two specific prophecies did Daniel give about life in the "latter days"?
    B. Are these two prophecies being fulfilled today? How can we know for sure? How are our times unlike any others?

Chapter 6:
No Pleasure in Wrath

1. If God really wants to bless us, then what most often explains the times when we don't see that blessing? What usually "short-circuits" the blessing of God?

2. What does God's "tough love" mean to you? How does his tough love come out of his holiness?

3. Read Lamentations 3:31–33.
   A. How does verse 31 show God's merciful nature?
   B. What does God "bring" in verse 32? What does he "show"? Why does he do this?

C. What is God's attitude when he brings "affliction or grief" to sinful human beings (v. 33)? How is this significant?

4. Read Hosea 11:8 and Matthew 23:37–38.
   A. What breaks God's heart, according to these passages?
   B. What do these verses teach us about the nature of God?

5. Read Jeremiah 2:14–19 and 18:7–8.
   A. What prompts God to sometimes bring disaster on his people?
   B. How could they avert such disaster?

6. Read Isaiah 55:7 and 2 Timothy 2:19.
   A. What does God ask his rebellious children to do in order to avert disaster?
   B. What does God expect of those who confess the name of the Lord?

7. Read Jeremiah 44:4–6.
   A. How often did God warn his people to turn away from their sin? How is this significant? What does it show us about his nature?
   B. What happened when the people refused to listen? Is this pattern the same today? Explain.

8. Read Amos 4:6–12.
   A. Name the six levels of God's escalating judgments as described in this passage.
   B. What does God's use of escalating judgments tell us about his character?

9. Read Romans 2:5–8 and Hebrews 10:31.
   A. What kind of judgment awaits those who refuse to listen to God?
   B. Why did the writer to the Hebrews say it is a "terrible thing" to fall into the hands of the living God? What does this mean?

10. Read Jeremiah 33:1–9.
    A. What judgment did God determine to pour out on Jerusalem because of its failure to repent (vv. 1–5)?
    B. What does the word "nevertheless" in verse 6 imply? What would God yet do for his people? What does this teach us about his nature?

Chapter 7:
Jesus: The Essence of Prophecy

1. Tim tells how he saw the red cross, even in communist China. What references to Jesus Christ do you often see in our own culture, outside of church? What symbols or reminders of him have you seen just today?

2. Why would secular people declare Jesus Christ to be the most influential person who ever lived? What is it about Jesus that impresses us two millennia after he died on a cross?

3. What do *you* think about Jesus? How would you describe him to someone who knew almost nothing about him?

4. Read Revelation 19:10.
   A. Why did the angel tell John to refrain from worshiping him?
   B. How did the angel relate Jesus to prophecy? What did he mean?

5. Read Micah 5:2 and Luke 2:1–5.
   A. What did Micah prophesy about the coming Messiah? Could that Messiah manipulate the prophecy? Explain.
   B. How did God fulfill Micah's prophecy? To what lengths did he go to fulfill it?

6. Read Psalm 41:9 and John 13:21–28.
   A. What prediction did Psalm 41:9 make?
   B. How was the prophecy fulfilled in Jesus' life? Does it ap-

pear that Jesus manipulated the fulfillment of this prophecy? Explain.

7. Read Zechariah 11:12–13 and Matthew 26:14–16, 27:3–9.
   A. What two messianic prophecies did Zechariah make in this passage?
   B. How were those prophecies fulfilled in Jesus' life?

8. Read Psalm 22:6–8, 16 and Matthew 27:43, John 19:34, 20:25–27.
   A. What two prophecies of the suffering Messiah do these verses from Psalm 22 highlight?
   B. How were the prophecies fulfilled in the life of Jesus? Could a merely human Jesus have manipulated the fulfillment of either of these prophecies? Explain.

9. Read Psalm 34:20 and John 19:33.
   A. What prophecy of the Messiah is given in the psalm passage?
   B. How was this prophecy fulfilled in the death of Jesus?
   C. What is especially significant about this prophecy? What connection does it have with Passover?

10. Read Psalm 16:10 and Acts 2:22–33.
    A. What prophecy of the coming Messiah did David make in Psalm 16?
    B. How was this prophecy fulfilled in the life of Jesus Christ? Why is this prophecy so central to the Christian faith?

Chapter 8:
Jesus: *The* Prophet

1. Why does Tim call Jesus Christ "the greatest prophet of all"? Why is he greater than Isaiah or Daniel or Moses?

2. What difference does it make if Jesus *is* the greatest prophet of all time?

3. Does the idea of Jesus as the greatest prophet in history change your perception or view of him? Why or why not?

4. Read Deuteronomy 18:17–19 and John 6:14; Acts 3:19–23.
    A. What kind of "Prophet" did Moses predict in Deuteronomy? What was special about this particular prophet?
    B. Whom does the New Testament identify as this special prophet? Why is this significant?

5. Read Mark 14:6–9.
    A. What prophecy did Jesus make about the woman who anointed him?
    B. How is this prophecy continuing to be fulfilled, even today?

6. Read Matthew 26:34, 74 and Luke 22:62.
    A. What did Jesus predict would happen to Peter on the night of Jesus' arrest? How did Peter react to this prediction?
    B. What happened to Peter on the night of Jesus' arrest? How did he react to his own failure? How do you think Jesus responded to Peter's failure? Why?

7. Read Matthew 12:40 and 16:4 and Matthew 28:1–7.
    A. What prediction did Jesus make concerning his own death and resurrection?
    B. Did Jesus' followers expect this prediction to come true? Explain.

8. Read John 21:18–22.
    A. What prophecy did Jesus give regarding Peter's death? How does tradition say this prophecy found fulfillment?
    B. What prophecy did Jesus give regarding John's life? How does tradition say this prophecy found fulfillment?

9. Read Matthew 11:21–24.
    A. What prophecy did Jesus give regarding the destinies of Capernaum, Korazin, and Bethsaida?

B. What do we know about the historical fortunes of these three cities?

10. Read Matthew 24:2.
    A. How impressed was Jesus with the beautiful temple grounds constructed by King Herod? What prophecy did he make regarding it?
    B. What happened in A.D. 70? In what way was Jesus' prophecy fulfilled to the letter?
    C. How do you, personally, respond to Jesus' many prophecies of events yet to come? Do they change anything in the way you live your life? Explain.

Chapter 9:
Jesus' Greatest Prophecy: The Church

1. Why does Tim consider Jesus' prophecy concerning the church to be his greatest prediction?

2. How would you describe your attitude toward the church Jesus said he would build? What shapes your attitudes toward the church?

3. Why do you think some people thought Jesus was John the Baptist? Why Elijah? Why Jeremiah or one of the prophets? What do you think tipped Peter off as to Jesus' true identity?

4. Read Matthew 16:18.
   A. What did Jesus say he would build?
   B. What opposition did Jesus predict would arise against his creation?
   C. What did Jesus predict would be the ultimate destiny of his creation?

5. Read Romans 10:9–10.
   A. Is it necessary to be born into the church in order to become a member? Explain.

B. How does the Romans passage instruct us to become a part of the church that Jesus is building?

6. Read Galatians 3:26–28.
   A. How does Jesus intend race, gender, or nationality to affect one's place in the church?
   B. How does this passage teach us to treat one another in the Body of Christ?

7. Read Ephesians 2:8–9.
   A. How "good" do we have to be before we qualify to become members of the church Jesus is building?
   B. If "good works" or a "cleaned-up life" can't get us into the family Jesus is putting together, what can?

8. Read 1 Corinthians 3:16.
   A. Why don't we have to go to Jerusalem or somewhere else to get close to God?
   B. Where does the Spirit of God live today? Does this include you? Explain.

9. Read Hebrews 4:16.
   A. Do we need a special priest or minister in order to come into God's presence? Why or why not?
   B. Are you taking full advantage of the free access you have to God through Christ? Explain.

10. How do you think you would react if someone demanded that either you deny Christ or be executed? Why do you think you would react this way? If you get the chance in heaven to speak with John Huss, William Tyndale, Girolamo Savonarola, or John Wycliffe—what would you most like to ask any of them?

Chapter 10:
Jesus' Scariest Prophecy: The Great Tribulation

1. Do the Bible's awesome descriptions of the coming Tribulation frighten you? Why or why not?

2. What do you think about God's method of using "extreme measures" to wake up men and women to their spiritual danger and to bring them into his kingdom? Do you think such a method shows his love? Explain.

3. If you have ever been through an earthquake, hurricane, torndado, or some similar awesome natural event, describe your feelings during the incident. Did it cause you to reevaluate your life or ponder eternity, even for a short while? Explain.

4. Read Joel 2:28–32 and Acts 2:14–21.
    A. What did Joel say God will do on the "day of the Lord"? What will be the result of this activity (v. 32)?
    B. What elements of Joel's prophecy were not fulfilled on the day of Pentecost as described in Acts 2? What must yet occur?

5. Read Revelation 7:3–4, 9–17.
    A. Although the "servants" described in this passage are never called evangelists, why does verse 9 suggest that they will be, in fact, powerful preachers of the gospel?
    B. Describe the people mentioned in verses 9 and 14. Who are they? How many are there? What does this suggest about the character of God?

6. Read Revelation 11:3–12.
    A. Describe the two men profiled in this passage. What will they do? What will be their mission?
    B. How are even the deaths of these two men designed to declare God's message to the whole world? What does this tell us about his character?

7. Read Revelation 12:1–6, 13–17.
   A. Whom does the "woman" symbolize in this passage (see especially verses 4–5)? Why is the devil so interested in persecuting her?
   B. How will God come to the woman's rescue? What will he do to help her? How will this show his merciful nature?

8. Read Revelation 14:6–7.
   A. Why is the activity described in this passage very unusual?
   B. Describe the message broadcast by the angel. How does this show the love and mercy of God?

9. Read Revelation 18:1–8.
   A. What is the destiny awaiting "Babylon" in this passage?
   B. What instructions will God give his people in verse 4? How will this show his mercy?

10. Read 2 Peter 3:3–9.
   A. What warning did Peter give in verses 3–4? How might this relate to our own day?
   B. What error did Peter point out in the thinking of those described in verses 3–4 (see verses 5–8)?
   C. How does God's delay in bringing judgment show his patience? What is God's desire for everyone? (v. 9) How does this show his love and mercy?

Chapter 11:
Jesus' Most Hope-Filled Prophecy: The Second Coming

1. In recent days, do you find yourself thinking more about the Second Coming than you used to? Explain. Have others recently engaged you in conversation about the Second Coming? If so, briefly describe the conversation(s).

2. How realistic is it for Jesus to tell us not to worry or be frightened about ominous world events? How could we practically follow his instruction?

3. What does it mean to you that God "has everything under control"? If he cannot commit evil, as the Bible clearly says (Hab. 1:13; James 1:13; 1 Pet. 3:12), then how can he remain in control while evil takes place?

4. Read Luke 12:32.
   A. What instruction did Jesus give us in this verse?
   B. On what basis did Jesus give us this instruction? What promise did he give? How is this supposed to help us comply with his instruction?

5. Read John 14:1–3.
   A. What command did Jesus give in the first part of verse 1? What instruction did he give us in the second part of the verse to enable us to comply with his command?
   B. What information did he reveal in verse 2 that ought to comfort us?
   C. What promise did he make in verse 3? How does this promise make you feel? Explain.

6. Read 1 Thessalonians 4:13–18.
   A. What prompted Paul to give his instruction in this passage (v. 13)?
   B. In your own words, describe the event Paul outlined in verses 14–17.
   C. How did Paul expect this revelation to affect his readers (v. 18)?

7. Read 1 Thessalonians 5:1–2 and Luke 12:39–40.
   A. According to these texts, when will the Lord return for his church?
   B. Given what these passages say about the timing of Jesus' return, what should we do to prepare for his arrival?

8. Read Matthew 24:29–30 and Daniel 7:13–14.
   A. How does the event described in these passages seem to differ from Jesus' "snatching away" of his church?
   B. In your own words, describe what this event will look like.

9. Read 1 Corinthians 11:26 and Matthew 26:28–29.
    A. How do these passages connect the celebration of the Lord's Supper with the second coming of Christ?
    B. How would it change your participation in the Lord's Supper if you were to consciously recall that it looks forward to Jesus' return?

10. Read Mark 13:35–37.
    A. What instruction did Jesus give us in this passage? What was the reason for his instruction?
    B. Are you complying with Jesus' instruction? If not, how could you do so?

Chapter 12:
God's Wonderful Plan for Your Present

1. When did you first hear the phrase, "God has a wonderful plan for your life"? How did you react to the phrase?

2. How can Bible prophecy be a practical help to you in your own life? How has it been so in the past?

3. Read 2 Corinthians 4:13–18.
    A. What fact gave the apostle Paul hope and confidence in the middle of trying times (v. 14)?
    B. What future fact described in verse 17 helped Paul not to "lose heart"?
    C. What must we do to take full advantage of this knowledge (v. 18)?

4. Read Matthew 18:21–35.
    A. Retell this story in your own words. What is the main point?
    B. What application did Jesus make to this story in verse 35? How does this make you feel? Explain.

5. Read 1 Corinthians 4:3–5 and Romans 14:9–13.
    A. What instructions do these two passages give us? What reasons do they give for their instruction?

B. Do you find this an easy instruction to follow, or do you struggle with it? Explain.

6. Read 1 Corinthians 6:1–8.
   A. What practice current among the Corinthians did Paul want to eliminate? Why did he want to eliminate it?
   B. What future events did he mention to show the Corinthians the error of their ways? Why should these events affect their behavior in the present?
   C. What makes it hard for some believers to comply with this instruction? Do you struggle with it? Explain.

7. Read 1 Thessalonians 5:9–11 and Hebrews 10:24–25.
   A. What two pieces of encouragement does 1 Thessalonians 5:9–10 give us? How did Paul want us to use this information to encourage one another?
   B. How did the writer to the Hebrews want us to encourage one another? Are you following his instruction? If so, explain how you do so. If not, why not?

8. Read 1 John 2:28 and 2 Corinthians 5:1–8.
   A. How did John suggest that we be confident and unashamed when Jesus returns? How can we do this, practically speaking?
   B. What reasons did Paul give for his confidence? How can these things give us confidence, as well?

9. Read 1 Corinthians 15:50–58.
   A. What future event did Paul describe in this passage?
   B. How did Paul expect that this event would give us the courage to work hard for the Lord? Does it have this effect in your own life? Explain.

10. Read Ephesians 5:3–7 and 2 Peter 3:10–12.
    A. How do these passages describe "holiness"? Why is it essential for those who profess the name of Jesus Christ?
    B. How does prophecy encourage us to live a lifestyle of holiness? How can it help you to live in a holy way?

Chapter 13:
God's Wonderful Plan for Your Future

1. If someone asked you to give your own view of the future, what would you say?

2. Read 1 Corinthians 2:9–10.
   A. What did Paul say about the future awaiting us?
   B. For whom has God prepared these things (v. 9)? Do you fit in this category? Explain.

3. Read Jeremiah 29:11–13.
   A. Describe the plans God said he has in store for his people.
   B. What promise did God give us in verse 13? How does this promise relate to his plans?

4. Read Revelation 20:1–10.
   A. What will happen to Satan during this thousand-year period? Why is this significant?
   B. Who will "reign" with Christ during this period?
   C. What will at the end of this period?

5. Read Isaiah 61:1–7.
   A. What activities will take place during the time described in this passage?
   B. What attitudes will reign during this period? Does it sound like a "fun" place to be? Explain.

6. Read 2 Corinthians 12:2–4.
   A. What happened to the man described in this passage?
   B. What was he unable to describe completely? Why was he unable to do so?
   C. How does even the "inexpressible" add to our anticipation of heaven?

7. Read Revelation 21:1–22:6.
   A. From your own reading of this passage, list all the things that *won't* be in heaven.

B. In the same way, list all the things that *will* be in heaven.

C. How does this passage make you feel? Explain.

8. Tim briefly lists the afterlife teachings of seven major religions or worldviews (Buddhism, Confucianism, Daoism, Existentialism/Secular Humanism, Hinduism, Islam, Judaism). Why does he claim that Christianity's understanding of the afterlife greatly surpasses any of them? Do you agree with him? Why or why not?

9. Read Titus 3:3–7.
   A. How did Paul describe the former way of life of his friends before they came to Christ?
   B. What changed their lifestyles and their destiny?
   C. What does it mean to be "heirs having the hope of eternal life"? How does this give one hope at the time of death? Do you have this hope? Explain.

10. Read Revelation 1:18.
   A. What claims did Jesus make in this verse?
   B. What difference to you do these claims make?

Chapter 14:
Lives Changed

1. Tim says that what one believes about God changes everything. What do *you* believe about God? How do *you* picture him?

2. How often do you approach God in prayer? When you do so, *how* do you do so? Confidently? Fearfully? Describe how you approach God.

3. Read 2 Corinthians 5:17.
   A. How did Paul describe "anyone [who] is in Christ"?
   B. What changes when someone places his or her faith in Christ? Has this been your own experience? Explain.

4. Recall Tim's statistics on what he calls the "prison recidivism rate."

   A. How likely is it that released prisoners who never come to faith in Jesus Christ will return to prison for another offense?

   B. How likely is it that released prisoners who come to faith in Christ while behind bars will return to prison for another offense?

   C. Why do you think there is such a huge difference between these two groups?

5. Recall Tim's story about Blue Lewis.

   A. Describe Blue Lewis before he placed his faith in Jesus Christ.

   B. Describe Blue Lewis after he placed his faith in Jesus Christ.

   C. What does this tell us about the power of God to change a person's life?

6. Read Revelation 20:11–15.

   A. Describe the event outlined in this passage.

   B. Why might this passage motivate some people to reconsider the courses of their lives and their eternal destinies? What effect does it have on you? Explain.

7. Recall Tim's story about Bob Fackler.

   A. What motivated Bob Fackler to get right with God?

   B. How do we know Bob's conversion was genuine?

8. Recall the "last words" of various individuals Tim quotes in this chapter.

   A. How would you characterize the last words spoken by the group of atheists Tim quotes?

   B. How would you characterize the last words spoken by Catherine Booth?

   C. What makes the difference in attitude between the two sets of quoted "last words"?

9. Recall Tim's story of the elderly Left Behind reader who committed his life to Christ.
   A. How had this man lived most of his life?
   B. What accounted for the change in the man at the end of his life?

10. Read Matthew 27:44 and Luke 23:42–43.
    A. How did both thieves crucified with Jesus react to the Lord at the beginning of the crucifixion?
    B. How did one criminal change his attitude? What do you think caused the change?
    C. How did Jesus respond to the criminal's change in attitude? What does this say about the nature of God?

Chapter 15:
Then They Will Know

1. How do you try to get those you love to know how you feel about them?

2. How has God tried to let you know how much he loves you?

3. Read Isaiah 43:10 and Jeremiah 16:21.
   A. What was God's great concern in these passages?
   B. How did God intend to fulfill the concern he expressed?
   C. What does this tell us about the nature of God?

4. Read Joel 2:21–27.
   A. List the things God promised to do for his people Israel in the future.
   B. Why will God do these things, according to verse 27?
   C. What does this show us about the nature of God?

5. Read Ezekiel 28:24–26, 34:30–31, 38:23, 39:28–29.
   A. What do all of these passages have in common?
   B. What does this show us about the nature of God?

6. Read Ezekiel 12:3 and Jeremiah 23:20.

A. To what lengths did God go in each of these passages to reach his people?

B. What does this show us about the character of God?

7. Read Isaiah 41:18–20.

A. What four terms did Isaiah use to show God's interest in helping us to know his identity and desire?

8. Recall the stories Tim told about the Arab dignitary, Andre Boshmakov, and the Rev. C. Kamalakar.

A. Which of the stories most interests you? Why?

B. What do these stories tell you about the lengths to which God is still going to get out his message?

9. Read John 7:1–44.

A. In what way did Jesus show us that God does things on his own *timetable* (vv. 1–8)?

B. In what way did Jesus show us that God does things in his own *way* (vv. 9–10)?

C. How does this account show us that God's plan cannot be stopped (v. 30)?

D. How does this account show us that God's message often gets mixed reactions (vv. 12, 31, 40–43)?

10. Read Exodus 18:9–11; 2 Kings 5:14–15; Acts 12:6–11.

A. Describe the similarity of reaction among the three men mentioned in these passages.

B. What prompted each of these men to respond as he did?

C. How about you? Can you say, "Now *I* know that the Lord is God"? Explain.

Chapter 16:
Seven Reasons Why Prophecy Matters

1. Try to name at least one area of life in which Bible prophecy has made a practical difference to you, then explain how it has made this difference.

2. Can Bible prophecy still make the difference between life and death, as in the case of the ancient Christians who fled Jerusalem before the Romans destroyed the city in A.D. 70? If so, how? If not, why not?

3. Read Isaiah 54:10 and Romans 8:31–39.
   A. How did God proclaim his love in these passages?
   B. How can this proclamation make a practical difference in your life?

4. Read Deuteronomy 7:9 and 1 Thessalonians 5:23–24.
   A. What did God say about his faithfulness in these passages?
   B. How can this truth make a practical difference in your life?

5. Read Numbers 14:18 and 2 Peter 3:9, 15.
   A. What do you learn about God's patience in these passages?
   B. How can this truth make a practical difference in your life?

6. Read Isaiah 8:12–14 and 1 Peter 3:14–15.
   A. What do these passages teach us about the security we have in Christ? What do they teach us about fear?
   B. How can knowledge of God's true character help you to feel secure, no matter what happens?

7. Read Romans 2:6–8 and 1 Timothy 5:24.
   A. What do you learn about the justice of God in these passages?
   B. Of what practical use is this knowledge to your daily life?

8. Read Micah 7:18 and Isaiah 55:7.
   A. What do these passages tell us about the mercy of God?
   B. How is the mercy of God to make a practical difference in our lives?

9. Read Romans 5:2–5.

   A. What do you learn in this passage about the hope that God wants to provide us?

   B. How can laying hold of the hope that God provides change your life in practical ways?

10. Read Revelation 1:3.

   A. What did God promise to those who read the prophetic Book of Revelation?

   B. Why do you think God promised this?

   C. Of what use is this promise? Do you avail yourself of it? Explain.

Chapter 17:
Can You Love a God Like That?

1. How do you greet most mornings—with a positive or a negative outlook? Explain.

2. Has your picture of God changed at all through reading Tim's book? Explain.

3. Read Luke 23:34.

   A. What request did Jesus make of his Father?

   B. Did God honor this request? How do you know for sure? (See Acts 2:23–38.)

   C. Have you asked God to forgive you of your sins? Explain.

4. Read Acts 13:38–41.

   A. Through what means is forgiveness made available to us?

   B. What warning does this passage give us? Have you heeded this warning? Explain.

5. Read Ecclesiastes 3:11.

   A. What has God placed in the heart of every man and woman?

B. How do you notice this divine gift in your own life? How does it make itself known?

6. Read John 3:36 and 5:24.
   A. What must one do to receive eternal life, according to these passages?
   B. What is the relationship between "believing" and "committing" one's life to Christ?
   C. Have you committed your life to Christ? Explain.

7. Read Deuteronomy 30:19 and 2 Corinthians 6:1–2.
   A. What choice is presented in these passages?
   B. What choice have you made? Explain.

8. How does Tim reply to those who say salvation by faith is "too easy"? How easy was it for Jesus to make our salvation possible?

9. Read Acts 8:26–40.
   A. Briefly describe in your own words the story recounted in the passage.
   B. Why did God send Philip to the Ethiopian?
   C. What does this episode teach us about the character of God?

10. What does this mean: "For the Christian, this life is as bad as it gets. But for the one who doesn't know Christ, this life is as good as it gets"?
    A. Can you trust a God who wants to bless you more than you want to be blessed?
    B. Have you trusted God with your life? Explain.

Notes

Chapter 1

1. Quoted from the screenplay available at http://members. tripod.com/~Adam_P_B/ghostbusters/script.html.
2. Not their real names.

Chapter 2

1. Charles G. Finney, *Memoirs of Rev. Charles G. Finney* (New York: 1876), 12–23.
2. Ibid.
3. Ibid.
4. Charles H. Spurgeon, *The Autobiography of Charles H. Spurgeon* (New York: Fleming H. Revell Co., 1898), I:102–104.
5. Ibid.
6. Ibid.
7. Ibid.
8. Ibid.
9. Some scholars think that the reference in Jonah 4:11 to "more than a hundred and twenty thousand people who cannot tell their right hand from the left" refers to young children. If this is correct, that would suggest a total Ninevite population of something like a million persons. Most ar-

chaeologists believe the walled city of Nineveh could not have sustained a total population of more than 175,000, and therefore believe the 120,000 figure refers to citizens that had lost their way morally.

Chapter 3

1. "101 Predictions & Prophecies for You and Your Loved Ones from World's Leading Seers and Psychics," *Sun*, 4 September 2001, 24–27.
2. Ibid.
3. See Dr. John F. Walvoord, *The Prophecy Knowledge Handbook* (Wheaton, IL: Victor Books, 1990).

Chapter 5

1. N. T. Wright, "Farewell to the Rapture," *Bible Review* XVII, no. 4, August 2001, 8, 52.
2. Ibid.
3. Ibid.
4. See Roy B. Zuck, *Basic Bible Interpretation: A Practical Guide to Discovering Biblical Truth* (Wheaton, IL: Victor Books, 1991), and Mal Couch, General Editor, *An Introduction to Classical Evangelical Hermeneutics: A Guide to the History and Practice of Biblical Interpretation* (Grand Rapids, MI: Kregel, 2000).
5. Josh McDowell, *Evidence that Demands a Verdict* (San Bernardino, CA: Campus Crusade for Christ, 1972), 290.
6. http://www.middleeast.com/sidon.htm, page 1.
7. Israeli Central Bureau of Statistics, www.cbs.gov.il/mifkad/tabBeng.htm.
8. See my book, *Are We Living in the End Times?* (Wheaton, IL: Tyndale House Publishers, 1999).
9. Wright, "Farewell to the Rapture," 8.

Chapter 6

1. Merrill C. Tenney, ed., *The Zondervan Pictorial Encyclopedia of*

the Bible, Vol. 4 (Grand Rapids, MI: Zondervan Publishing House, 1976), 443, 445.

2. Robert Byrne, ed., *1,911 Best Things Anybody Ever Said* (New York: Fawcett Columbine, 1988), 138.

Chapter 7

1. David Barrett and Todd Johnson, *World Christian Trends*, William Carey Library, global diagram 16, "Evangelization through martyrdom;" http://www.gem-werc.org.
2. Josh McDowell, *Evidence that Demands a Verdict*, 175.
3. See Matthew 1:17, 11:2–6, 16:16, 24:5, 26:63–64; John 1:41–42, 4:25–26, etc.
4. David Barrett and Todd Johnson, *World Christian Trends*.
5. See Isaiah 53:10–11; Psalm 22:22–31; Zechariah 12:10; and so on.

Chapter 8

1. See Matthew 12:40, 16:4, 21, 17:22–23, 20:17–19, 26:2, 27:63; Mark 8:31–32, 9:31–32, 10:33–34; Luke 9:22, 44, 18:31–34; 24:5–8; John 2:18–22; 12:20–36.

Chapter 9

1. David Barrett and Todd Johnson, *World Christian Trends*.
2. David Barrett and Todd Johnson, *World Christian Trends*.
3. Mark O'Keefe, "Christian Persecution: Widespread, Complex," *Sunday Oregonian*, 25 October 1998, A7.
4. Story and quotes from Michael Cunningham, "A Changed Man," *JSOnline: Milwaukee Journal Sentinel*, http://www.json line.com/packer/news/oct10100901.asp; appeared in the *Milwaukee Journal Sentinel* 10 October 2001.
5. Ibid.
6. Ibid.
7. Ibid.
8. Ibid.

Chapter 11

1. For a more comprehensive treatment of the Rapture and the Glorious Appearing, see some of my previous books on prophecy: *Are We Living in the End Times?* (Wheaton, IL: Tyndale House Publishers, Inc., 1999); *Rapture Under Attack* (Eugene, OR: Harvest House Publishers, 1998); *Tim LaHaye Prophecy Study Bible* (Chattanooga, TN: AMG Publishers, 2001); *Understanding the Last Days* (Eugene, OR: Harvest House Publishers, 1998); *Charting the Future* (Eugene, OR: Harvest House Publishers, 2001) contains fifty color charts and descriptions that graphically outline Bible prophecy; *Perhaps Today: Living Every Day in the Light of Christ's Return* (Wheaton, IL: Tyndale House Publishers, 2001), a ninety-day devotional based on Second Coming passages.

2. Tim LaHaye, "Jesus, the Spirit of Prophecy," a sermon given at First Baptist Church of Houston, Houston, TX, on April 23, 2001.

Chapter 12

1. John Piper, *Desiring God,* 10th Anniversary Expanded Edition (Sisters, OR: Multnomah Books, 1996), 144.

Chapter 13

1. Josephson Institute of Ethics, resources—quotes, "The Future, Fate, Change, Security," http://www.josephsoninstitute.org/quotes/quotefuture.html.

2. Future Quotes—Quotation Guide, http://www.annabelle.net/topics/future.html.

3. Ibid.

4. Ibid.

5. George Orwell in *The Portable Curmudgeon*, ed. Jon Winokur (New York: NAL Books, 1987), 105.

6. International Revival Network, http://www.openheaven.com/community/library/history/wales.htm.

7. *Eerdman's Handbook to the World's Religions,* (Grand Rapids, MI: Wm. B. Eerdmans Publishing Co., 1982), 230–235.

8. *Eerdman's Handbook to the World's Religions,* 246–251.

9. Ibid., 250–254.

10. Quotes found at http://library.thinkquest.org/16665/afterlifeframe.htm.

11. *Eerdman's Handbook to the World Religions,* 170–196.

12. Mohammed Marmaduke Pickthall, trans., *The Meaning of the Glorious Koran,* (New York: Mentor Book), 384, 385.

Chapter 14

1. Taken from http://www.cwfa.org/library/_familyvoice/2001-07/34-37.shtml.

2. Ibid.

3. Herbert Lockyer, *All the Last Words of Saints and Sinners* (Grand Rapids, MI: Kregel Publications, 1969), 131.

4. Ibid., 132.

5. Ibid, 133.

6. Ibid.

7. Ibid., 134.

8. Ibid., 53.

Chapter 15

1. Ezekiel 6:14, 7:27, 12:16, 25:11, 17, 26:6, 28:23, 24, 26, 29:9, 16, 21, 30:8, 25, 26, 32:15, 33:29, 34:30, 35:15, 36:38, 38:23, 39:28.

2. Luis Palau, *Everything You've Longed For* (New York: Doubleday, 2002), chapter 1.

3. Ibid.

4. Phillips Brooks in *How Great Thou Art: 365 Reasons Why God Is Awesome,* ed. Steve Halliday and William Travis (Sisters, OR: Multnomah Books, 1999), 345.

Chapter 16

1. Walter Wessel, "Mark" in *The Expositor's Bible Commentary, Vol. 8*, gen. ed. Frank E. Gaebelein (Grand Rapids, MI: Zondervan Publishing House, 1984), 749. See also D. A. Carson, "Matthew," in the same volume, page 501.
2. Eusebius, *Ecclesiastical History*, 3.5.3.
3. "What the world needs now is love," 1971, lyrics by Hal David, music by Burt Bacharach.
4. Myrna Alexander, *Behold Your God* (Grand Rapids, MI: Zondervan Publishing House, 1978), 89, 90.
5. Ibid.
6. Norval Geldenhuys, *Commentary on the Gospel of Luke: The New International Commentary on the New Testament* (Grand Rapids, MI: Wm. B. Eerdmans Publishing Company, 1951), 527.
7. "Mercy" in *The Random House College Dictionary*, Revised Edition (New York: Random House, 1988), 836.
8. Story compiled from various news reports, including: Dave Northfield and Doug Irving, "Teen driver gets two days in jail after negligent homicide plea," NWCN.com, December 14, 2001; Scott Wike, "Man responsible for Oregon Police deaths will plead guilty," http://stacks.msnbc.com/local/kmtr/M126597.asp?cpl=1, December 14, 2001.
9. Charles R. Swindoll, *Hope: Our Anchor of the Soul* (Portland, OR: Multnomah Press, 1983), 15.

Chapter 17

1. John Bartlett, *Familiar Quotations*, 10th Edition, 1919, quote #3087.

Appendix A

1. William R. Macklin, "Judgment Day fails to arrive on time," *The Sunday Oregonian*, 2 October 1994.
2. "Tips from the product merchandising staff," Spring Arbor.
3. See my book *Are We Living in the End Times?* (Wheaton, IL: Tyndale House Publishers, 1999).